CROSS-CULTURAL PERSPECTIVES ON
EARLY CHILDHOOD

Education at SAGE

SAGE is a leading international publisher of journals, books, and electronic media for academic, educational, and professional markets.

Our education publishing includes:

- accessible and comprehensive texts for aspiring education professionals and practitioners looking to further their careers through continuing professional development

- inspirational advice and guidance for the classroom

- authoritative state of the art reference from the leading authors in the field

Find out more at: **www.sagepub.co.uk/education**

CROSS-CULTURAL PERSPECTIVES ON
EARLY CHILDHOOD

Edited by
Theodora Papatheodorou
Janet Moyles

Los Angeles | London | New Delhi
Singapore | Washington DC

SAGE Publications Ltd
1 Oliver's Yard
55 City Road
London EC1Y 1SP

SAGE Publications Inc.
2455 Teller Road
Thousand Oaks, California 91320

SAGE Publications India Pvt Ltd
B 1/I 1 Mohan Cooperative Industrial Area
Mathura Road
New Delhi 110 044

SAGE Publications Asia-Pacific Pte Ltd
33 Pekin Street #02–01
Far East Square
Singapore 048763

Library of Congress Control Number: 2011927612

British Library Cataloguing in Publication data
A catalogue record for this book is available from the British Library

ISBN 978-1-4462-0754-3
ISBN 978-1-4462-0755-0 (pbk)

Typeset by Dorwyn, Wells, Somerset
Printed in India by Replika Press Pvt Ltd
Printed on paper from sustainable resources

*In memory of Pam Nason whose commitment to give voice to all
and bridge community and academia
will continue to inspire us*

Contents

Acknowledgements

There are many people to whom we are totally indebted for the compilation and completion of this volume. First of all, we would like to thank all the contributors to this volume and the anonymous reviewers of the proposal for their constructive feedback and support for this publication. Second, we would like to acknowledge and thank Jude Bowen and Alex Molineux, at Sage Publications, for their help and advice throughout this project. Finally, we would like to acknowledge the financial support, received by The British Academy (grant award number CSG: 55280), for the funding of an international conference at Anglia Ruskin University on 25–27 March 2010 and the many people who organised, attended and made this such a lively and informative event. This volume includes a small selection of the papers presented at that conference.

About the editors and contributors

The editors

Theodora Papatheodorou, PhD, is an early years educator and researcher. Her teaching and research interests are in the area of early childhood pedagogy and curriculum, children's behaviour, social inclusion, multicultural education and bilingualism. She is the author of *Behaviour Problems in the Early Years* (2005) and co-editor (with Janet Moyles) of *Learning Together: Exploring Relational Pedagogy*, both published by Routledge. She is also the co-author (with Paulette Luff and Janet Gill) of *Child Observation for Learning and Research* (2011), published by Pearson.

Janet Moyles is Professor Emerita, Anglia Ruskin University and a play/early years specialist. She has worked as an early years teacher, head and HE tutor and has written and edited widely, including *Just Playing?* (OUP, 1989), *The Excellence of Play* (OUP, 2009) and *Effective Leadership and Management in the Early Years* (OUP, 2007). She has directed several research projects including *Jills of All Trades?* (ATL, 1996), *Too Busy to Play?* (Esmee Fairbairn Trust/University of Leicester, 1997–2000), *SPEEL (Study of Pedagogical Effectiveness in Early Learning)* (DfES, 2002) and *Recreating the Reception Year* (ATL, 2003).

The contributors

Ronit Alin works in the field of maths education, currently teaching in teacher development courses and designing maths learning activities, in part computer-assisted. For the last 10 years, she has been working as a lecturer in Ohalo Regional Teacher Training College, Israel. Ronit teaches pre-service kindergarten teachers the basics of mathematics, cognitive psychology of early childhood in maths study and the didactics of mathematics. The focus of her doctorate was maths education in the early years.

Linda Cooper gained a first-class honours degree in Education and Childhood Studies. As part of the Anglia Ruskin Undergraduate Student Research Placement Scheme, she worked as a co-researcher with Mallika Kanyal. Linda's main areas of research include children's participation, mothering and feminism. The focus for her doctoral research is on generational changes in the way women access higher education.

Julia Druce is Senior Lecturer in Education Studies and Pathway Leader for the sector-endorsed Foundation Degree in Early Years Childcare and Education at Anglia Ruskin University. Julia's professional development and post-graduate studies have centred mainly on practice-based play therapy, with a particular focus on supporting children's social and emotional (holistic) development. The focus of her doctorate is play therapy.

Hasina Banu Ebrahim is currently Professor and Head of the discipline of Early Childhood and Foundation Phase Education (ECFPE) in the Faculty of Education, University of the Free State, South Africa. Her particular interest lies in the development of Early Childhood Foundation Phase Education (ECFPE, birth to 9 years) through a research focus and publications on early care and education, teacher development and policy priorities with special reference to the developing world context. She has been involved in research involving early literacy, barriers to learning in early childhood, knowledge transfer in the early years and indigenous models of early care and education.

Sue Gascoyne is an educational trainer and published author, focused on embedding sensory play experiences in the learning environment. She has led research projects, successfully provided mentoring, training and consultancy services for over 12 years, and founded early years educational resources supplier, Play to Z Ltd. A primary school governor and mother of two young children, many of Sue's activities and resources are based on observations of her own children's play.

Anne Hunt is a member of the Early Childhood Research and Development Team at the Early Childhood Centre, University of New Brunswick. This team has developed the New Brunswick Curriculum for Early Learning and Childcare and continues to work with early childhood educators to develop curriculum support documents. Anne has had a long career as an entrance class teacher in public schools and has also taught courses in early literacy, play, children's literature and curriculum at both the Universities of New Brunswick and St Thomas in Canada.

Mary James is the founding director of LETCEE, a non-profit organisation based in Greytown, KwaZulu Natal, South Africa. LETCEE's vision is for every South African child to develop in a nurturing environment with access to early education. To achieve this, LETCEE works to build the skills and confidence of adults who work with vulnerable young children. The organisation also implements home- and family-based early education programmes in deep rural communities. Mary trained as a teacher and moved into this work 20 years ago. She was awarded an honorary Doctorate in Education from Anglia Ruskin University in 2009.

Hazel Jennings is a Training and Development Officer for mpowernet, Faculty of Education, Anglia Ruskin University, with a previous background in teaching and development. She is a lead for the Early Years Professional Status (EYPS) programme and facilitates the development of consultants for this programme, assessment, mentoring, tutoring and also both internal and external moderation. She collaborates with other mpowernet staff on research projects, potential markets for professional development and business development. Hazel is currently studying for an MA in Children's Book Illustration and has a particular interest in the arts and creativity in education and learning.

Mallika Kanyal is Senior Lecturer and a social researcher at Anglia Ruskin University. She teaches across a range of early childhood undergraduate programmes and has been engaged in research in the areas of children's peer relationships, children's participation, blended learning in higher education and using virtual learning environments as a pedagogic tool in higher education. She has presented research papers and run workshops at both national and international conferences in education.

Athina Kammenou has studied psychology and educational sciences at the University of Geneva and obtained a postgraduate degree in special education. She has taught in the Faculty of Kindergarten Teachers in the canton of Geneva. She is currently a lab assistant at the Department of Preschool Education of the Technological Educational Institute (TEI) of Athens. She is responsible for creating and implementing individualized programmes for the integration of children with special needs.

Lilian G. Katz is Professor Emerita of Early Childhood Education at the University of Illinois (Urbana-Champaign) and a member of the Clearinghouse on Early Education and Parenting (CEEP). Lilian served as director of the ERIC Clearinghouse for 33 years and as past president of the National Association for the Education of Young Children. As well as all the states of the USA, Australia and Canada, she has lectured in 55 countries internationally. She is editor of the first online peer-reviewed, open-access, bilingual early childhood journal, *Early Childhood Research and Practice*.

Sara Knight is Senior Lecturer at Anglia Ruskin University, and has taught on professional training courses for nursery nurses. Sara has worked with a leading environmental charity, taking programmes into primary and special schools to develop children's awareness of ecological and sustainability issues. Sara's doctorate is about pedagogical principles of Forest School. Her publications include *Forest Schools and Outdoor Play in the Early Years* (2009), *Risk and Adventure in Early Years Outdoor Play* (2011) and *Forest School for All* (edited, 2011), all with Sage Publications.

Patricia H. Kostell has taught from preschool through to graduate level, including work with children with special education needs. After earning her doctorate (from the University of South Carolina) and working as an

Assistant Professor (at Winthrop University, South Carolina), she started her own consultancy business. She offers professional development and works with teachers in their classrooms. She has held a national board position in the Association for Childhood Education International (ACEI) and presented numerous papers internationally.

Paulette Luff is Senior Lecturer in Early Childhood Studies at Anglia Ruskin University. Her professional interest is early childhood education, with a particular focus on adults' roles in children's care and learning. Paulette's doctorate explored early years practitioners' use of child observation. She has presented and published work on this topic nationally and internationally. Paulette has worked in the field of early childhood for more than 20 years, as a teacher, foster carer, school–home liaison worker and as a childcare and education lecturer in further education.

Eva Maagerø is Associate Professor in Norwegian language at Vestfold University College, Norway. She teaches and researches linguistics, language development, literacy, text theory, semiotics and multimodality on bachelor and masters programmes. Together with Birte Simonsen, she has recently completed a project in kindergartens in Norway where English as a foreign language was introduced to children from 3 to 6 years.

Pam Nason was a member of the Faculty of Education at the University of New Brunswick (UNB), Canada. The Chelmsford Conference and this article were her last academic contributions. She died in September 2010. Pam used her knowledge and writing skill to bring the voices of children, families and early childhood educators into the academic circle. Her deep commitment to a society where there are no privileged voices has shaped the thinking that has emerged throughout the last several years of research at the Early Childhood Centre, UNB. She was also committed to taking the academy out into the community, founding the University Children's Centre as a place to give early childhood education students practical experience, to foster innovative practice, and, through this, to reach out to the wider community.

Natassa Papaprokopiou holds a PhD in Education. She studied psychology and pedagogics in Paris at the University of Paris V-Rene Descartes. She is Associate Professor and head of the Department of Preschool Education at Athens Technological Educational Institute. She has taught pedagogics and psychology at university level. She has also sat on European research committees for many years. Over recent years she has been systematically engaged in studying educational innovations and in-service training of educators. Her research work has been published in academic journals and presented at international conferences.

Jill Sachs has extensive experience in early childhood development. She held the position of Early Childhood Development (ECD) manager for the KwaZulu Natal Provincial Department of Education. Now as Education Programmes Manager, she is the designer and developer of all the Early

Years Education (eYe) training programmes offered by the arts-based, accredited South African Caversham Centre. Jill studied at the University of South Africa for a Higher Education Diploma in ECD and a further Diploma in Education Guidance and Counselling.

Carolyn Silberfeld has been actively involved in developing and leading early childhood studies undergraduate programmes for 18 years, the past 11 of which have been at the University of East London. She has a background in children's nursing, midwifery and health visiting. She is a founder member of the Early Childhood Studies Degrees Network. Carolyn has a particular interest in international student exchange programmes and reflective learning.

Birte Simonsen has practised as a primary and secondary school teacher for 25 years. Since 1993, she has been a lecturer for student teachers at Agder University, Norway, in the field of education. She is now Dean of the Teacher Education section. She has participated in different development and research projects connected to ICT and school, and has published articles in books and journals on early language teaching and learning.

Christine Such is Senior Lecturer in Education Studies and Pathway Leader for Early Childhood Studies programmes at Anglia Ruskin University. She has taught both in further and higher education and previously worked in the voluntary sector in welfare advice. Christine is completing a doctorate in education focusing on professional leadership for graduate early years practitioners. Her research into the use of dialogic teaching and learning to support undergraduate students' inquiries into early years practice, led her to evaluate conditions for peer collaboration.

Maulfry Worthington is engaged in doctoral research into the emergence of children's mathematical graphics in play (Free University, Amsterdam). Maulfry taught young children for many years, was a National Numeracy Consultant in England and has lectured on primary and early years mathematics and pedagogy. Maulfry's publications include *Understanding Children's Mathematical Graphics,* (OUP, 2011) co-authored with Elizabeth Carruthers. They were commissioned to write *Children Thinking Mathematically* (DCSF, 2009) and are co-founders of the international *Children's Mathematics Network* (www.childrens-mathematics.net/).

Hazel Wright has trained women to work in childcare for many years – in Adult, Further and Higher Education contexts. She is currently Senior Lecturer at Anglia Ruskin University, and lectures on both BA and MA courses. Hazel's research into the lives of mature women studying for a Level 3 qualification in childcare was part of a doctoral study adapted for the publication, *Women Studying Childcare: Integrating Lives Through Adult Education* (Trentham, 2011).

List of figures, photographs and tables

Introduction

Theodora Papatheodorou and Janet Moyles

Overview

The 21st century started with early childhood being at the top of national and international policies, initiatives and regulations with aspirational outcomes and targets for children, their families, communities and societies. From being a service to the child, early childhood provision has been acknowledged as a service to families and communities aiming to achieve societal economic well-being, cohesion and stability. While such policies offer many opportunities for improved practice, they have not been without challenges.

In this introduction, we will first provide an overview of the commitments and policies of supranational entities that have promoted and increased early childhood provision by referring to the relevant research. We will then discuss the challenges and opportunities created by them for practice and research, considering a socio-historical and cultural perspective. Finally, we will conclude by presenting the structure and organisation of this volume, offering a coherent argument for its compilation.

In today's knowledge-based societies, the notion of *brain power* forms the intangible *human capital* required to achieve long-term competiveness, social cohesion and equity (Commission of the European Communities, 2006; Keeley, 2007). Supranational and national entities have now recognised that, in order to increase individual and societal competitiveness and quality of life, there is a need for significant investment in education that starts early on in children's lives. These claims have been well substantiated by a significant body of evidence which has demonstrated the long-term benefits of high quality early childhood services for young children, their families and the wider community (Kilburn and Karoly, 2008; Heckman, 2006; Sylva et al., 2004; Wylie and Thompson, 2003; Schweinhart et al., 1993). A review of longitudinal studies has established that quality early years provision has lasting effects – especially for children living in poverty – than any other educational innovations implemented at later stages (Schweinhart, 1994). Evidence from neuroscience has also supported these arguments by confirming the importance of early stimulation on brain development (Woodhead, 2006; Shonkoff and Phillips, 2000).

The Commission of the European Communities (2006: 3) has explicitly acknowledged these benefits by stating that '... pre-primary education has the highest rates of return of the whole lifelong learning continuum, especially for the most disadvantaged, and the results of this investment build up over time'. Similarly, the Jomtien Declaration *Education for All* and the subsequent Dakar *Framework for Action* have mandated the expansion and improvement of early years education and care, by declaring that learning starts at birth (UNESCO, 1990, 2000). The OECD reports *Starting Strong* and *Starting Strong II* have further reiterated the importance of flexible services and provision to accommodate the diverse needs of children and their families (OECD, 2001, 2006), while earlier, the *United Nations Convention on the Rights of the Child* set out universal values and aspirations for children's development and well-being (UNICEF, 1989).

As a result, the 21st century began with many international and national commitments and policies which set out aspirational outcomes and benefits for children, their families and the wider society. These have explicitly emphasised the place of early childhood provision within the wider global agenda and established it as a cornerstone for individual and societal well-being, by tackling inequality and disadvantage early on in children's lives through education (Eurydice Network (EACEA), 2009; Kilburn and Karoly, 2008; UNICEF, 2008; Keeley, 2007; UNESCO, 2000, 1990; OECD, 2001).

These policies, however, have also prompted further continuing debates and disputes regarding their philosophical underpinnings and the way they have informed and shaped curricula frameworks and pedagogical practices. Arguably, these policies envisage the global child whose learning and development is subject to universal truths and laws, and potentially ignoring the influence of socio-political and economic factors, power structures and values within communities and societies (Moss, 2008; Dahlberg et al., 2007; Cannella, 2005). They continue to foster debates such as child-centred versus outcomes-based provision; playful learning versus systematic instruction; developmentally versus culturally/contextually appropriate practice; debates which tend to take a polarised and dichotomised stance. They ignore the diversity that exists across the globe and within countries and the complexity and dynamic interactions of many factors that impact on child development and learning (Papatheodorou, 2010; Katz, 1999; Bredekamp, 1987).

The focus on such dichotomised debates, however, can hide the great variations that exist between these polarised stances. It is argued here that if such variation and complexities are not explicitly acknowledged, understood, critiqued and negotiated, policy commitments may lead to disadvantaging, marginalising and even pathologising certain childhoods, despite their well-meant intentions and aspirations. With these arguments in mind, an international conference was organised by Anglia Ruskin University, supported by The British Academy[1] in 2010. The conference, entitled *Early Childhood Curriculum, Policy and Pedagogy in the 21st Century: An International Debate*, aimed to:

- bring together academics, researchers, policy makers and early childhood professionals for a series of purposeful talks and discussions
- open up the debate and bridge a potential philosophical, theoretical and practice chasm that may exist
- interpret the underpinning philosophies of policy into practice that is relevant to different situations across countries.

The papers presented and the discussions generated during the conference supported the view that there is much variation within polarised debates. They reminded us that policies and practices are not always uncritically accepted; instead they are critiqued with reference to 'cultural scripts', that is 'the shared beliefs, attitudes, norms and values of a given socio-cultural community' (Rosenthal, 2003: 104). They are determined by cultural values and a set of norms, which we hold, for example, about children, families and communities; the purpose and role of education and care institutions; the philosophical perspectives and traditions of educational practice; and the use of educational and cultural tools we have available. To recall Bruner (1990), our cultural values and set of norms make meaning public and shared and offer us procedures that give meaning to practices when they depart from these norms. For Bruner, the human mind, actions and life are as much a reflection of culture and history as they are a product of biology and physical resources.

Culture, however, is not static or rigidly framed. It is fluid, multi-layered and continually evolving. Over time, new ideas and practices that have been appropriated and accommodated within our cultural frames of mind have, in turn, transformed and changed them. The dynamic interrelationships between old and new, the familiar and the strange and tradition and innovation have changed the ways of our cultures. For example, at one level, policy makers, practitioners and researchers tend to understand and accommodate new ideas (e.g. policy recommendations, good practice suggestions and research perspectives) in the light of existing cultural scripts. At another level, existing cultural scripts are transformed and changed by the influence of these new ideas. Evidently, there is a relational and dialectical relationship between existing knowledge and the enactment of new ideas that lead to negotiated and appropriated practices which, in turn, lead to transformation and change. Our cultural frames of mind determine our activity and learning as much as our activity and learning transforms our cultural scripts. As a result, our cultural milieu evolves and changes over time. These ideas reflect a socio-historical and cultural perspective on human learning (Lave and Wenger, 1991).

These ideas are well-illustrated in the chapters included in this volume. Drawing from the long-standing European traditions and history of early childhood care and education and the work of early pioneers (such as Froebel, Pestalozzi, Montessori and Isaacs), Sue Gascoyne and Sara Knight (Chapters 1 and 2, respectively) reiterate the importance of sensory play and the value of children's access to the outdoors and nature. Informing their work from contemporary notions of children's agency and their participation as co-constructors of knowledge, Maulfry Worthington (Chapter 3) and Mallika Kanyal and Linda Cooper (Chapter 4) present innovative ways of working with children. It may appear that holding on to traditional educational cultures and the introduction of new ideas and concepts create tensions but it is the negotiation of the space between them that leads to the transformation of our understanding of children's learning cultures. As MacNaughton has argued:

> In between the new and the familiar are competing and contested understandings of what is 'best', 'right' and ethical for children, and these understandings bring choices: choices about which knowledge is 'best' and 'right' to form and motivate the everyday business of early childhood. (2005: 1)

Similarly, in Chapter 5, despite a policy commitment for integration and inclusion of ethnic minority groups, Birte Simonsen and Eva Maagerø explore the subtle power of majority culture and caution readers of the dangers of uncritically accepted policies. In Chapter 6, Mary James and Hasina Ebrahim provide an exemplar of pedagogical practice that invests in existing human capacity to meet the mandate for universal education and care for young children. When in the wider context centre-based education and care, delivered by trained adults, is the norm, the particular local circumstances mean that provision should utilise and rely on young people's skills and capacities. In the chapter that follows, Anastasia Papaprokopiou and Athina Kemmenou illustrate the struggle of introducing more formal methods of communication with parents and induction practices in a culture where informality remains the norm of communication. These chapters signpost new cultures of pedagogy that are innovative and questioning and, at the same time, enable negotiation of both traditions and new expectations.

The impact of supranational and national policies is nowhere else more evident than in the development of curricula frameworks and their implementation and in requirements to monitor children's progress. One of the editors (Papatheodorou, 2010) has argued that outcomes-driven curricula have been a challenge for the early years workforce who, for a long time, have embraced, and been educated in, a child-centred approach. The other editor (Moyles, 2010) has argued for reflection-based practices in early childhood to ensure continual improvements to pedagogy and curriculum implementation. Yet, curricula frameworks are seen as the level playing field for all children and especially those who have limited experiences and opportunities to reach their potential. Three chapters in this volume take on the challenge of curricula and assessment demands. In Chapter 8, Ronit Alin refers to the introduction of mathematical concepts, drawing upon theories of child development and traditions of pedagogy to introduce teaching practices that are culturally appropriated. The next chapter on literacy, written by Pat Kostell, starts from and extends children's cultural experiences and learning through the reading of books and related experiences. Finally, Paulette Luff's chapter on children's assessment provides a balanced critique on the issues, making reference to the English context and policy. Once again, these chapters illustrate how a dialogical engagement with what is known and what is required creates new perspectives on curriculum implementation and triggers thinking and action.

The nature of early childhood education and care continues to be at the forefront of debates but an overarching concern is the potentially limited number of well-trained and educated people in the workforce. Policy commitments for quality early years provision demand a workforce that is well trained and appropriately equipped with skills and knowledge to achieve positive outcomes for children (Sylva et al., 2004). Such policies also require the development of conceptual and structural frameworks with common core principles to retain and preserve cultural meanings and connotations (European Commission, 2007). While in many European countries a graduate qualification is a requirement for working with young children, in many countries this remains an aspiration (Oberhuemer et al., 2010).

Efforts made to enhance the skills and knowledge of the existing workforce have brought to the fore many challenges and dilemmas but have also provided opportunities for exploring empowering models of education and training. These are illustrated in the last part of this volume where, in Chapter 11, Anne Hunt and Pam Nason discuss how top-down policies in Canada expose the profession to colliding discourse that threaten their professional identity; while in Chapter 12, Jill Sachs demonstrates that a South African training approach that invests in *the individual as an inspiration* becomes an empowering learning experience. International experiences and access to professional discourses are discussed by Carolyn Silberfeld (Chapter 13) and by Chris Such, Julia Druce and Hazel Jennings (Chapter 14) as powerful examples of changing practice. Chapter 15, with Hazel Wright's focus on crossing the family culture to enter professional cultures, substantiates the importance of democratising access to higher education for the early years profession. The challenges and opportunities faced by the field of early childhood education and care are summed up in the final chapter by Lilian Katz, who also sets out a vision for the future of early childhood education and care internationally.

Clearly, there is no single way to pursue global outcomes for children. These can and are achieved by practices which are embedded in local cultures, values and ideals and, at the same time, informed by external influences.

Interrogating these influences and balancing diverse perspectives may be demanding but equally rewarding, when children are endowed with roots and wings, that is, a strong identity with culture and place (roots) and knowledge, skills and competencies (wings) to deal with new, different and unfamiliar challenges presented by a rapidly changing world (Duhn, 2006).

Undoubtedly, universal policies have greatly impacted in changing structures, procedures and cultures in early childhood. However, they are also seen as reflecting and seeking to impart the values and ideals of dominant and powerful sections of society. A dialectical and dynamic relationship between policy and practice can potentially combat such partial influences and afford greater cultural coherence and cohesiveness. It is the critical examination of underlying principles of ideas and theories that makes dogmatism redundant (Dewey, 1997). Therefore, to recall and paraphrase Freire (1998), it is the human capacity to compare, judge and decide to intervene, or not, that gives, or takes away, opportunities for equality for all; not practice that is conditioned by policy and statutory requirements. We are reminded that '... education is not a technical matter, nor an "experts" issue, but a human process in which teachers are core agents, and they have much to say and to do' (InterGuide, 2002: 106).

These ideas are nowhere better expressed and reflected than in the discourse and debate about early years professionalism which is defined by practitioners being intuitive, reflective, responsive and effective in creating empathetic engagement and personal involvement with children, their families and communities. The most effective practitioners will hold strong beliefs and feelings based on clear reflection and a deep commitment to the protection and support of children. A passionate commitment remains the core value of the profession (Katz, Claxton, Freire in Osgood, 2006).

Acting with professionalism and fired by passion (Moyles, 2002), the early childhood workforce strives to establish reciprocal communication between interested parties, i.e. practitioners, policy makers, academics and researchers, so that they are empowered by each other and, in turn, empower children to receive their entitlement for the most effective care and education, becoming fulfilled, potent and contented citizens of today and tomorrow. This was a consistent, aspirational and inspirational message communicated by the conference delegation and it is reflected in the selection of papers included in this volume which responds to UNESCO's call for:

> Equitable exchange and dialogue among civilizations, cultures and peoples, based on mutual understanding and response and the equal dignity of all cultures [which] is the essential prerequisite for constructing social cohesion, reconciliation among peoples and peace among nations. (2003)

The structure and content of the book

This volume is a compilation of practice-focused research papers written by academics and researchers, practitioners and trainers, all of whom work in the field of early childhood. The chapters address a range of issues pertinent to the field and explore arguments and messages that have significance for local and global childhood communities. Our aim, as editors, was to:

- embrace different voices and bridge the gap between practice and research

- signpost to a roadmap enabling pedagogical cultures and encounters

- provide a framework for systematic documentation, monitoring and evaluation in order to establish evidence-based early childhood education and care.

The chapters are organised under four main themes:

- children's learning cultures

- cultures of pedagogy

- cultural perspectives on curricula

- cultures of professional development.

These themes form the four parts of the volume which are outlined in the section introductions.

The inclusion of a range of very diverse chapters is intentional, as we endeavour to give voice and value to the experiences of various knowledgeable and able individuals who serve the field of early childhood. We are committed to listening to and valuing all these voices – those who come directly from practice and those of academics and researchers. We want to democratise knowledge and explore new practices, new ideas and new challenges, as these are articulated by all stakeholders in the field of early childhood.

The volume has a dual purpose: (1) the applicability of discussed practices and (2) challenging thinking and ideas. The reader will find chapters from which the intention is that they gather some ideas about how to do things; others might inspire an exploration of different approaches.

Some chapters have been written by non-native English speaking authors. As editors, we have attempted to streamline concepts and terminology used in the English literature. However, we acknowledge that this was not always easy without misrepresenting the concepts behind the terminology. We would expect that the reader will appreciate the cultural/local nuances which may result.

Each chapter of the book starts with an overview and concludes with questions for discussion. It also includes recommended further reading, which is **emboldened** in the reference lists.

Summary

In this introductory chapter, we have attempted to set out the scene for what follows in this volume. We have provided an overview of key supranational policies and referred briefly to research that has been the cornerstone for increasing demand and provision of early childhood education and care. We have highlighted some of the polarised debates raised about professional practice as a result of such policies and argued that most of the practice presents a variation within the extreme polar opposites of the debate, attempting to negotiate conflicting and competing discourses. Finally, we have presented the structure of the book, offering a coherent thread of argument for its compilation and format.

Questions for discussion

1. What are the main influences on your professional practice?
2. What cultural beliefs and values underpin your professional practice?
3. Are there any conflicting and competing messages that impact on your professional practice and, if so, how?

Note

[1] Award Number CSG: 55280.

References and suggested further reading

Entries in bold are further reading.

Bredekamp, S. (1987) *Developmentally Appropriate Practice in Early Childhood Programmes*. Washington, DC: NAEYC.

Brooker, L. and Edwards, S. (2010) *Engaging Play*. Maidenhead: Open University Press.

Bruner, J. (1990) *Acts of Meaning*. Cambridge, MA: Harvard University Press.

Cannella, G.S. (2005) Reconceptualizing the Field (of Early Care and Education): If 'Western' Child Development is a Problem, Then What Do we Do? In N. Yelland (ed.) *Critical Issues in Early Childhood Education*. Maidenhead: Open University Press.

Commission of the European Communities (2006) *Communication from the Commission to the Council and the European Parliament: Efficiency and Equity in European Education and Training Systems (COM 2006, 481 final of 8 September)*, Brussels. Available online at http://ec.europa.eu/education/policies/2010/doc/comm481_en.pdf (accessed 22 March 2011).

Dahlberg, G., Moss, P. and Pence, A. (2007) *Beyond Quality in Early Childhood Education and Care: Languages of Evaluation*. London: Routledge.

Dewey, J. (1997) *Experience and Education*. New York: Touchstone. (Initial publication in 1938 by Kappa Delta Pi.)

Duhn, I. (2006) The Making of the Global Citizen: Traces of Cosmopolitanism in the New Zealand Early Childhood Curriculum, Te Whariki. *Contemporary Issues in Early Childhood,* 1(3): 191–202. Available online at: www.wwwords. co.uk/ciec/content/pdfs/7/issue7_3.asp#1 (accessed 23 March 2011).

European Commission (2007) *Common European Principles for Teacher Competencies and Qualifications*. Available online at: www.see-educoop.net/education_ in/pdf/01-en_principles_en.pdf (accessed 23 March 2011).

Eurydice Network (EACEA) (2009) *Tackling Social and Cultural Inequalities Through Early Childhood Education and Care in Europe*. Brussels: Education, Audiovisual and Culture Executive Agency.

Freire, P. (1998) *Pedagogy of the Oppressed* (20th anniversary edition). New York: Continuum.

Heckman, J.J. (2006) *Investing in Disadvantaged Young Children is an Economically Efficient Policy*. Available online at: www.ced.org/images/library/reports/education/ early_education/report_2006prek_heckman.pdf (accessed 23 March 2011).

InterGuide (2002) *A Practical Guide to Implement Intercultural Education at Schools*, Sócrates Comenius 2.1 INTER Project, no. 106223-CP-1–2002-1-COMENIUS-C21. Available online at: http://inter.up.pt/docs/guide.pdf (accessed 23 March 2011).

Katz, L. (1999) *Curriculum Disputes in Early Childhood Education*. ERIC Digest (ERIC Identifier: EDO-PS-99–13). Available online at: www.ericdigests.org/2000–3/ disputes.htm (accessed 23 March 2011).

Keeley, B. (2007) *Human Capital: How What you Know Shapes your Life*. Paris: OECD.

Kilburn, R.M. and Karoly, A.L. (2008) *The Economics of Early Childhood Policy: What the Dismal Science Has to Say About Investing in Children*. Santa Monica, CA: RAND Corporation.

Lave, J. and Wenger, E. (1991) *Situated Learning: Legitimate Peripheral Participation*. Cambridge: Cambridge University Press.

MacNaughton, G. (2005) *Doing Foucault in Early Childhood Studies: Applying Poststructural Ideas*. Abingdon: Routledge.

Moss, P. (2008) Meeting Across the Paradigmatic Divide. In S. Farquhar and P. Fitzsimons (eds) *Philosophy of Early Childhood Education: Transforming Narratives*. Malden, MA: Blackwell.

Moyles, J. (2002) Passion, Paradox and Professionalism in Early Years Education. *Early Years: Journal of International Research and Development,* 21(2): 81–95.

Moyles, J. (2010) *Thinking About Play: Developing a Reflective Approach*. Maidenhead: Open University Press.

Oberhuemer, P., Schreyer, I. and Neuman, M.J. (2010) *Professionals in Early Childhood Education and Care Systems: European Profiles and Systems*. Opladen and Farmington Hills, MI: Verlag Barbara Budrich.

OECD (2001) *Starting Strong: Early Childhood Education and Care*. Paris: OECD.

OECD (2006) *Starting Strong II: Early Childhood Education and Care*. Paris: OECD.

Osgood, J. (2006) Professionalism and Performativity: The Feminist Challenge Facing Early Years Practitioners. *Early Years: An International Journal of Research and Development,* 26(2): 187–99.

Papatheodorou, T. (2010) Being, Belonging and Becoming: Some Worldviews of Early Childhood in Contemporary Curricula, *Forum on Public Policy Online*, 2 (September). Available online at: http://forumonpublicpolicy.com/spring2010.vol2010/spring2010archive/papatheodorou.pdf (accessed 23 March 2011).

Rosenthal, M. (2003) Quality in Early Childhood Education and Care. *European Early Childhood Education Research Journal*, 11(2): 101–16.

Schweinhart, L.J. (1994) *Lasting Benefits of Preschool Programs. ERIC Digest* (ERIC Identifier: ED 365478). Available online at: www.ericdigests.org/1994/lasting.htm (accessed 23 March 2008).

Schweinhart, L.J., Barnes, H. and Weikart, D. (1993) *Significant Benefits: The High/Scope Perry Preschool Study Through Age 27*. Monograph of the High/Scope Educational Research Foundation, 10. Ypsilanti, MI: High-Scope Educational Research Foundation.

Shonkoff, J. and Phillips, D. (2000) *From Neurons to Neighborhoods: The Science of Early Childhood Development*. Washington, DC: National Academy Press.

Sylva, K., Melhuish, E.C., Sammons, P., Siraj-Blatchford, I. and Taggart, B. (2004) *The Effective Provision of Pre-School Education (EPPE) Project Technical Paper 12*. London: DFES/Institute of Education, University of London.

UNESCO (1990) *World Declaration on Education for All and Framework for Action to Meet Basic Learning Needs* (adopted by the World Conference on Education for All: Meeting Basic Learning Needs, Jomtien, Thailand, 5–9 March). Paris: UNESCO. Available online at: www.unesco.org/education/pdf/JOMTIE_E.PDF (accessed 23 March 2011).

UNESCO (2000) *World Education Forum: The Dakar Framework for Action. Education for All: Meeting Our Collective Commitments* (adopted by the World Education Forum, 26–28 April). Paris: UNESCO. Available online at: http://unesdoc.unesco.org/images/0012/001211/121147e.pdf (accessed 23 March 2011).

UNESCO (2003) *Statement on Intercultural Dialogue*. Available online at: www.unesco.org/en/dialogue/intercultural-dialogue (accessed 25 March 2011).

UNICEF (1989) *United Nations Convention on the Rights of the Child*. Available online at: www2.ohchr.org/english/law/crc.htm (accessed 23 March 2011).

UNICEF (2008) *Childcare in Transition: A League Table of Early Childhood Education and Care in Economically Advanced Countries*. Florence, Italy: Innocenti Research Centre.

Woodhead, M. (2006) Changing Perspectives on Early Childhood: Theory, Research and Policy. Background paper prepared for the *Education for All Global Monitoring Report 2007 – Strong Foundations: Early Childhood Care and Education* (ref. 2007/ED/EFA/MRT/PI/33/REV). Paris: UNESCO. Available online at: http://unesdoc.unesco.org/images/0014/001474/147499e.pdf (accessed 23 March 2011).

Wylie, C. and Thompson, J. (2003) The Long Term Contribution of Early Childhood Education to Children's Performance – Evidence from New Zealand. *International Journal of Early Years Education*, 11(1): 69–78.

Part 1

Children's Learning Cultures

Introduction

Janet Moyles and Theodora Papatheodorou

The Education for All: Strong Foundations Report states: 'Early childhood sets the foundations for life … [it] is a highly sensitive period marked by rapid transformations in physical, cognitive, social and emotional development' (UNESCO, 2006: 7). It is also a period in which children – already undergoing massive changes physiologically and cognitively – acquire understanding of different cultures. From the culture of the home and community, children in many parts of the world move into a culture of early childhood education and care (ECEC) which requires significant new learning if the child is to adapt to the new context and all its underlying complexities and expectations.

The culture of settings and schools requires quite different understandings from both children and their parents/carers; they have to be acculturated into such aspects as routines, expectations of the people involved, what is permitted and what is not, how one is supposed to behave in this new context and whether the children can play!

Children's play is a universal phenomenon in development and learning that is culturally grounded and is the basis of many early childhood education settings and curricula. As Wood says:

> By emphasizing the socially and culturally situated nature of learning, children can be understood as active participants in cultural communities … Participation also provokes situated agency – children actively engage in the social construction of their own identities and subjectivities. (2010: 11)

Needless to say, observing and interpreting children's learning and play differs from culture to culture because of individual norms within cultures. For example, the individualistic nature of western cultures means children are expected to achieve as individuals whereas the more collective societies of, for example, the Far East and Africa advocate more collective outcomes.

We all have a culturally shaped mindset. It is clear that how we interpret children's play, learning and development differs from culture to culture (Brooker and Edwards, 2010). Solitary play, for example, was once thought to be the province of only very young children but the culture of today's media-based societies means that this is historically and culturally outmoded because all ages of children now seem to spend much solitary time on computers and gadgets (Marsh, 2004).

That said, it has also long been acknowledged that children's learning is multi-dimensional: children learn through every aspect of their senses and this enables them to make meaning of the experiences they encounter in an ongoing way. Heuristic play is just one such form: 'heuristic' means helping to find out or discover; proceeding by trial and error, which is described by Esgate and Groome as 'if you can think of it, it must be important' (2004: 12). Such importance is afforded particularly in the first chapter constituting this section, written by Sue Gascoyne about her experiences of developing a sensory play continuum, used in the UK but with implications for global ECEC practice. Sue begins with the concept of treasure baskets and heuristic play as the basic sensory stimulation for babies and toddlers but then develops the argument for use with older children to encourage creativity, problem solving and trial and error learning. She explores the research and practitioner training she has undertaken to verify her assertions regarding the need for high quality sensory experiences for children.

In Chapter 2, these experiences are broadened to include outdoor sensory experiences for children through a chapter about Forest School and the importance of a culture of outdoor play provision in several European countries, written by Sara Knight. This experience provides yet another different cultural context for learning, with further norms, rules and considerations, for example to do with safety and risk but also learning about the natural environment and sustainability. The Forest School context also provides extended and different opportunities for children to play and problem-solve. Under Article 31 of the UN *Conventions on the Rights of the Child*, (UNCRC) play – and in this case outdoor play – is the right of every child and something, one could argue, that we ignore at our peril given the current challenges in the western world with regard to children's health and well-being (Albon, 2011), as well as their capacity as capable learners.

This takes us neatly to Chapter 3, in which Maulfry Worthington writes absorbingly about her research into graphicacy in early childhood, acknowledging the centrality of the child's perspective that enables each child to explore a complex interplay of meanings in ways that are powerful and personally relevant. Graphicacy, in this instance, is described as a concept similar to 'mark making' in early childhood education where these 'marks' incorporate children's multi-literacies, crossing all curricular barriers. They are the 'graphics' which children produce and which convey great meaning. Maulfry stresses that this perspective rests on a poststructural view of the child as a co-constructor of knowledge, culture and identity and recognises all children as capable and intelligent with the support of informed, committed and reflective practitioners (Moyles, 2010). This chapter shows clearly how the culture of formalised learning differs greatly from the culture of child-oriented and initiated learning, the 'situated agency' outlined by Wood above. Many international countries are now recognising the agency of the child since the UNCRC, and Maulfry's findings are applicable internationally.

That children are agents in their own learning and are instrumental in developing their own cultures of learning is evidenced in the final chapter of this section by Mallika Kanyal and Linda Cooper. Fascinating research carried out by these two writers delved into 5- and 6-year-olds' perceptions of their socially and culturally different school experiences and children's perspectives. Being carried out in India and England, the study offers a view of differences and similarities in practices and children's perceptions of their environment. The chapter also explores a range of methods for gathering child-focused data which has worked across cultures and shows links with the previous chapter.

In the next section, we move the focus to the cultures of pedagogy that support children's play, learning and development.

References

Albon, D. (2011) Promoting Children's Health and Well-being in Primary Schools. In J. Moyles, J. Georgeson and J. Payler (eds) *Beginning Teaching Beginning Learning* (4th edn). Maidenhead: Open University Press.

Brooker, L. and Edwards, S. (2010) *Engaging Play*. Maidenhead: Open University Press.

Esgate, A. and Groome, D. (2004) *An Introduction to Applied Cognitive Psychology*. New York: Psychology Press.

Marsh, J. (ed.) (2004) *Popular Culture, Media and Digital Literacies in Early Childhood*. London: Routledge.

Moyles, J. (2010) *Thinking about Play: Developing a Reflective Approach*. Maidenhead: Open University Press.

UNESCO (2006) *Education for All Global Monitoring Report: Strong Foundations*. Available online at: http://unesdoc.unesco.org/images/0014/001477/147794e.pdf (accessed 14 March 2011).

Wood, E. (2010) Reconceptualizing the Play–Pedagogy Relationship: From Control to Complexity. In L. Brooker and S. Edwards (eds) *Engaging Play*. Maidenhead: Open University Press.

1

Seeing the wood for the trees: adults' roles in supporting sensory play

Sue Gascoyne

Overview

Over the last century, Steiner, Dewey, Montessori and Malauzzi have all made the case for the numerous benefits of sensory play. With evidence that children's access to sensory play is in decline, the treasure basket can potentially offer a tool for increasing sensory stimulation, especially when the three stages of play set out in the *Sensory Play Continuum* are followed. Treasure baskets are used for simple exploration, problem solving and domestic role play (see Goldschmied and Jackson, 2004); older children use them in pretend and goal-oriented symbolic play, where the objects became something new, reflecting and portraying children's ideas and thoughts; when combined with other resources, the potential for creativity and problem solving significantly increases. Adults have a crucial, yet subtle role in maximising quality sensory play opportunities from play with a treasure basket across all three stages of the *Sensory Play Continuum*. This chapter explores whether treasure baskets can help compensate for children's limited access to multi-sensory experiences and, if so, what role adults have.

Picture a children's play area on a wet and cold day with a group of toddlers excitedly jumping in muddy puddles. Their delight is apparent but what remains a mystery is what each individual child is most enjoying or gaining from this sensory-rich experience – be it the satisfyingly noisy splash, the striking cold feel of the water gushing into their wellies, the swirly patterns as their feet stir the mud into the puddle, feeling 'at one' with nature, exploring and discovering 'cause and effect', the liberating feeling of space, time and freedom or a myriad of other unique sensations and experiences. The author observed this group for approximately 20 minutes: the puddle sustained their interest while some nearby play equipment remained conspicuously empty. The children were 'enjoying some fresh air' with enlightened childminders but what of their parents' reactions to their mud-encrusted clothes later that day? Some may have reminisced about similar experiences from their childhood, others may have reflected upon the amazing learning potential of a puddle and still others may have simply sighed at the thought of all that washing! This snapshot succinctly illustrates two key strands to this chapter: (1) the importance and appeal of sensory-rich play for children and (2) the role of adults in supporting and encouraging such experiences.

The benefits of sensory stimulation

Ask an adult about their typical childhood play memories and chances are they might reflect upon days spent exploring, climbing trees, building dens, lighting fires and making mud pies and rose petal perfume! If you can relate to this happily, you are not alone: these were just some of the vivid childhood play memories that 146 parents and practitioners retold as part of the national Sensory Play Research project (Papatheodorou, 2010).

Those lucky enough to share such memories will probably understand why children get so much from sensory-rich play and why it is important. Watch children's concentration, focus, determination, problem solving and social skills as they play with natural materials. Not only is it hugely satisfying for children but it's often free, requiring little or no preparation. The value of sensory experiences (both inside and outdoors) and benefits for children's learning have been highlighted by a raft of respected philosophers and educationalists over more than a century (for example, Steiner, Dewey, Montessori and Malaguzzi).

We now know that the human brain is made up of billions of cells called neurons. These remain at rest until a stimulus occurs when an electrical signal passes from one neuron to another, relaying information about everything we see, hear, taste, touch and smell (Wartik and Carlson-Finnerty, 1993). When we experience a sensory input, a new 'pathway' is formed. The more times these connections are made and reinforced, the thicker this 'pathway' becomes, and the faster signals travel, helping us to think and recall more accurately and swiftly. Picture a multi-pack of plant seeds. The scene on the packet is bursting with verdant foliage, colourful flowers and a wide variety of exotic vegetables. Within the packet are several tiny envelopes, each containing a different seed variety. Like the neurons in a baby or child's brain, each tiny seed is packed with amazing potential but unless the seeds are planted and regularly nourished with water, sunlight and nutrients from the soil, they will not grow. Even if a seedling forms, without constant nourishment this will wither and die. So, too, it is only through repeated sensory stimulation of the brain cells and through connections being made with other parts of the brain, to transform the sensory stimulation into action and ultimately feedback (MacIntyre, 2010: 87), that neurons and pathways survive the ruthless pruning that takes place in the human brain and children's talents have the opportunity to blossom and grow. Just suppose that one of the tiny envelopes of seeds is accidentally left in the packet and not planted alongside the other seeds. The seeds themselves may be perfect but they will not yield magnificent vegetables or flowers without the required conditions and nourishment. So it is with the brain: a child's eyes may be perfect in every way but if the necessary connections have not been made with the ocular part of the brain, they will be incapable of actually seeing. The importance of sensory experiences as a mechanism for establishing these vital connections could not be clearer.

From birth, children use all their senses to make meaning from the world around them. Our brains are constantly decoding patterns (in sensory information) to help us understand the world, shaping children's brains and influencing development and learning. As we will see in Chapter 2 in this volume, sensory play experiences like Forest Schools offer children the freedom to become 'discoverers' (Tomkins and Tunnicliffe, 2007: 155; see also Knight, 2009) and the opportunity to experience and experiment. Resources featuring colour, pattern, creativity, physical involvement and fun will appeal to both hemispheres of the brain, enhancing learning. Sensory stimulation is great for kinaesthetic, tactile, visual and auditory learners, so given that a good treasure basket offers all these attributes, it's not hard to imagine some of the fascination and delight they promise.

Crawley and Eacott (2006) made the links between memory recollections and early sensory experiences, particularly visual, touch and smell. A fact supported by the Sensory Play research as 68% of adults' most vivid childhood memories involved sensory-rich play outdoors (Papatheodorou, 2010). Closely related to this is the link between the development of language and sensory experiences. Crowe (1984: 39) claims that 'Words are connectors ... children's senses cry out to be used first to provide the experiences that they will later need in order to connect. Children must feel the world, listen to it, see it, taste it, smell it, "know" it. That takes time and a great deal of silent investigation in peace and privacy'. Memory is clearly an integral factor in giving meaning to words and in helping to link together the complex architecture of the brain. A young child playing with a treasure basket (see below) may discover that some things feel cold to touch but can warm up if held and only much later attach the words 'cold', 'warm' and 'metal' to the experience.

Given the importance and appeal of sensory play to children and our vivid memories of these as adults, it is striking that nearly 82% of adults surveyed felt that play has changed. Their prevailing childhood memories included: *being* outdoors, *feeling* and *making* things, contrasting strongly with the finding that, nowadays, children's toys are predominantly plastic, manufactured and commercialised, with screen-based entertainment increasingly dominant (Papatheodorou, 2010). When combined with more structured, age-segregated lives and less free play outdoors, young children's exposure to multi-sensory experiences appears to be declining.

Play with treasure baskets – a sensory-rich resource

Plentiful access to freely available natural resources is obviously paramount but sensory play isn't just about getting mucky and playing outside. The carefully selected items within a treasure basket can happily engage young babies to primary age children and children with special educational needs (SEN). Adults may struggle to see the appeal of this resource – a sturdy basket, containing about 50 objects, picked for maximum sensory appeal, including a mix of shapes, colours and objects that move in different ways and have different weights, textures and properties (see Figure 1.1). But children absorbed in play for an hour or longer suggests something special is taking place. When working in orphanages in 1940s Italy, Elinor Goldschmied observed babies' fascination for household objects – the things commonly found in a utensil drawer, and the idea of a treasure basket, for babies, was born.

A treasure basket will normally include:

Small cardboard box, mini board book	Teaspoon, wooden spoon
Pastry, shaving, mini bottle, nail brush	Wooden eggcup, napkin ring, pegs, juicer, coaster
Metal tin, thick length of chain, measuring spoons/bowl, coaster, whisk	Mini glass jam jar, mini flower pot
Pine cone, stone, shell, dried whole orange, wicker ball, loofah, large cork	Bean bag, knitted ball, crocheted mat, flannel

Figure 1.1 Objects commonly found in a treasure basket

A treasure basket of 'open-ended' resources which can be played with in countless ways and literally grow with a child, clearly resonates with the *Reggio Emilia* (Rinaldi, 2006) approach. Key to its success is the careful sourcing of stimulating objects and allowing children time and space to explore these fully and freely. The adults' role in treasure basket play is to sit nearby, attentive, responsive and unobtrusive. The baby or child gets to make their own choices about which objects to explore and how, without interference or feeling encumbered by a right or wrong way of playing. Although originally conceived for babies, there is growing recognition of their value for children across the ages as well as for children and adults with SEN. Great for developing literacy and numeracy, encouraging sorting and learning about the properties of materials – for example, hot and cold, heavy and light, big and small, floats and sinks – a treasure basket introduces surprisingly sophisticated concepts that help unlock secrets to how the world works.

The research highlighted children's particular enjoyment of exploring and investigating the different textures, smells and noises associated with a treasure basket and their great interest and focus. Tomkins and Tunnicliffe (2007: 150) note that children are most attracted to items which have a 'novel nature or appearance, have aesthetic attributes, display some responsiveness to them, engage with their previous experience, or elicit affective feeling'. Clearly, a carefully sourced treasure basket provides babies and children with sensory-rich stimulation and a deeply satisfying experience from the opportunity to explore and to discover things for themselves (Arnold, 2003). It may also compensate for children's limited access to multi-sensory experiences and even prepare them to get the most from other sensory-rich opportunities.

The benefits of treasure baskets

Free play with a treasure basket is believed to offer a host of benefits for children across the ages, including:

- developing fine motor skills and hand–eye coordination
- stimulating all the senses, including the lesser known proprioceptive and kinaesthetic senses, necessary for providing positional feedback
- creating vital connections in the brain
- encouraging exploration and discovery
- increasing concentration and focus
- developing shoulder, arm and back muscles
- building confidence and self-esteem
- firing imagination
- encouraging problem solving and creativity
- helping develop speech and language.

So how does a collection of ordinary objects become a basket of awe and wonder? It's the very fact that the basket doesn't include any toys, and like that muddy puddle or the proverbial cardboard box, every treasure is packed with open-ended play potential. So a knitted purse becomes a bag, a dolly's hat, a submarine or even a hot air balloon basket. These open-ended resources with no right or wrong way of being played with, encourage children to explore, problem solve, create and discover to their hearts' content. Although patterns of play can be seen, there are differences too, with babies playing for over an hour simply with one object, be it a woven maize coaster or a heavy metal chain; toddlers repeatedly transporting a metal chain between a tin and bowl; or older children preparing 'magnificent meals'.

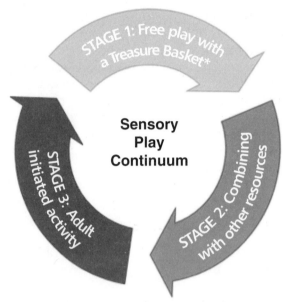

Figure 1.2 The Sensory Play Continuum
*Fits with original Goldschmied concept (Goldschmied and Jackson, 2004)

The Sensory Play Continuum

For Elinor Goldschmied, the treasure basket was perfect for babies not yet mobile, with limited scope for choosing what they play with. However, a greater potential of treasure baskets can be seen if one observes children of different ages playing side by side. For the older child, the basket of disparate objects offers intrigue, exploration and problem-solving opportunities. A baby might focus on 'What is this object like?' while an older child moves quickly to 'What can I do with it?' and 'What can it become?' This behaviour, and in particular a return to mouthing (the earliest form of problem solving), is not unusual when older children encounter unfamiliar objects. Based on observations of treasure basket play, the Sensory Play Continuum has been developed (Gascoyne, 2008).

The continuum is a fluid and transitory process, with iterative cycles of repetition and flexibility over the order in which the stages are accessed. For example, one reception class teacher introduced the treasure basket via an adult-initiated activity (i.e. Stage 3) in order to model appropriate use and respect for the resources. The children then progressed to free play. Similarly, other practitioners have used the activity structure to enable older children or those with SEN to access the resource. Through play with peers and familiarisation with the objects, they then play with the objects freely.

The three stages of the Continuum (see Figure 1.3) are a tool for increasing sensory-rich play opportunities and helping adults to stay detached. The stages are indicative of how children play with a treasure basket and are not prescriptive. Central to the Continuum is the hypothesis that a child's play may vary not just because of their age and developmental needs but also in terms of how the treasure basket is presented, i.e. the stage of the Continuum. Unlike other forms of heuristic play characterised by lots of similar objects, a treasure basket presents richly diverse objects in close proximity, providing multiple challenges and problem-solving opportunities. Similarly, the use of the objects in an unexpected way, for example with another resource such as sand, water or magnets in Stage 2 or as part of an adult-initiated activity in Stage 3, helps to 're-frame' the resources.

Figure 1.3 The three stages of the Sensory Play Continuum

The following three observations illustrate how a child (R, aged 2 years and 1 month) played with a treasure basket at each of the three stages of the Continuum. Attention is drawn to the changing role of the adult through-out.

Stage 1 – Free Play with a Treasure Basket

Context
The treasure basket was positioned in the book corner where R particularly liked to sit.

Practitioner observation
R picked up objects one at a time, looked at them, waved them and placed them next to him. He chatted to himself whilst doing this. The words were mainly unrecognisable, but occasionally they were recognisable words such as 'ball'. All his chatter was very animated with a range of intonation.

He then moved on to playing with objects together. He picked up the pan, put the metal whisk in the pan and then tried other metal objects together. He tried to put the wooden whisk into the pan – this didn't fit so he went back to emptying and investigating objects randomly one at a time.

Two other children joined. R left the treasure basket then quickly returned and continued emptying objects one at a time. He then started reading the mini book to himself. When he finished reading the book, he said 'bye bye book' and continued emptying objects one at a time from the basket, each time chatting to himself as if explaining what he had got or was doing.

Another child joined – no interaction between children. R continued investigating objects and placing them next to him. R returned to the book, put it back in the treasure basket when he had finished reading it, then put the other objects back in the basket, chatting as if he was naming the objects as he did it. R left the activity and went to play in the home corner.

Learning points and adults' roles

This session is characterised by a good range of vocabulary, verbalising, concentration and focus. Examples of domestic role play and pretend play were evident as was problem solving, as R discovered that some objects didn't fit and tried other objects instead. The photos suggest that R 'sorted' the objects into different piles but his commentary gave no indication of their meaning or relevance. R appears to be commenting on his play, for his own ends – private speech (Vygotsky, 1986) – rather than engaging in conversation. The practitioner's knowledge of R and his preference for playing with books, influenced where and how the treasure basket was offered.

Stage 2 – Combining with Sand

Context

The session was observed by an experienced nursery practitioner who placed a treasure basket containing most of the objects next to the sand tray. There were no other resources in the sand, however these were in containers next to the sand where children could have freely accessed them as usual.

Child C (aged 2 years and 8 months) very rarely plays in the sand tray, preferring the mark-making area and small world where he generally plays without any commentary or communication with others, however he has good vocabulary and willingly talks to adults when they initiate conversation or asks for approval from adults.

Practitioner observation

9:45   Two children came to the sand tray.

R chose the pan, metal egg cup and wooden spoon: he tried filling both the pan and egg cup with sand using the wooden spoon. R put the peg into the pan, then picked up the tin and attempted to place it on top of the objects in the pan. He played in silence, not attempting to communicate with me, other children or make any utterances during his play. The other children were talking during play. R then got the whisk, saying 'mix, mix' several times.

9:50   Child C joined the other two in the sand tray. He attempted to fill the metal egg cup several times before choosing the jar to fill.

R got the jar, attempted to put the whisk inside, abandoned the whisk when it did not fit, then tried the tin lid before finding the jar lid and successfully put it on top of the jar. He then got the pan and brush, saying 'mixing'.

9:55   R left the sand tray and went to play with the construction toys. Child C then spent a further 50 minutes playing with the resources in a range of ways:

- filling the metal containers with sand and using the brush to carefully brush the sand
- play changed to pretend play and he started to comment on his own play. He filled the metal egg cup with sand, saying 'wait a minute need egg'. Then filling the pan with sand: 'making tea now'. He went on to fill the tin with sand and showed me, saying: 'Sand inside of it, see'
- using the pastry brush to brush the sand off the sides of the sand tray

(Continued)

(Continued)

and off his hands, repeating 'brush, brush, brush', then singing 'brush, brush, brush it off, it clean now, it not got any sand on it anymore'

- burying objects in the sand, saying 'where's it gone?', then finding it and saying, 'here it is'.

The session eventually drew to an end as the rest of the room was tidied up.

Learning points and adults' roles

The almost absence of language contrasts markedly with the previous session where R commented throughout his play. The addition of sand may account for his play in silence (possibly a sign of deep concentration). In fact, this stage was typically found to be the most creative stage of play. Interestingly, C's play was also noteworthy as he played in a focused way for 70 minutes, never needing an adult to sustain his play. This is all the more remarkable given his age and the fact that he was playing with sand, a medium with which he rarely chooses to play. Several of his actions – for example, filling the tin with a spoon, smoothing the top, using the brush in the sand – bear striking similarities with those of other children observed playing with a treasure basket and sand. Both R's and C's play were experimental, involving much trial and error as they explored what objects would fit or work for the task they seemingly had set. This is typical of other sessions observed both at Stage 1 and 2 of the Continuum, where the child appears to have set themselves a challenge, be it tossing a chain in a pot or fitting an object inside another, and perseveres with this without frustration. This type of explorative play was also described by Goldschmied and Jackson (2004: 120–1) when reflecting upon heuristic play.

Both R's and C's play evolves into pretend play, perhaps showing Hughes' stages of play (2006) in accelerated fashion. C creates his own song mirroring his actions and then appears to invent his own game of hiding the objects. Another observation of 4-year-olds revealed more games. The three children filled a mini flower pot with sand and, on discovering that the sand had disappeared (through the seldom noticed hole), developed a game of 'who can run the furthest around the garden before the sand disappears'. Although apparently playing independently, Child C communicates what he is doing to both the practitioner and other children. In fact, the practitioner remarked upon how C was very vocal, commenting on his own play.

Stage 3 – Adult-initiated Activity

Context

The *Huff Puff Houses* activity was selected with R in mind although other children initially joined in. All the children joined in with the huff, puff and blow your house down and enjoyed blowing during the story.

Practitioner observation

R started helping sort the objects (to make the three houses) but quickly went back to the story poster and started retelling the story in his own words, pointing to all the pigs, naming them and showing me that the wolf had fallen down. He repeated 'bang' and clapped at the picture of the wooden house falling down.

He then started playing with the treasure basket toys as he had done in previous observations, getting the pan and whisk, saying 'mix, mix'. His play with the treasure basket toys changed compared to previous observations he seemed to link his play with the story. He placed the felt toy on top of the loofah, saying 'night, night', and pointed to the picture of the wolf lying on the floor at the end of the story.

He then found the mini book in the basket, started reading it and naming objects in the pictures. He then handed it to me to read to him. He returned to the story poster pointing to pictures and retelling the story to himself before leaving the area.

Learning points and adults' roles

The practitioner picked an activity about a book to build upon R's special interest. The relevance of this is borne out by the recurring theme and subsequent social sharing of the book. Crucially, the practitioner responded flexibly when R changed the focus. Although the activity itself did not sustain R's interest, it does appear to act as a catalyst for enjoying and re-enacting the story on another level. R's focus shifts from the story to domestic role play, back to the story (this time using the objects), to the mini book, before finally retelling the story. Although R's focus appears to flit, the treasure basket/Huff Puff activity remain common threads throughout. R revealed great confidence and mastery in remembering and retelling the story, and again was very vocal. Examples of domestic role play, pretend play and highly creative 'compositional play' (Papatheodorou, 2010: 27) were evident as R linked the objects to the story and used a felt 'gingerbread person' to represent the wolf and a piece of loofah for a bed.

Emerging themes

Several key themes emerged from the research, many of which are supported by observations generally:

Simple to complex play

Play becomes increasingly complex with children's age/developmental level and familiarity with the resource. Children are frequently seen moving from single-object play to more complex play with multiple objects (Garvey, 1977). However, even sessions featuring problem solving and pretend play involved very few objects. In an hour-long session, a 3-year-old used just a few simple objects. Similarly, three 4-year-olds generated exceptional problem solving, peer mentoring, creativity and scientific exploration through play with sand and just two objects. There is also evidence that the Continuum functions in 'multiple cycles of actions' whereby the experience from Stage 3 is internalised to lead to free play (Stage 1) and play with a combination of other materials and resources (Stage 2). This was especially true when other children were involved where there was 'evidence of peer (subtle and unconscious) facilitation' (Papatheodorou, 2010: 34). For example, in one pre-school observation (not part of the research), a treasure basket was offered to a girl with separation anxiety to occupy and distract her when her mother left. Not only did the treasure basket totally and happily absorb her for about an hour but, after being joined by a group of peers using the objects for pretend play, her play changed significantly from single-item exploration to using multiple objects for domestic role play.

Concentration and focus

In several of the sessions, play was 'moved on' by practitioners and not allowed to take its natural course. Where this did evolve, extended focus and concentration were evident. In one session, an 8-month-old playing with the treasure basket and sand 'ignored other children crawling through the sand tray and continued spooning'. She continued, 'attempt[ing] to spoon around another child sat in the sand tray and then [finally] moved away'. Although this session was truncated, this child, like so many others observed, displayed amazing levels of focus and concentration.

Language and communication

The effect of treasure basket play on language is an area worth further investigation. An 8-month-old babbled excitedly when playing with the basket in Stage 1; was quiet in Stage 2; and was described as laughing and chortling in Stage 3. Similarly, R babbled incessantly in Stage 1, with some decipherable words; was largely silent in Stage 2; and verbalised continuously in Stage 3. Compare this with C, normally quiet during play, who commentated and communicated eloquently at Stage 2 and some interesting language responses are evident.

Imagination, creativity and problem solving

Problem solving emerged as a key theme throughout many of the 77 observations – from mouthing of objects; experiments with gravity, trial and error, cause and effect; discovering different properties (such as the need to add water to sand) and the effects of change. In all cases, children were deeply absorbed in their endeavours. On its own, a treasure basket was used for exploration, problem solving and domestic role play. Older children used the objects in pretend and goal-oriented symbolic play, where they were used to produce something new, reflecting and portraying children's ideas and thoughts. In some instances, 'compositional play' was evident where 'the synthesis and composition of resources portrayed something new that went beyond the original qualities and attributes of the resources' (Papatheodorou, 2010: 27). Simple, open-ended resources like treasure baskets are powerful agents for firing children's imagination and creativity. The fact that there are no right or wrong ways of playing appears a huge contributory factor.

 Summary

By observing children playing, we gain a valuable insight into their interests, developmental levels, schemas and personalities – essentially what children enjoy doing and how. Children's propensity for imagination, problem solving, creativity and social skills are apparent from the exploration and play themes that emerge. Although we cannot yet quantify the value-added of children's play with a treasure basket, observations appear to support this. Perhaps of greater interest is not what children learn (most appear hard-wired to get what they need from sensory-rich play) but rather what we as adults can learn from them. Just like those childminders who made it possible for that muddy puddle to be fully and freely enjoyed, adults play a vital, albeit subtle role in supporting (or, conversely, limiting) sensory-rich play. In reflecting upon a fun winter walk through a wood, three children aged 4–10 years relayed how they'd enjoyed exploring, looking, listening, discovering, finding out, creating, imagining and challenging themselves: 'All the things that we do every day'. And what of adults' roles in this? Giving children the opportunity, space and time to engage in a wide range of experiences and, crucially, watching, listening and learning through children's eyes.

Questions for discussion

1. How best can you offer a play environment conducive to quality play, in terms of space, time, opportunities and mindset?

2. How can you select resources and activities which have meaning for children?

3. How can you support children's learning when you're not actively involved in the play?

4. How can you promote quality play with curriculum outcomes, rather than being curriculum driven?

References and suggested further reading

Entries in bold are further reading.

Arnold, C. (2003) *Observing Harry.* Buckingham: Open University Press.

Crawley, R.A. and Eacott, M.J. (2006) Memories of Early Childhood: Qualities of the Experience of Recollection. *Memory and Cognition*, 3(2): 287–94.

Crowe, B. (1984) *Play is a Feeling.* London: Allen and Unwin.

Garvey, C. (1977) *Play: The Developing Child.* Glasgow: Fontana/Open Books.

Gascoyne, S. (2008) *The Continuum of Sensory Play* (self-published).

Goldschmied, E. and Jackson, S. (2004) *People under Three: Young Children in Day Care.* London: Routledge.

Hughes, A. (2006) *Developing Play for the Under 3s: The Treasure Basket and Heuristic Play.* London: David Fulton.

Knight, S. (2009) *Forest Schools and Outdoor Learning in the Early Years.* London: Sage.

MacIntyre, C. (2010) *Play for Children with Special Needs: Supporting Children with Learning Differences, 3–9* (2nd edn). London: Routledge.

Papatheodorou, T. (2010) *Sensory Play.* Report submitted to Play to Z. Chelmsford: Anglia Ruskin University.

Rinaldi, C. (2006) *In Dialogue with Reggio Emilia: Listening, Researching and Learning.* London and New York: Routledge.

Tomkins, S. and Tunnicliffe, S.D. (2007) Nature Tables: Stimulating Children's Interest in Natural Objects. *Journal of Biological Education*, 41(4): 150–5.

Vygotsky, L.S. (1986) *Thought and Language* (translated by A. Kozulin). Cambridge, MA: MIT Press.

Wartik, N. and Carlson-Finnerty, L. (1993) *Memory and Learning.* New York: Chelsea House Publishers.

2

Valuing outdoor spaces: different models of outdoor learning in the early years

Sara Knight

Overview

For the first time in 2007, the new English Early Years Foundation Stage (EYFS) curriculum stated that outdoor spaces are as important to young children's learning as the indoor environment and that they should be outside for some part of every day. Forest School (FS) is impacting on early years provision in the UK, valuing an engagement with wilder spaces. It is still less pervasive than the *Friluftsliv* tradition is in Sweden and Norway (Dahle, 2003), or *Udeskøle* is in Denmark (Bentsen et al., 2009), which seem to symbolise a love of the environment embedded into the culture of those countries. In other countries, particularly the 'developed' ones, many academics and practitioners are concerned to re-engage children with natural places, seeing this as a link to health and well-being, as well as engaging children with issues around climate change and respect for the environment. In less 'developed' countries, many children still spend significant periods of the day outside and there is a tension between a desire for the formalisation of learning and a recognition of the value of what exists. This chapter examines the regard early years practitioners have across the world for outdoor provision in the early years.

Attitudes to the importance of outdoor play in the healthy development of young children have varied between countries and between times. The European traditions that probably started with Rousseau, Pestalozzi, Froebel and Steiner (Knight, 2009b: 62) have embedded, in some countries, a cultural norm that regards outdoor experiences as importance for all, and I will discuss *Friluftsliv* as one such tradition informing current practice in northern Europe.

It is interesting that outdoor play seems to have engaged the minds of educators and thinkers in the western world in the later half of the 19th century, at the point at which there was a population shift into urban settings (Knight, 2009: 3) and a subsequent drop in opportunities to utilise the outdoor environment as a natural part of family life. Thus, it seems to be that in societies where this shift occurred later or not at all, many children have maintained their connection to the outdoor environment, making explicit the link between outdoor spaces and healthy development. Formalising contact with the outdoor environment has not been necessary until creeping modernity in the shape of the electronic age has reached the youngest in those societies (Meade, 2006). I will discuss this below with reference to approaches in different countries.

The prevailing weather also seems to affect whether policy makers deem it appropriate to specify the need for outdoor experiences in early years settings, as the models of outdoor learning in the early years seem to be developed furthest in northern countries where adults might think that staying indoors would be preferable. So it is that, in Italy, the model developed by Montessori (Montessori UK, undated) and the *Reggio Emilia* approach (Maynard et al., 2008) emphasise the value of beautiful objects and the importance of natural materials without expressly linking these to outdoor spaces (Knight, 2009b: 63) and yet, on further reading, this link is apparently implicit. As these models are spreading in popularity, I will refer to them again.

An interesting thread linking these themes is the growing popularity for providing wilder play for young children, largely expressed in the UK through contact with Forest School (Knight, 2009), an ethos espousing managed risk and child-led contact with outdoor spaces. I will identify Forest School, *naturbørnehaven* and *Waldkinder* as examples of environments for wilder play.

The majority of the best quality settings in the UK, whatever methodology they espouse, now have gardens and/or wild spaces and sessions planned for those spaces. This is in a large part due to recent changes to the early years curricula in England, Scotland, Ireland and Wales. I will be discussing the first of these, and whether it is a governmental response to the winds of change or foresight on the part of the policy makers.

Alongside all of these traditions in early years care and education is a growing concern with academic standards being expressed in the media in some European countries. These seem to focus on standards of behaviour, of the development of speech and of formal education. This concern seems to be creating a three-way tension between a desire for progress, a recognition of the value of what exists and a desire to return to a more formal educational style at a younger age. In this debate, the quality of the education of our youngest children seems to be under threat. An appreciation of the value of play-based learning, including outdoor learning, seems to need to be defended again.

Outdoor play in the English Early Years Foundation Stage

The Early Years Foundation Stage is the first stage of the National Curriculum. It was reinvented in 2007 (and reviewed in 2010/2011) to include children of all ages from birth to 5 years old. It is intended to be play-based but still has learning goals, culminating in an Early Years Profile (QCA, 2003) which is used as a baseline for more formal schooling after children's 5th birthday. These two aspects can be in opposition when less able staff are trying to plan for play and plan for assessment simultaneously. It therefore came as a shock to some practitioners when the EYFS documentation contained a requirement that children should have access to the outdoors on a daily basis (DCSF, 2007a: 35).

Why the policy makers have taken this step is not fully explained in the EYFS statutory documentation but there is a practice sheet for practitioners (DCSF, 2007b) with links to theory and there has been an increasing amount of literature documenting the benefits of outdoor experiences. Concurrently, different disciplines such as health and social care have created a wave of pressure that has resulted in the current emphasis on providing outdoor spaces for all children and young people in England through the Play Strategy (DCSF, 2008a).

Educators and academics cite the work of pioneer Margaret McMillan (Bradburn, 1995), who took the writings of Steiner and applied them to ameliorate the environment for preschool children in the poor area of Deptford in London with good effect. She created nurseries that were gardens, green spaces in an industrialised area, demonstrating the positive effects they had on the development of those children. McMillan was a member of the then New Labour movement, which also started the Woodcraft Folk movement in 1925, an association for children and young people fostering social and emotional skills (see www.woodcraft.org.uk). Perhaps it is no coincidence that the new EYFS and the *Learning Outside the Classroom Manifesto* (DfES, 2006) were published during a Labour government. This early work, together with the popular methodologies of Montessori and *Reggio Emilia* mentioned above, constituted pressure from the academic perspective on early years provision.

Health professionals added another set of pressures around obesity (Ellaway et al., 2006) and around well-being (Knight, 2009a) and highlighted the need for regular exercise outside (Natural England, 2009). They drew on research from the health sector to highlight access to the outdoor environment as a key factor in addressing these issues (Knight, 2009a). In addition, Wilson (1984), an evolutionary biologist, argues that we have a genetic need to spend time in wild places, a need which he termed 'biophylia'.

Yet more pressure came from playworkers who, while focusing their attention on older children, were linking outdoor play to improving the behaviour of children and young people (SkillsActive, 2006). The 10-year Play Strategy then emerged in December 2008 (DCSF, 2008b, *Every Child a Talker*), the strategy focusing not just on the places where children play, including parks and green spaces, schools and children's centres, but also on communities and neighbourhoods, to make them more child-friendly. In its first two years, many local councils have taken the opportunities for funding to create better outdoor spaces for children. The pressures here included voices from the voluntary sector.

The impact on English early years provision has been to create an acceleration in training and publications, both on the development of spaces in settings, and on support for practitioners. For the children, there are more, and better, opportunities to get outside. It would seem that a governmental response to the winds of change has come from foresight on the part of those who influence the policy makers. Recent reports (Rose, 2009; Alexander, 2009) are recommending that some of these values are recognised in the curricula for 5–7-year-olds in England, as has already happened in Wales.

Friluftsliv in Norway, Sweden and Denmark

Other countries have traditions that were not as affected by an industrial revolution, in particular in Scandinavia. The deep cultural links between people and nature can be seen in their folk stories and the earliest expressions of religion, which have those links at their core. How they are maintained are accidents of history and geography. With populations spread more thinly and many industries linked to the land (for example, paper, hydro-electric power), the Scandinavian countries have kept closer links to their environment for longer (Dahle, 2003). In 1859, Ibsen coined the term *Friluftsliv* (fri = free, luft = air, liv = life) to describe the cultural expression of this link which is still an important movement today (Henderson and Vikander, 2007: 10). As Norway had been joined to Denmark from 1536 to 1814 and then to Sweden till 1905, these countries, too, have inherited this term, although its expression differs in different areas. The outcome of this for young children is that daycare in these countries includes the norms of access to the outdoor environment that we in the UK are aspiring to as a matter of course, and there are settings which offer more than this. For example, in *naturbørnehaven* (Knight, 2009b) in Denmark, children spend more time outdoors than in, and in all weathers (Bentsen et al., 2009).

In these countries, however, there is recognition that modern life is eroding this long-standing tradition. Research (Martensson et al., 2009) is helping practitioners to ensure that there is a conscious development of outdoor opportunities in preschool settings (Brügge, 2007).

The spread of outdoor play

Iceland and Finland share the same cultural links with *Friluftsliv* as the Scandinavian countries. The spread of the popularity of *Friluftsliv* to countries in Eastern Europe, such as Czechoslovakia, has been more recent (Martin et al., 2007). In Germany, a similar tradition has created *Waldkindergarten*, preschools whose link with the outdoors is similar to that described in Scandinavia above and to that of Forest School in the UK (Konijnendijk, 2008). My research points to similarities across the rest of northern Europe.

We have noted above how the traditions of Montessori and *Reggio Emilia* incorporate outdoor learning but in the southern part of Europe outdoor provision is not given the same focus, which I suspect is a combination of a concern for the effects of heat on small children and, in rural areas at least, an assumption that outdoor play still occurs naturally.

Of course, individual countries across Europe have very different approaches to the care and education of their younger children. The first differences will be the age of the children encompassed by similar provision, statutory or non-statutory. For example, in many countries in Europe (Eurydice, 2009), it is usual for children to be cared for in a home environment until they are 3 years of age, with group care in a playful setting until school starts for the children at 6 or 7 years of age. Even this is misleading as many countries expect children to start school with a play-based curriculum rather than a formal one (Play England, 2007).

Recognition of the importance of outdoor experiences is also growing in America (Louv, 2010) and Canada (Tucker and Irwin, 2009). In Australasia, too, there is evidence of debates and research on the importance of outdoor play (Meade, 2006). As in Europe, it seems to be in response to concerns about the impact of modern life on children's development, and the perception is that it is appropriate to start with preschool children.

In less industrialised countries, many children still spend significant periods of the day outside, so the sense that this might be an issue to confront is still in its infancy. But in some of the fast-growing economies, change is on its way. In India (Kanyal and Cooper, 2009) and Japan

(Takano, 2002), for example, there is an awareness of the importance of outdoor play for young children, without a clearly expressed sense of why this is important, as yet.

Why is outdoor provision important for early childhood policy and pedagogy in the 21st century?

In the sources referenced above, there is a recognition that, as a species, we need to be connected to our environment for our health and well-being and for that of the planet, and that this should start as soon as possible in the life of the child. For young children, this will mean through playful activities. Furthermore, the most valuable play is that which is 'freely chosen, personally directed and intrinsically motivated' (Conway, 2008) and, where possible, gives opportunities to engage with the wilder elements of their environment. Reading the materials cited so far will give a clear sense of the value of such play.

To unpick that value a little more, it is useful to consider a diagram similar to that created by Bronfenbrenner (1979), with the child in the centre of concentric circles (see Figure 2.1). In this case, I will put around the child their immediate family, then the community in which they are growing up and, round the outside, the whole of humanity.

To start with the child, something all early years practitioners aspire to do, is central to my theme. That central child consists of overlapping elements, indicating that no single aspect of their development occurs in isolation but is an integrated interacting whole. However, I will attempt to look at the elements in turn, leaving the reader to synthesise them into a whole and growing small person.

One element – an obvious one – I will call the developing body. As well as nourishment, it requires air and exercise. Clearly, there is fresh air outside, and that air is usually cleaner and fresher in wilder places. This is also true of exercise – opportunities for running and such like, occur happily outdoors but they are more diverse, flexible and exhilarating where uneven, irregular and diverse. Providing only tamed spaces is not enough – Forest School practitioners tell me of 2-year-olds afraid to walk on grass or on a beach because they have no experience of walking on uneven surfaces. Growing bodies develop better bone density, better heart and lung function, and better muscle tone when they are stretched and tested. I have observed that children are more likely to undertake exercise that does this in more holistic ways when motivated by climbing a tree or moving a log than they are by carefully planned exercise routines. The value of outdoor play here is in helping to reverse the estimated decline in longevity due to a sedentary lifestyle (Olshansky et al., 2005).

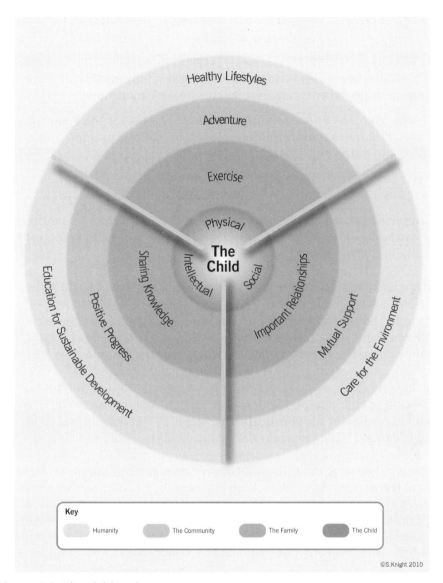

Figure 2.1 The child at the centre

Consider now the developing mind. Evidence strongly indicates (O'Brien and Murray, 2007) increases in the following key areas when children in the UK are given opportunities for Forest School:

1. Confidence: self-confidence and self-belief from freedom, time and space to learn, grow and demonstrate independence.

2. Social skills: increased awareness of the consequences of their actions on other people, peers and adults and an ability to work cooperatively.

3. Language and communication: more sophisticated written and spoken language prompted by their sensory experiences at Forest School.

4. Motivation and concentration: a keenness to participate in exploratory learning and play activities, an ability to focus on specific tasks for extended periods of time.

5. Physical skills: improved stamina and gross motor skills through free and easy movement, fine motor skills by making things.

6. Knowledge and understanding: increased respect for the environment, interest in natural surroundings, observational improvements – identify flora and fauna and changing seasons, etc.

7. New perspectives: for teachers and other adults seeing children in different settings, giving understanding and identifying learning styles.

8. Ripple effects: asking to go out at weekends and holidays, parents' interests and attitudes to Forest School and the environment changing (see Knight, 2009b: 43).

Item 5 was considered in the previous paragraph and 7 and 8 will be considered later. I would therefore like to discuss 1, 2 and 4. The UNICEF report that put the UK bottom of a table of 21 rich countries for child well-being (Innocenti Research Centre, 2007) has been criticised for its methodology but, as an indicator of the effects of a society where access to outdoor play has been in decline, it is worrying. The social and emotional benefits listed above indicate one value of outdoor play to be a working towards improving the well-being of children. In addition, if we apply Maslow's hierarchy of needs to children and add the effects of items 1, 2 and 4 to items 3 and 6, we can see the learning potential as another value of wilder outdoor play.

There is a growing focus in academic debates on the nature of learning around the importance of dispositions to learning. Claxton has been working with Gardner and Craft (Craft et al., 2008), building on his earlier work on dispositions; Alexander (2009) considered the relative importance of learning to learn; and Waite and Davis (2007) link this to outdoor experiences. The value of outdoor experiences as defined in item 6 seems to be in providing a congenial place to learn, full of stimuli whilst being relaxing and fun.

The English government is currently exercised by evidence that many children have poor language skills and have launched a scheme to aid practitioners in early years settings – *Every Child a Talker* (DCSF, 2008b). Practitioner research (Falch-Lovesey and Seal, 2007) lends support to links between opportunities in wilder outdoor play and literacy. It would seem that the value of outdoor play as expressed in item 3 is to provide an environment where children find something to say and a need to say it.

Consider the impact that our smarter and fitter children could have on their family. O'Brien and Murray (2007) include this as items 7 and 8. Adults working with children in outdoor settings, or hearing them talk about their experiences, re-engage with them on new terms. As one head teacher said to me, 'I get to know them as people'. And parents and carers find that they are being encouraged by their children to go outside and engage with nature themselves, developing a micro-culture of *Friluftsliv* from the bottom up. In addition, difficult-to-reach parents and carers are coming into settings to volunteer to be outside and to donate outgrown outdoor clothing. This is supporting stronger community cohesion around the settings.

There is a potential for research on wider effects. Children who are engaged with their environment are more likely to respect it. In one village in the UK where children are involved by the school in growing trees to plant in their community wood, there is almost no vandalism (see www.greenlighttrust.org). This has not been researched but the indicators are positive. The village is also linked to one in Papua New Guinea and the children seem to engage with the problems of living in a threatened rainforest, giving a global dimension to their learning. So I would argue that there is a potential for education for sustainable development, learning about the environment and our place in it on a global scale from outdoor experiences as young children grow older.

 Summary

In summary, my argument is that we have evidence that the value of outdoor experiences in the early years is recognised and supported by research from a range of sources across the world. It is also intuitively recognised by many practitioners, and is becoming acknowledged more widely by policy makers and government departments. However, there is still not enough hard evidence to protect the place of outdoor learning in our curricula, be it early years or beyond.

There is a need to develop methodologies by which practitioners and academics can validate what they find. In particular, there is a need to find a valid model with which to influence policy makers (Beunderman, 2010). I have experimented with using the Foundation Stage Profile to compare results from children who had, or had not had, Forest School experiences in their early years settings, but that was flawed, and only served to reject that route (Knight, unpublished).

 Questions for discussion

1. Is it better to use an imposed method with which to measure success, or to ask the children?
2. How can a qualitative measure become robust enough to convince politicians?
3. What are the worldwide questions we should be considering?

Useful website

Woodcraft Folk. Available online at: www.woodcraft.org.uk (accessed 1 February 2011). Through activities, outings and camps, Woodfolk helps members to understand important issues like the environment, world debt and global conflict and, in recent years, has focused on sustainable development.

References and suggested further reading

Entries in bold are further reading.

Alexander, R. (ed.) (2009) *Children, Their World, Their Education: Final Report and Recommendations of the Cambridge Primary Review.* London: Routledge.

Bentsen, P., Mygind, E. and Randrup, T. (2009) Towards an Understanding of Udeskøle: Education Outside the Classroom in a Danish Context. *Education 3–13,* 37(1): 29–44.

Beunderman, J. (2010) *People Make Play.* London: Play England.

Bradburn, E. (1995) Margaret McMillan 1860–1931. *International Journal of Early Childhood,* 27(2): 69–73.

Bronfenbrenner, U. (1979) *The Ecology of Human Development.* Cambridge, MA: Harvard University Press.

Brügge, B. (2007) Friluftsliv with Preschool Children. In B. Henderson and N. Vikander (eds) *Nature First: Outdoor life the Friluftsliv Way.* Toronto: Natural Heritage Books.

Conway, M. (2008) The Playwork Principles. In F. Brown and C. Taylor (eds) *Foundations of Playwork.* Maidenhead: Open University Press.

Craft, A., Gardner, H. and Claxton, G. (2008) *Creativity, Wisdom and Trusteeship: Exploring the Role of Education.* London: Sage.

Dahle, B. (2003) Norwegian 'Friluftsliv': Environmental Education as a Lifelong Communal Process. In A. Watson and J. Sproull (eds) *Seventh World Wilderness Congress Symposium.* Fort Collins, CO: US Department of Agriculture.

Department for Children, Schools and Families (DCSF) (2007a) *EYFS Statutory Framework.* Nottingham: DCSF.

Department for Children, Schools and Families (DCSF) (2007b) *The Early Years Foundation Stage – Effective Practice: Outdoor Learning.* Nottingham: DCSF.

Department for Children, Schools and Families (DCSF) (2008a) *The National Play Strategy.* Nottingham: DCSF.

Department for Children, Schools and Families (DCSF) (2008b) *Every Child a Talker: Guidance for Early Language – Lead Practitioners.* Nottingham: DCSF.

Department for Education and Skills (DfES) (2006) *Learning Outside the Classroom Manifesto.* Nottingham: DfES.

Ellaway, A., Kirk, A., Macintyre, S. and Mutrie, N. (2006) Nowhere to Play? The Relationship Between the Location of Outdoor Play Areas and Deprivation in Glasgow. *Health and Place,* 13(2): 557–61.

Eurydice (2009) *Compulsory Age of Starting School in European Countries.* Slough: NFER. Available online at: www.nfer.ac.uk (accessed 8 March 2010).

Falch-Lovesey, S. and Seal, N. (2007) *Using a Forest School Experience as a Stimulus for*

Speaking and Listening with a Focus on Raising Achievement in Boys' Writing using ICT: A Joint Broad Futures and Norfolk County Council (Environmental Education Service and Literacy Team) Project. Available online at: www.schools.norfolk. gov.uk (accessed 12 March 2010).

Henderson, B. and Vikander, N. (2007) *Nature First: Outdoor Life the Friluftsliv Way.* Toronto: Natural Heritage Books.

Innocenti Research Centre (2007) *An Overview of Child Well-being in Rich Countries.* Florence, Italy: UNICEF.

Kanyal, M. and Cooper, L. (2009) Young Children's Perceptions of their School Experience: A Comparative Study Between England and India, in the 2009 *Proceedings of the World Conference on Educational Sciences.* Available online at www.sciencediect.com (accessed 12 March 2010).

Knight, S. (2009a) A Pilot Study to Test the Correlation between Forest School Experiences in the Foundation Stage and Results from the Foundation Stage Profile in English Schools. Paper presented at the ENSEC 2nd Conference, Turkey, September.

Knight, S. (2009b) *Forest Schools and Outdoor Learning in the Early Years.* London: Sage.

Knight, S. (2011) *Risk and Adventure in Early Years Outdoor Play.* **London: Sage.**

Konijnendijk, C. (2008) *The Forest and the City: The Cultural Landscape of Urban Woodland.* Netherlands: Springer Science + Business Media.

Louv, R. (2010) *Last Child in the Woods* (2nd edn). London: Atlantic Books.

Martensson, F., Boldemann, C., Söderström, M., Blennow, M., Englund, J-E. and Grahn, P. (2009) Outdoor Environmental Assessment of Attention-Promoting Settings for Preschool Children. *Health and Place,* 15(4): 1149–57.

Martin, A., Turčová, I. and Neuman, J. (2007) The Czech Experience: Turistoka and Connections to Friluftsliv. In B. Henderson and N. Vikander (eds) *Nature First: Outdoor Life the Friluftsliv Way.* Toronto: Natural Heritage Books.

Maynard, T., Waters, J. and Cridland, J. (2008) *Exploring Reggio Outside: Children Playing and Learning in the Outdoor Environment.* Swansea University (unpublished).

Meade, A. (2006) *The Importance of Outdoor Space.* Wellington, New Zealand: University of Wellington College of Education.

Montessori UK (undated) *The Environment.* Available online at: www. montessori.org.uk/whatismontessori/the_environment (accessed 1 February 2011).

Natural England (2009) *Our Natural Health Service.* Nottingham: HMSO.

Nilsson, K., Sangster, M., Gallis, C., Hartig, T., de Vries, S., Seeland, K. and Schipperijn, J. (eds) (2011) *Forests, Trees and Human Health.* **London: Springer.**

O'Brien, L. and Murray, R. (2007) Forest School and its Impacts on Young Children. *Urban Forestry and Urban Greening,* 6: 249–65.

Olshansky, S., Passaro, D., Hershow, R., Layden, J., Carnes, B., Brody, J., Hayflick, L., Butler, R., Allison, D. and Ludwig, D. (eds) (2005) A Potential Decline in Life Expectancy in the US in the 21st Century. *The New England Journal of Medicine,* 352: 1138–45.

Play England (2007) *Free Play in Early Childhood.* London: NCB.

Qualifications and Curriculum Authority (QCA) (2003) *Foundation Stage Profile.* Nottingham: QCA.

Rose, J. (2009) *The Independent Review of the Primary Curriculum: Final Report.* Nottingham: DCSF.

SkillsActive (2006) *Playwork in Extended Schools Services: A Guide for Local Authorities and Advisors.* London: SkillsActive.

Takano, T. (2002) Essence of Friluftsliv: Outdoor Education in Alaska and Japan. In *The Proceedings of the 2002 International Seminar in Education: Frifultsliv, Oslo.* Edinburgh: University of Edinburgh.

Tucker, P. and Irwin, J. (2009) Physical Activity Behaviours during the Preschool Years. *Child Health and Education,* 1(3): 134–45.

Waite, S. (2011) *Children Learning Outside the Classroom.* London: Sage.

Waite, S. and Davis, B. (2007) The Contribution of Free Play and Structured Activities in Forest School to Learning Beyond Cognition: An English Case. In B. Ravn and N. Kryger (eds) *Learning Beyond Cognition.* Copenhagen: Danish University of Education.

White, J. (2008) *Playing and Learning Outdoors.* London: Routledge.

Wilson, E.O. (1984) *Biophilia: The Human Bond with Other Species.* Cambridge, MA and London: Harvard University Press.

3

The power of graphicacy for the young child

Maulfry Worthington

Overview

This chapter explores graphicacy in early childhood, acknowledging the centrality of the child's perspective that enables them to explore a complex interplay of meanings in ways that are powerful and personally relevant. This perspective rests on a view of the child as a 'co-constructor of knowledge, culture and identity', assuming 'that children are knowers of their worlds and that, therefore, their perspectives and understandings can provide valuable insights' (Janzen, 2008: 291–2) – a poststructural view. It recognizes all children as capable and intelligent, providing an image of the child that changes in a 'pedagogy of listening' (Dahlberg et al., 2007: 102), and that teachers have the potential to make a difference (Yelland and Kilderry, 2005: 247). Examples of children's drawings, writing, maps and their *mathematical graphics* included in the chapter were gathered from nursery and reception children (aged 3–4+ years) during the course of data collection for doctoral research[1].

This chapter explores the power of young children's graphics as they draw on home knowledge and experiences to communicate personal meanings for various purposes. It raises questions about traditional (school) perceptions of drawing, writing and mathematical notations, arguing for recognition of the child's agency and identity as they explore and develop understanding of the complexity of multiliterate texts.

The research on which the chapter draws investigates the emergence of *children's mathematical graphics* within play, and takes a Vygotskian, social semiotic perspective of children's imagination and symbolic tools (Carruthers and Worthington, 2011; Worthington, 2010a; Van Oers, 2005; Kress, 1997; Vygotsky, 1978). It points 'to a "natural history" of graphical signs' (Worthington, 2009): children's meanings and cultural knowledge are at the heart of this semiotic perspective. It is premised on the belief of the necessity of a new discourse around children's multiliteracies based on a positive view of young children as learners.

Graphicacy: becoming multiliterate

The term 'graphicacy' was originated by Balchin and Coleman (1966) who describe it as 'an intellectual skill' that is necessary for communication. It includes a range of literate texts and is increasingly used in place of 'mark making' in early childhood education. Children's graphicacy can be viewed within the context of 'mutiliteracies', explained as 'the multiplicity of communications channels and increasing cultural and linguistic diversity in the world today [that] call for a much broader view of literacy than portrayed by traditional language-based approaches' (The New London Group, 1996: 60). These various 'literacies' (e.g. linguistic, scientific, digital, mathematical, visual) are all narratives through which children tell their stories, choosing modes that best communicate their meanings. They provide 'a vehicle for learning that makes children's thinking visible' (Larson and Peterson, 2003: 306, citing Gallas, 1994). Unsworth (2001) proposes that they 'can be differentiated not only on the basis of the channel and medium of communication (print, image, page, screen), but also according to field or subject area (history, geography, science, maths, etc.)' (p. 10).

Lancaster argues that 'when we talk about whether writing evolves from drawing, or is an essential precursor to writing, or simply ask whether children's early marks can be identified as drawing, writing, or enumerating … we are operating from sets of assumptions about graphic signs and systems, from our literate adult consciousness, that very young children cannot possibly share' (2007: 130). Whilst our research shows that at an early age many children make and distinguish between contexts and their purposes, any distinctions between the different graphical genres or literacies made in this chapter are not intended to be rigid interpretations.

Developing agency; developing identities

Rather than becoming dependent on adults for direct instruction, children's own literacies empower them, affirming their sense of agency and identity. In the context of this research, this refers to the capacity for children to make personal choices, to shape their learning and have their voices heard. The child's personal feelings of self-worth contribute to their beliefs, enabling them to see themselves capable and confident, and able to initiate and communicate through graphicacy.

There is increasing evidence that teachers in schools in England experience considerable 'top-down' pressures that often result in a narrowing of children's experiences and can limit their personal beliefs about their self-worth. Thompson proposes that: 'Historically our schools have been predicated on the belief that it is the outsider's knowledge that is *sovereign*. Local, state and national curriculum guidelines are examples of knowledge that is handed down, not created *by* the mind of the learner, *in* the mind of the learner' (2003: 188, italics in the original). In the current educational climate, the 'traditional' values and pedagogies persist, ensuring that beliefs of what counts as acceptable drawings, writing and mathematical notation in schools endure.

Our research into *children's mathematical graphics* and wider aspects of graphicacy (Carruthers and Worthington, 2011) grew from the democratic approaches to learning we espoused in our own classrooms and settings. This perspective views the child as a 'co-constructor of knowledge, culture and identity', assuming 'that children are knowers of their worlds and that, therefore, their perspectives and understandings can provide valuable insights' (Janzen, 2008: 291–2). It enables children to develop 'cultural capital' (Bourdieu, 1992) and has implications for early childhood pedagogy. Recognizing all children as capable and intelligent provides an image of the child that changes in what Dahlberg and Moss (2005: 102) describe as 'a pedagogy of listening'. Moss (2007: 7) proposes that 'democracy creates the possibility for diversity to flourish. By so doing, it offers the best environment for the production of new thinking and new practice'.

In 1930 Vygotsky argued that whereas 'writing is taught as a motor skill and not as a complex cultural activity … writing should be meaningful for children, that an intrinsic need should be incorporated into a task that is *necessary and relevant for life … reading and writing should become necessary for her in her play*' (Vygotsky, 1978: 117–18, italics added). Vygotsky's words appear significant today for all children's literacies. Vygotsky was writing about children of kindergarten age (3–7 years in Russia) and 80 years later the challenge must surely be to support effective play and graphicacy, so that such 'intrinsic needs … are "*necessary and relevant*" in the lives of all young children'.

Examples from practice

Vygotsky believed 'that make-believe play, drawing and writing can be viewed as different moments in an essentially unified process' (1978: 116), therefore it makes sense to view children's multiliterate endeavours within the context of their play. The main section of this chapter explores children's sense of identity and agency through their multiliterate texts. Some relate to themselves and to their place in their family or peer group; other children use graphics to assert and justify their views and position; to communicate rules within play; to confront anxieties, to persuade and to pretend new technologies.

Developing abstract symbols

Children's active involvement enables them to make and communicate a range of personal meanings. For example, playing in the sand outside her nursery class, Aman combined two visual signs signifying 'boat' and 'water', thereby creating a hybrid symbol that effectively communicated her meaning (see Photograph 3.1). Combining and transforming symbols allows children to create and communicate complex meanings (Kress, 1997). Pahl proposes that 'by using one idea the children are driven by internal links within them to explore other possibilities ... The meanings change and grow inside their minds ... These meanings then develop as they move from one concept to another' (1999: 20–1).

Photograph 3.1 Aman's 'boat-water' symbol

By 2 years of age, many children understand that meaning can also be communicated through highly abstract visual symbols, and in the nursery are already communicating personal meanings through their own. At one nursery, three boys were playing a ball game outside. As their game progressed, they began to invent a complex range of symbols, using them to keep track of their progress and to communicate the complexity of their rules to each other. Hearing Henry explain 'A cross means you lose', Joe generated a new symbol, explaining 'This is where you *double* lose' (Photograph 3.2). Their nursery nurse Mandy watched their sign making, occasionally engaging in sensitive discourse with them about their symbols.

Photograph 3.2 'This is where you *double* lose'

Multiliterate narratives

This semiotic knowledge is powerful and allows children to explore personal narratives which Engel (1995: 10) regards as central to their lives, allowing them to 'structure and communicate social experiences'. Moll et al. write of children's 'funds of knowledge' as 'historically accumulated and culturally developed bodies of knowledge and skills essential for household or individual functioning and well-being' (1992: 133). Such knowledge also provides rich resources that young children draw on in their play (Riojas-Cortez, 2001). The relationship between children's funds of knowledge and the narratives they explore, is evidenced by other educators such as Paley (1986) and Kress (1997).

Children's social and cultural experiences are revealed through the graphical, multiliterate narratives in this chapter, whether the role of name badges in a nursery setting, the seats occupied by various family members in the car or memories of a family visit to a fairground. They are highlighted in a child's assertion of his position in his peer group when he is almost 4 years of age, by another exploring personal anxieties relating to a computer game or a child playing out his ideas of electronic security systems.

Representing the self

Nathan was playing shops with some friends and decided to make name badges such as those he'd seen visitors to the nursery wearing. He used simple scribble marks to signify the various names and his marks suggested writing, rather than being an attempt to write any specific names on each. As Nathan focused on the function and role of name badges, he drew on his cultural knowledge and experiences, enabling Nathan and his peers to become part of this shared cultural practice (see Photograph 3.3).

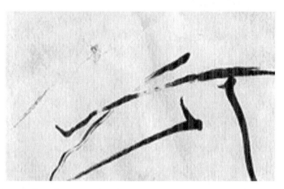

Photograph 3.3 Nathan's name badge

Hamzah loves cars and his drawing is connected to his feelings about being with his family, enabling him to revisit and reflect on journeys in the family car with his parents. This was the second of two drawings that Hamzah made about cars on the same occasion; in the first he represented his idea of the *exterior* of cars (Worthington, 2010a). In this example (Photograph 3.4 opposite), Hamzah focused on the *interior* of the car. Pointing to the four sections within the grid, he explained that these were where members of his family sat: his father in the front (the lower-right section) with the 'driving wheel', his mother at the back (the top-left section) and himself next to her (pointing to the lower-left section). Finally, Hamzah added two dots at the foot of his car for wheels, and wrote 'H' several times to signify the first letter of his name, also an important feature of young children's self-identity.

Assertion

Finnian was discussing his age with his peers: the other children in his group were already 4 years of age and in his estimation were 'bigger'. His mum had told him his current age and in the nursery he explained 'I'm *not* three, I'm three and *three quarters*!' and making some personal letter or number-like symbols on a whiteboard, he explained 'Look! *This* is how you write three and three quarters' (top and centre of Photograph 3.5). Then beneath this he wrote more symbols, explaining 'And this is how you write three and a half'.

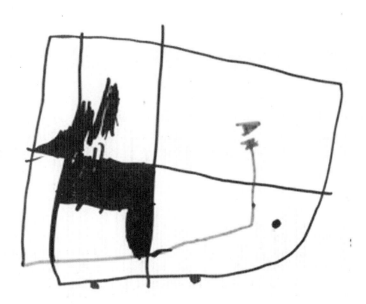

Photograph 3.4 Hamzah's car

Photograph 3.5 Finnian – '*This* is how you write three and three quarters ...'
'And this is how you write three and a half.'

These were Finnian's personal symbols for something that was extremely important to him and the collaborative dialogue with his peers and teacher was vital to his sense of belonging. The discussion continued over several weeks, the children making 'many more examples of their very own fractions' (Carruthers and Worthington, 2009: 24), helping Finn assert his position as a confident and equal member of the group.

Confronting anxieties

Three-year-old Tore explained his energetic marks as a 'shark' (Photograph 3.6): his drawing appears to be what Luquet (2001) refers to as 'fortuitous realism' in which the child notices something in the marks he has made. Perhaps Tore's marks suggested to him a shark moving rapidly in rotation; perhaps the dots and short vertical lines suggested 'teeth', although such drawings can be difficult for adults to understand without further explanation. Matthews (1999: 90) argues that: 'Far from being chaotic actions and random "scribblings" children's use and organisation of visual media exhibits semantic and structural characteristics from the beginning'. Tore used his marks to explore something he was excited about and possibly a little afraid of: we can see that his drawing allowed him to explore his feelings in a safe context where *he* was in control of the shark.

Photograph 3.6 Tore's shark

Pretending new technologies (Wohlwend, 2009)

Multiliteracies embrace cultural changes and modern technologies, new media and a popular 'superhero' culture that impact on children's play, drawings and model making (Worthington, 2010b; Wohlwend, 2009; Marsh, 2005; Pahl, 1999; Dyson, 1997; Paley, 1984), as the next two examples show.

James's complex storying arose through his interest in 'robot (fighting) games' – console games he plays with his 10-year-old brother. Drawing on a large sheet of card, James used a combination of intersecting lines, circles and figurative drawings to narrate his story (Photograph 3.7).

Photograph 3.7 James's 'robot game' narrative

James's drawing appears to be both a means of addressing and controlling the rather frightening content of the computer game, and is as much a relevant form of narrative as writing. James explained that his brother had drawn some of the photographs (top left): the four nearest the top are ducks, one of which James had drawn. Pointing to various features of his drawing, James explained 'The ducks built a snowman' (the figure immediately below the ducks). To the left of this group is 'A man drinking a milk-shake – he's scared of the ducks and the snowmen!' The large circular shape in the centre was 'a house' and to the right of it the cross with extending lines is 'an aeroplane with things that go round' (propellers). The remaining shapes (most of which are identical to the aeroplane) are 'grenades to fight the king who lives in the house – to fight everyone!'

James continued his narrative on the reverse of the same sheet of card, using an equally complex drawing that extended and concluded his narrative.

Isaac was interested in security systems and one day set about creating a 'business card swipe machine' for the gate to the large outside sandpit at his nursery. He stuck a large label on the fence and wrote instructions on it (Photograph 3.8), saying 'You have to have a business card to swipe in' and explained that he didn't need one as 'I've got my special hands'. Soon, another child entered the sand area without a 'business card' and Isaac wrote another instruction: 'This is a bell in case you don't have a card.' Later, he attached a third notice to the centre of the gate: 'This is for delivery vans. It's a camera and it opens the gate automatically.'

Photograph 3.8 Isaac's security notice

Isaac's friend Oliver had been quietly watching, interested in the power that Isaac's notice had in encouraging children to 'swipe' cards to gain access. Oliver decided to write his own instructions and, pointing to his sign, explained: 'This means you're not allowed to come in this way, but two ticks means you can – I've drawn two.' Oliver watched as several other children listened to his rules, observing the influence of his signs on their behaviours.

Isaac's interest in security arose from home and is something that he explored in his play throughout the entire year. For a long time, his favourite 'bedtime story' at home had been a builders' trade catalogue which included cable locks and padlocks. During a visit to his home, Isaac was keen to show me his favourite locks in one of the catalogues and to discuss them with me. Isaac's father worked in the building trade and through his involvement and many discussions and practical experiences with his dad, Isaac had gleaned considerable knowledge about safes and combination locks; electronic entry systems; safety signs to warn of road works; surveillance cameras; designated entry points for fire engines and police speed cameras – in addition to his knowledge of tools and practices of the building trade.

Isaac made and talked about the various combinations of numbers on a lock he made for a 'safe' created during play; wrote 'no entry' signs; invented an elaborate system to record everyone coming through the door into the nursery and made police speed cameras. Isaac's teacher Emma commented on how he increasingly used graphicacy to communicate in his play.

Persuasion

At home, children's drawing is often free of adult expectations and agendas (Anning and Ring, 2004) and they are likely to use them to embody a rich range of experiences and feelings. Megan had made several drawings about fairground rides, including a Ferris wheel and 'a runaway train'.

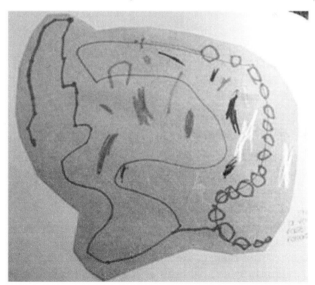

Photograph 3.9 Megan's 'very big fast roller-coaster'

Photograph 3.9 suggests the route the roller coaster took with its undulating and rapid movement and includes its many seats: not a conventional 'picture', it may also be 'read' as a map. Megan told her mum: 'This is a very big fast roller coaster!', as she recalled some of the different rides from her previous visit with excitement and used the drawings as a means of persuading her family that they should take her again. Megan's mother explained: 'Megan was thinking about how much she'd love to go to a funfair again'.

Whilst playing with blocks, Isaac heard Jaydon remark that there were no more hammers. He decided to write a letter to Oliver who was using the only available hammer that was much in demand. Isaac explained: 'I'm writing a letter to Oliver to give Jaydon the hammer. It says "let me have the hammer"' (Photograph 3.10).

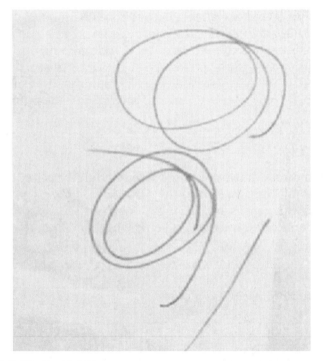

Photograph 3.10 Isaac's letter

Both Isaac's letter and Nathan's name badge (Photograph 3.3) are *indicators* of 'writing' within the context of their play. Such examples are likely to be accepted by teachers who 'understand more deeply how children's intentions, multiple approaches to text meaning, children's worlds and multiple discourses can be used as resources for curriculum purposes ... and may begin to address educational equity (Gallas, 1997)' (Larson and Peterson, 2003: 307). One of the factors identified during the period of data collection for this research, was the extent to which effective teachers appeared to focus on the children's own meanings about their symbolic tools (in play and in their graphics) through sensitive, collaborative dialogue, helping mediate the children's understanding. Bringing their 'pedagogy of listening' enables adults not only to focus on the child's embodied meanings but also to bring their (adult) insights to the semiotic discourse.

Contrasting cultures: challenging literacies

Lancaster emphasizes that: 'Each of the [literate] systems which they develop and use is not so much a stage on the way to realism, as a system which continues to evolve and to remain useful, nothing is wasted' (Lancaster, 2003: 151). However, Anning and Ring (2004) have argued that children's drawing continues to be poorly understood, and that this can be particularly evident in school. Van Oers highlights that:

> An overwhelming mass of studies can be cited to show that schooling is a decisive factor in cognitive development and identity formation, in the distribution of cultural capital and power, as well as in the innovation of culture. It has become clear that the way the teacher organizes classroom activities is crucial for the empowerment of the pupils. (2005: 165)

My research suggests that in the transition from home or nursery to school, children's personal explorations of the symbolic languages of *writing* and *mathematics* reveal an even greater disjoint than drawings. Young children's emergent writing and *mathematical graphics* may not always be viewed as conventional or 'comfortable': they may not always conform to adults' expectations and, as a result, are likely to challenge established perceptions. This suggests that whereas, in school, teachers may more readily accept the examples of drawings as those shown in this chapter, children using their early marks and symbols for writing and mathematics are likely to be led down a 'transmission' path resulting in their passive involvement. This has important implications for issues of continuity as children move from nursery to school, and from their reception class into Key Stage 1 and, since multiliterate texts play a significant role across all areas of the curriculum, pedagogy that fails to privilege democratic learning cultures can only restrict children's developing understandings of diverse literacies.

Recent research by Alexander (2010) has identified some possible causes of the tensions that exist in classes with children of 4–5 years in reception classes in England. She found that teachers and practitioners in the Foundation stage (birth to 5 years) had contrasting views of young children, and that these views were dependent on the type of setting in which they taught. Teachers in Children's Centres (with children up to 4 years of age) viewed 'successful' children in terms of communication and relationships, persistence in self-initiated activities and resilience, whereas those working in schools (with children of 4–5 years of age) 'tend to see successful children as compliant, understanding the rules and able to get on with their learning [tasks] in a relatively independent way' (2010: 114). These differing views impacted on the practitioners' pedagogical and organizational practices and was characterized by different experiences for the children.

Alexander observes that whilst staff in all early years settings are informed by the same accountability regime and curriculum documents for the Foundation stage, 'schools seem to feel the weight of this accountability more heavily than other settings' due to 'the tremendous pressure on schools to conform to accountability measures, targets and standards' (2010: 116).

 Summary

This chapter reveals young children as active, competent, powerful thinkers and meaning makers, co-constructing meanings and cultures. They show how young children use their drawings, maps, writing and their *mathematical graphics* to explore anxieties and be in control. They develop, negotiate and justify their sense of belonging in their family and peer group and use graphics for other genres and communicative purposes, including persuasion. These multiliterate texts also highlight the children's developing understanding of the power of symbolic (graphical) tools to signify and communicate specific meanings, at home and in the nursery.

Young children need to be supported to build personal 'cultural capital' (Bourdieu, 1992). Within democratic learning cultures, children develop both a strong feeling of agency and personal identity, strengthening and empowering their understandings of the various literacies they explore: this should be within the reach of *all* early childhood settings. Yelland and Kilderry emphasise that postmodernism 'enables educators to view students and teachers, their teaching, the educational setting and the greater cultural context in ways that they may not have considered before', inviting teachers to consider such a 'vision of literacies or mutiliteracies in early childhood education' (2005: 243, 246). Thompson concludes: 'the way to reintroduce the sovereignty of the learner into the school is to create environments for authentic enquiry ... Student curiosity itself should be the force that defines the school curriculum' (2003: 188) so that they develop 'a strong and positive sense of self-identity' that the curriculum requires (DfES, 2007: 45).

This chapter shows how children's meanings combine with culture to shape their narratives and inform different symbol systems, emphasizing an alternative construct of young children as powerful agents of their own learning. It challenges established views of children's drawings in early childhood and, particularly, perceptions of what constitute 'writing' and 'written' mathematics in school. These narratives reveal the power of multiliteracies and surely demand understanding throughout the most significant period of children's lives.

Questions for discussion

1. To what extent are you aware of young children's purposes and meanings in the various graphical texts they create? How might you develop your understanding?
2. What are *your* views of a 'successful' child?
3. How close do you think the beliefs, values and cultures of the setting in which you teach (either nursery or school) are to those of the setting to which the children will move? How might you begin to explore the views of staff in both settings, and come to some shared understanding?

Note

[1] With thanks to Open University Press (Carruthers and Worthington, 2011, Broadhead et al, 2010) and to the editors of the *Psychology of Education Review* and *Nursery World* for their kind permissions to include examples first included in their publications.

References and suggested further reading

Entries in bold are further reading.

Alexander, E. (2010) A Successful Child: Early Years Practitioners' Understanding of Quality. *Early Years*, 30(2): 107–18.

Anning, A. and Ring, K. (2004) *Making Sense of Children's Drawings*. Maidenhead: Open University Press.

Balchin, W. and Coleman, A. (1966) Graphicacy Should Be the Fourth Ace in the Pack. *The Cartographer*, 3(1): 23–8.

Bourdieu, P. (1992) *Language and Symbolic Power*. Oxford: Basil Blackwell.

Carruthers, E. and Worthington, M. (2009) Marking Time. *Nursery World*, 1 October: 24–5.

Carruthers, E. and Worthington, M. (2011) *Understanding Children's Mathematical Graphics: Beginnings in Play*. Maidenhead: Open University Press.

Dahlberg, G. and Moss, P. (2005) *Ethics and Politics in Early Childhood Education*. London: RoutledgeFalmer.

Dahlberg, G., Moss, P. and Pence, A. (2007) *Beyond Quality in Early Childhood Education and Care: Languages of Evaluation*. London: Routledge.

Department for Education and Skills (DfES) (2007) *Practice Guidance for the Early Years Foundation Stage*. London: DfES.

Dyson, A.H. (1997) *Writing Superheroes: Contemporary Childhood, Popular Culture and Classroom Literacy*. New York: Teachers College Press.

Engel, S. (1995) *The Stories Children Tell: Making Sense of the Narratives of Childhood*. New York: Freeman and Company.

Gallas, K. (1994) *The Languages of Learning: How Children Talk, Write, Dance, Draw and Sing their Understanding of the World.* New York: Teachers College Press.

Gallas, K. (1997) Story Time As A Magical Act Open Only to the Initiated: What Some Children Don't Know About Power and May Not Find Out. *Language Arts,* 74(4): 248–54.

Janzen, M. (2008) Where is the (Postmodern) Child in Early Childhood Education Research? *Early Years,* 28(3): 287–98.

Kress, G. (1997) *Before Writing: Rethinking the Paths to Literacy.* London: Routledge.

Lancaster, L. (2003) Moving into Literacy: How it All Begins. In N. Hall, J. Larson and J. Marsh (eds) *Handbook of Early Childhood Literacy.* London: Sage.

Lancaster, L. (2007) Representing the Ways of the World: How Children Under Three Start to use Syntax in Graphic Signs. *Journal of Early Childhood Literacy,* 7(2): 123–54.

Larson, J. and Peterson, S.M. (2003) Talk and Discourse in Formal Learning Settings. In N. Hall, J. Larson and J. Marsh (eds) *Handbook of Early Childhood Literacy,* London: Sage.

Luquet, G.H. (2001) *Children's Drawings.* London: Free Association Books.

Marsh, J. (ed.) (2005) *Popular Culture, New Media and Digital Literacy in Early Childhood.* London: RoutledgeFalmer.

Matthews, J. (1999) *The Art of Childhood and Adolescence: The Construction of Meaning.* London: Falmer Press.

Moll, L., Amanti, C., Neff, D. and Gonzalez, N. (1992) Funds of Knowledge for Teaching: Using a Qualitative Approach To Connect Homes and Classrooms. *Theory into Practice,* 31(2): 131–41.

Moss, P. (2007) Bringing Politics into the Nursery: Early Childhood Education as a Democratic Practice. *European Early Childhood Education Research Journal,* 15(1): 5–20.

Pahl, K. (1999) *Transformations: Meaning Making in Nursery Education.* Stoke-on-Trent: Trentham Books.

Paley, V.G. (1984) *Boys and Girls: Superheroes in the Doll Corner.* Chicago: University of Chicago Press.

Paley, V.G. (1986) *Mollie is Three.* Chicago: University of Chicago Press.

Riojas-Cortez, M. (2001) Preschoolers' Funds of Knowledge Displayed Through Sociodramatic Play Episodes in a Bilingual Classroom. *Early Childhood Education Journal,* 29(1): 34–40.

The New London Group (1966) A Pedagogy of Multiliteracies: Designing Social Futures. *Harvard Educational Review,* 66(1): 60–94.

Thompson, D. (2003) Early Childhood Literacy Education, Wakefulness and the Arts. In L. Bresler and M. Thompson (eds) *The Arts in Children's Lives: Context, Culture and Curriculum.* London: Kluwer Academic Publishers.

Unsworth, L. (2001) *Teaching Multiliteracies across the Curriculum.* Buckingham: Open University Press.

Van Oers, B. (2005) Teaching as a Collaborative Activity: An Activity Theoretical Contribution to the Innovation of Teaching. *Mind, Culture and Activity,* 12(2): 165–7.

Van Oers, B. (2010) Emergent Mathematical Thinking in the Context of Play. *Educational Studies in Mathematics,* 74(1): 23–37.

Vygotsky, L.S. (1978) *Mind in Society: The Development of Higher Psychological Processes*. Cambridge, MA: Harvard University Press.

Wohlwend, K. (2009) Early Adopters: Playing New Literacies and Pretending New Technologies in Print-Centric Classrooms. *Journal of Early Childhood Literacy*, 9(2): 117–40.

Worthington, M. (2009) Fish in the Water of Culture: Signs and Symbols in Young Children's Drawing. *Psychology of Education Review*, 33(1): 37–46.

Worthington, M. (2010a) Play is a Complex Landscape: Imagination and Symbolic Meanings. In P. Broadhead, L. Wood. and J. Howard (eds) *Play and Learning in Educational Settings*. London: Sage.

Worthington, M. (2010b) 'This is a *Different* Calculator – With Computer Games On': Reflecting on Children's Symbolic Play in the Digital Age. In J. Moyles (ed.) *Thinking About Play: Developing a Reflective Approach*. Maidenhead: Open University Press.

Yelland, N. and Kilderry, A. (2005) Postmodernism, Passion and Potential for Future Childhoods. In N. Yelland (ed.) *Critical Issues in Early Childhood Education*. Maidenhead: Open University Press.

Young children's perceptions of their classroom environment: perspectives from England and India

Mallika Kanyal and Linda Cooper

Overview

This chapter explores the use of different participatory methods to enable us to understand children's perceptions of their school experience. It is based on a study carried out with 12 5–6-year-old children from a primary school in south-east England and 15 5–6-year-old children from a school in northern India. The chapter's aims are twofold: first, to discuss the use of qualitative participatory methods – children's drawings, children's pair interviews and photographic/video evidence of different areas of the class/setting, taken/videoed by children themselves – as a means to understand children's perceptions of their classroom experience and, second, to interpret children's meaning making of their classroom experience using the cultural-historical framework of understanding human behaviour.

Growing awareness and understanding of children as actors in their own right is becoming widely accepted within societies and education communities (Kellett, 2011). This potentially enables us to ascertain the needs of the child through their own eyes and not necessarily only through adult interpretation. By gaining the insights of the children themselves into their school environment, we can explicitly address the individual and collective needs of children. The creation of a learning environment developed in collaboration with children is, therefore, more likely to be sympathetic and responsive to their needs and aspirations.

Lancaster (2006) believes that children's experiences and voices must be understood as perceived by the child and not how adults infer or interpret them. Practitioners may, however, find it challenging to attend to a number of voices in the classroom. Integral to the challenge is the knowledge of using appropriate methods, both visual and verbal, to encourage *all* children to participate in discussions affecting their experiences at school. Further to this is the intersection of unique personality traits which may differ for confident, vocal children to those of quiet, shy children. These traits influence children's will and level of participation and also the explicit and implicit expression of ideas within the classroom. The explicit voices are relatively easier to attend to but the implicit voices may need some form of adult interpretation. This then raises the question of whether some form of subjectivity is bound to emerge if we are to fully understand the explicit and/or implicit voices of children.

Children's participation is, therefore, a contested notion. One way of simplifying this is to consider participation as being conceived and constructed within the social-cultural context of any given society. The social constructs, for example, of childhood, vary among communities. They influence our policies and practices and how we encourage and guide children to participate in decisions affecting their lives. The implications of these policies to practice are that children's participation may range from tokenism to intermediate and true to partnership experiences.

Since our study is based on two different socio-cultural contexts, the English and the Indian, it is important to first look closely at the two educational contexts. In the current English system, there are a range of frameworks to guide children's agency and participation in different social and educational institutions, for example the English Early Years Foundation Stage (DCSF, 2008a) and Every Child Matters (ECM) (DCSF, 2003). Together, such programmes or frameworks are intended to be representative of cultural beliefs and values, attempting to put children at the heart of everything that professionals do with young children. These beliefs and values can then be seen as being passed on to the younger generation through opportunities for guided participation (Rogoff, 2003). Critics have, however, expressed their concern over the difference between real participation and tokenism where children and children's images can be used merely for decoration purposes (Hart, 1997). Also, there is no guarantee that such policies will empower children's position as there could be other external and internal constraining factors which may influence the translation of national policies into local practice.

India, on the other hand, could be perceived as going through a phase of change, both socially and educationally. The education system is in the process of implementing the newly conceived National Curriculum Framework (NCF, 2005) which is receiving a mixed response from the professionals concerned. It is welcomed by some (for example, Kumar, 2005) but, at the same time, critics have questioned the translation of this framework into reality due to the weak infrastructure of schools (Deepa, 2005; Sharma, 2000).

The differences in such social contexts influence the opportunities for guided participation and interaction that children may experience within their communities. These opportunities are expressed through everyday routine practices, for example in the school and family, which can be perceived as positive or negative (depending upon our ethnocentric views). However, on the precautionary side, it is important to remember that it is not fair to label people solely according to their membership of perceived cultural community(ies). These processes often intersect with children's individual personality and influence the way they behave and learn.

Why should we listen to children?

We believe that the recognition of children's agency and children's voices is a direct result of the ratification of the *United Nations Convention on the Rights of the Child* (UNCRC, 1989) by all major countries in the world (except the USA and Somalia). It has been a major milestone in creating an attitudinal shift which emphasises the need to listen to children. Articles 12, 13 and 14 of the UNCRC quite specifically acknowledge children's legal right to participate in their own learning and how they should be given autonomy as a recognised group of social actors in their own right (UNCRC, 1989). But despite this recognition of children as social actors and their legal entitlement to participate in activities that affect their lives, there is still contention about children's meaningful participation in their own education and related processes (McNaughton et al., 2007). There is scepticism, especially about young children's lack of competence and experience to participate. This, on the other hand, could be interpreted as a lack of adults' confidence and will to share their authority with children. Such resistance often creates barriers in developing children's participative capacity. Adoption of this idea into reality and everyday practice, therefore, can challenge our familiar ways of thinking about adult–child relationships. It can demand new role expectations for adults who take care of children (Woodhead, 2005).

Relating this argument to the education context, various authors have used different approaches and metaphors to describe levels of children's participation, such as the *Mosaic Approach* (by Clark et al., 2003), *Ramps* (by Lancaster, 2006) and *Ladder* (by Hart, 1997). These models could be understood and applied both at the policy and practice level. For example, *Ramps* and *Ladder* could be used as an evaluative framework to help institutions and practitioners guide their own policies and practice. The *Mosaic Approach*, on the other hand, can give practitioners practical ideas on how to encourage and include children in planning and designing their own learning environments.

With this in mind, our study uses both traditional and contemporary methods to identify children's perceptions of their learning environment. This can be seen as the first step for planning and implementing any change to the classroom learning environment. Environments thus created in conjunction *with* children and *for* children are believed to be much more sympathetic and responsive to their needs.

Ethical issues were duly considered, especially those involving the children's consent, given the nature of the study's focus.

Listening to children's voices: some interactive methods

This section outlines our small-scale study, carried out in summer 2009, involving 12 5–6-year-old children from a primary school in south-east England and 15 5–6-year-old children from a school in north India. Our aim, as the title suggests, was to capture young children's perceptions of their classroom environments in these two culturally different countries and compare these views using the socio-cultural perspective of understanding human behaviour. Three qualitative participatory methods – children's drawings, photographic/video evidence of different areas of the class or setting recorded by children themselves and children's pair interviews – were used. It was believed that this triangulation of participatory methods would give children multiple opportunities to express their perceptions of the school environment and also give our study findings validity.

Method 1: Children's drawings

Children's drawings have been a subject of controversy in the academic community. Martindale (2008) argues that children's drawings cannot possibly be viewed as a reliable source of information, including children's perceptions of themselves, or anything else. He believes that, through their drawing, children may not always represent their perceptions but, rather, a 'wish'. But other researchers have shown the effectiveness of children's drawings in helping educators and other professionals to understand the lives of children in school and related settings (for example, Walker, 2008; Anning and Ring, 2004; Bonoti et al., 2003; Weber and Mitchell, 1995). These settings form part of children's cultural locale which informs their meaning making (Kendrick and McKay, 2004). Hence, children's drawings are much more than a simple representation of what they see before them and can be better understood as ways in which they are making sense (Anning and Ring, 2004).

We, therefore, believe that children's drawings can be a very useful tool to help us capture individual children's perceptions of their school experience. It also enables us to listen to the voices of children with different personalities, both vocal and shy. Martindale's (2008) perspective of children's drawing as representative of their 'wish' and not 'perception' is also a useful one. We believe that it is imperative for a practitioner to actually acknowledge both children's 'perceptions' and 'wishes'. By doing so, they get the opportunity to enter into children's mental spaces of their 'ideal school' experience.

With this in mind, children in settings in both England and India were asked to draw two pictures using a research instrument designed by Armstrong (2007). This included a picture of:

- their 'actual school experience'

- what they anticipate as their 'ideal school experience'.

It was suggested to the children that, in both drawings, they put themselves, their teacher and a friend or two. Children were asked to make sure that everyone was shown to be doing something and also, if possible, to label the people in their drawing. This guidance was intended to be *facilitative* to encourage children to draw various aspects of their experiences. There is some contention about adult manipulation of children's voices to adhere to an adult-dominated agenda of quality and performance. The idea here was to capture children's thinking while they were engaged in the process of drawing their pictures. The children were only given guidance and were free to draw what they liked to represent their thinking about their 'actual' and 'ideal' school experiences. The narratives from children about their drawings were recorded whilst they were actively engaged in the process.

Method 2: Photographic and video evidence

The use of cameras and video cameras has been a popular method of engaging children with contemporary research. There are clear benefits of using such methods as they can be fun for children and informative for adults. It can also help to overcome the limitation of drawing by capturing the action(s), which is not always possible to capture through drawings (Punch, 2002).

The children in our research were given disposable cameras to take pictures of different areas within their classroom and school – inside or outside – capturing areas which they particularly liked or disliked. Areas of the school which repeatedly appeared in the photographs were placed into the broad categories of 'learning environment' and were later used as prompts during the interview process. The running commentaries (video recordings) were also carefully noted, identifying children's likes and dislikes and the reasons behind these. The whole process of taking photographs aimed at encouraging children's participation and active involvement. It was framed by an approach using visual methodologies which recognise that young people are experts in their own worlds and have distinctive ways of seeing (Burke, 2005).

Whilst recognising the value of contemporary research instruments, it is important to note that such photographs/video clips can be representative of only the current learning theme which may not necessarily last for the whole year. Therefore, it is advisable to integrate similar tools into routine evaluative plans, for example to collect children's views each time there is a change in the theme of classroom learning environment. Not every setting, however, will be in a position to buy such expensive equipment. There are other interactive methods, like interviews or small group work, which could be equally effective in understanding children's perceptions of their classroom environment.

Method 3: Interviewing young children

Interviews with young children can yield valid results, provided attention is paid to certain preconditions (Brooker, in Macnaughton et al., 2004; Formosinho and Araújo, 2006). Four such preconditions which we would like to refer to are, first, the context in which interviews are carried out; second, the number of children to be interviewed at a given time; third, the medium used for the interview; and fourth, the number of questions asked.

Applying these principles to our research, interviews were carried out with children in the school context (within their classroom). This is perceived to have favoured the interview process as a familiar environment elicits better interview utterances (longer, clearer, more complex, more thoughtful). Children were also interviewed in pairs by using a toy telephone as the interview medium. The interview was kept short to a minimum number of questions (three in this case) and children's voices were tape-recorded to allow researchers to revisit their response at a later stage. The questions asked were as follows:

1. Why do you think you come to school?

2. What do you like about coming to school or into your class?

3. Is there anything you do not like about your school or your class?

Being reflexive: interpreting an essential component of listening

Listening, as Clark et al. (2003) suggest, is not all about hearing but also interpreting, constructing meaning and responding. Therefore, it is essential to interpret the findings and develop a shared understanding of the information gathered by using different participatory methods with young children. It is a reflexive process which can only promote good practice.

Analysis and interpretation of children's drawings in both countries indicate that their 'actual school experience' is academically driven, representing a traditional view of classrooms where the teacher takes the authority position and children comply with instructions (Lodge, 2007; Weber and Mitchell, 1995). The majority of the children drew their 'actual' experience as sitting inside the classroom and doing 'class work' (mostly literacy and numeracy activities) whilst the teacher was sitting at the front of the classroom, taking the authority position. A few children drew their actual experience as 'playing' outside with friends, with the teacher being in close vicinity. The teacher was viewed as either 'watching', 'playing', 'guiding' or 'helping' them in their play activities. This could be argued to represent their implicit acceptance of a teacher's significant role, even in peer-dominated play experiences. The children's 'actual' experiences are, therefore, influenced by both the explicit and implicit presence of a teacher who seemed to be illustrating both dominating and facilitative roles in shaping children's everyday school experiences.

The ideal school experience portrays a mixed image of children's perceptions in the schools in England and India. In England, children unanimously express their wish to be outside, engaged in a range of activities with their teacher and friends. Children in India, however, gave a mixed response, some expressing their wish to be outside, just like children in England, whilst others struggled to draw the difference between the actual and ideal school experience. This can be perceived as the gap in their understanding about the abstract term 'ideal school', which may be a result of the lack of opportunities and experiences available to them to draw upon, or else they were 'conditioned' to believe this is what happens within the 'ideal' context. Their representations were more focused on the structure variables and facilities, such as an ICT room, good quality fans and lighting, general cleanliness, etc., which brings our attention to the environment and well-being issues.

Considering these findings from a pedagogic position, children at school in India did not demonstrate variation in child–teacher interaction through their ideal school drawings. The teacher was still the central figure taking the traditional authority role, whereas the children at school in England, through their ideal school experience drawings, showed the teacher either in a supervisory role or as non-existent in their drawings. This shows that the children took our instructions for their drawings as guidance only as they still chose not to include teachers in their ideal school drawings. Children's ideal school experiences, therefore, could be depicted in an emancipation continuum where some chose to be free from the frameworks of school and teacher and others chose to imagine their experiences within the given structures and boundaries of school.

The second method, the photographic and video evidence, was used to categorise the learning environments, which constituted the themes shown in Table 4.1.

Table 4.1 Categorising the learning environment: classroom/school areas as photographed or videoed by children at schools in India and England

S. no.	Class/school area (England)	Class/school area (India)
1	The white board	The blackboard
2	The book area	The teachers' sitting area (desk and chair)
3	Phonics area	Play area (one climbing frame)
4	Outside (playground)	Outside (playground)
5	(Various) class displays	(One) display area
6	Work table	Reading/writing on the desk
7	Colouring time/area	Colouring time
8	Craft area	Fans and tube lights
9	Computer area	Windows
10	Puppet area	Friends (friendship)
11	Coat peg area	Bottle (and lunchbox)

After categorising photographs into the themes in Table 4.1, children were then asked whether they liked/disliked or were not sure about that area. A majority of the children in England liked all these areas in the classroom and the outside space, with a few not being sure of some displays as 'they were old'; the white board as 'it may involve reading'; the peg area as 'it is boring'; the phonics area as 'it involves sounding out letters'; the puppet area as 'it is boring'; the book area as 'it involves reading'; and the work table as 'it involves studying'.

The majority of the children in India also liked all class/school areas, with a few not being sure of some areas like windows as 'they are not clean'; the outside area as 'it becomes mucky'; and fans and tube lights as 'they throw hot air and the room looks dark at the time of power cut'.

However, both in England and India, there was no resounding dislike for any of the areas. Children's perceptions of why they liked these areas was a general like towards activities that underpinned the working of these areas, such as colouring, making a display, reading interesting books, playing football and doing art and craft activities.

Analysis thus drawn from their identified theme areas suggests that children at school in England appear to be having access to a range of activities/areas, whereas children at school in India have few things that constitute their learning environment. These perceived affordances could limit or encourage children's interaction with the environment, which is believed to shape children's perceptions of their everyday school experiences.

My friends Yasmin and Anna are sitting around the table with me. We are putting our hands up
to answer the question by the teacher. Teacher is teaching the class and standing by the white board.

Figure 4.1 'Actual' school drawing, England

In this picture I am outside with my friends. Caitlin and Ella are playing outside near the swings.
I am getting on the roundabout. Teacher is watching us play outside.

Figure 4.2 'Ideal' school drawing, England

The teacher is teaching us and we are sitting on desks and chairs.
My friends are playing in the classroom.

Figure 4.3 'Actual' school drawing, India

In my ideal school there are nice trees, table, fans and my books.

Figure 4.4 'Ideal' school drawing, India

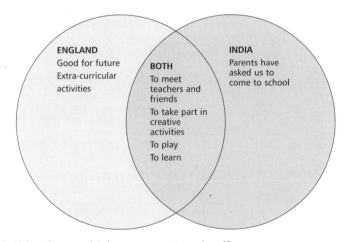

Figure 4.5 Why do you think you come to school?

On the basis of the third and our last method, interviews, it is clear that children's perceptions of why they attended school ranged from adult-imposed reasons (to improve their future or to comply with parents' wishes) to reasons which might be of benefit to themselves (self-gratifying or educational). Interestingly, when questioned on their views on likes and dislikes at school, all of the children expressed suggestions of particular activities in which they like to take part. However, no explicit dislikes were expressed, although mention was made of factors which might cause them physical or emotional harm (mild aggression or discomfort). Findings from both settings are represented in the Venn diagrams below, showing the similarities and differences in children's responses to the interview questions.

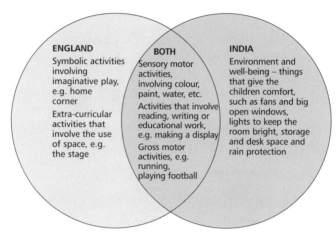

Figure 4.6 What do you like about coming to school or into your classroom?

The responses from the interviews indicate children's liking towards the learning environment, both the objects/people and the processes undertaken by them with their peers and teacher(s).

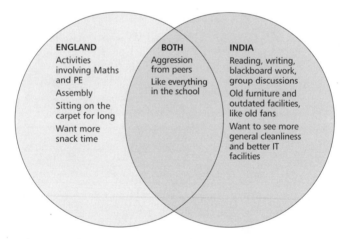

Figure 4.7 Is there anything you don't like about your school or classroom?

Children's perceptions: a socially constructed phenomenon

Children's perceptions of their school experiences in two different sociocultural contexts (England and India) are analysed using Rogoff's (2003) three planes of analysis (see Figure 4.8).

The *first plane* is at the personal level where individual children's perceptions are considered at an *intra*personal level. By giving each child the opportunity to take photographs, draw pictures and talk in their own words, we provided them with the tools to participate in expressing their views about the classroom environment. It can be perceived as providing the children with a sense of their own agency, enabling them to control and present their viewpoint to us. Concomitantly, it allowed us to capture their understanding of the school environment, which potentially could be used as a reflective tool to plan (more) responsive and meaningful learning environments for the children.

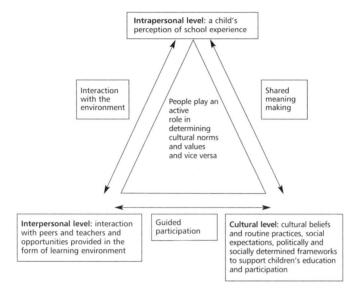

Figure 4.8 Insights into children's participation using Rogoff's three planes of analysis

To gain an insight into the wider factors that affect the development of children's perceptions, Rogoff's *second plane* of analysis, called the social or *inter*personal level, is used. This includes children's involvement in socially constructed collective activities (Rogoff, 2003). Children actively make meaning from the experiences gained by interacting with their environment (as shown in Figure 4.3). The environment can take the shape and form of structures, for example the external building and its surroundings (Thelin and Yankovich, cited in Carney-Strange and Banning, 2001) and the processes involved when different objects and/or people interact within this environment. Interaction with the environment can range from *over* stimulation to minimal or *no* stimulation. These interactive operations are highly important as it is during these processes that intersubjectivity, or shared understanding, is established between participants. But these joint purposes and goals can only be realised when children's views are heard. Such guidance principles can now be perceived as universal, though their precise forms vary from community to community.

This brings us to the *third* and *final plane* of analysis which is at the *cultural* level. At this level, children are believed to learn their cultural practices and tools through guided participation in cultural endeavours (Rogoff, 2003). We must, therefore, recognise the cultural nature of everyday practices, including pedagogical processes. The forms of these processes vary within different societies resulting in different sets of experiences for its groups of people. However, we must not forget that individuals (including children) have agency and that they can choose how to behave (Rogoff, 2003). This suggests that culture is not always a linear phenomenon; it can 'create people' but, at the same time, can be modified or changed by the action of its groups of people.

Implications for practice

At the pedagogic level, our findings from this small study lead us to suggest:

- Our methods to understand children's perceptions of their school experience are relatively easy to replicate.

- Drawings, small group interviews and digital technology can be used effectively to capture children's perceptions about their (learning) environments.

- These resources allow a dialogue between the teacher and the group of children to give them agency to participate.

- Attending to voices does not always mean that a process needs to be changed or that final decisions are to be made by the children. Instead, it means that children are being given opportunities to enter into relational dialogic spaces with adults, the purpose of which is to make them feel confident and valued members of the group.

- Children are active people, capable of engaging in the development of their own learning, which occurs at three different levels: intrapersonal, interpersonal and cultural.

- Adults need to provide opportunities through guided participation to encourage children to develop shared understanding about the cultural tools and norms of their community but, at the same time, be aware of the fact that an individual can belong to multiple communities.

- Rather than looking at culture as a static social process, we must focus on individual people's involvement and participation in cultural communities.

Summary

From a practical viewpoint, the findings from the research highlight the importance of understanding children's voices as perceived by the child and not by how adults infer. However, attention must be paid to both the explicit and implicit voices of children.

We feel there is a need to celebrate good practice. The fact that the children did not cite explicit dislikes may be a favourable reflection on the environment that was created for them. This positive response from the hardest critics of all – the children – should empower practitioners. In a context which is bombarded with reporting, paperwork and inspections to measure improving outcomes, this can only be a good thing.

Questions for discussion

1. In what ways are you able to give children a voice in their learning and environments?

2. What do you think you would learn from children if they made drawings of their environment and relationships? How might this enable you to understand children's perceptions of their learning environment?

3. What other media/method do you think could be used effectively to encourage children to enter into the dialogic relation space with their teacher(s) to share their views about their learning environment, both in its structures and processes?

References and suggested further reading

Entries in bold are further reading.

Anning, A. and Ring, K. (2004) *Making Sense of Children's Drawings*. Maidenhead: Open University Press.

Armstrong, D. (2007) *Classroom Visions: Efficient and Effective Ways to Differentiate Education*. Available at: www.classroomvisions.com (accessed 10 January 2011).

Bonoti, F., Plousia, M. And Fotini, G. (2003) Graphic Indicators of Pedagogic Style in Greek Children's Drawings. *Perceptual and Motor Skills*, 97: 195–206.

Burke, C. (2005) Play in Focus: Children Researching Their Own Spaces and Places for Play. *Children, Youth, Environments*, 15(1): 27–53.

Carney-Strange, C. and Banning, J.H. (2001) *Education by Design*. San Francisco, CA: Jossey-Bass.

Clark, A., McQuail, S. and Moss, P. (2003) *Exploring the Field of Listening to and Consulting with Young Children*. London: DfES Research Report 445.

Deepa, A. (2005) *New Curriculum Framework: A Few Chapters Short*. Available online at: www.indiatogether.org/2005/dec/edu-ncf2005.htm (accessed 14 November 2009).

Department for Children, Schools and Families (DCSF) (2003) *Every Child Matters*. Available online at: http://www.dcsf.gov.uk/everychildmatters/about/aboutecm (accessed 12th November 2009).

Department for Children, Schools and Families (DCSF) (2008) *Statutory Framework for the Early Years Foundation Stage*. Nottingham: DCSF.

Formosinho, J. and Araújo, S.B. (2006) Listening to Children as a Way to Reconstruct Knowledge about Children: Some Methodological Implications. *European Early Childhood Education Research Journal*, 14(1): 21–31.

Hart, R.A. (1997) *Children's Participation: The Theory and Practice of Involving Young Citizens in Community Development and Environmental Care*. London: Earthscan.

Kellett, M. (2011) Accessing Children's Voices and Experiences. In J. Moyles, J. Georgeson and J. Payler (eds) *Beginning Teaching, Beginning Learning* (4th edn). Maidenhead: Open University Press.

Kendrick, M. and McKay, R. (2004) Drawings as an Alternative Way of Understanding Young Children's Constructions of Literacy. *Journal of Early Childhood Literacy*, 4(1): 109–28.

Kumar, K. (2005) *New Curriculum Framework: A Few Chapters Short*. Available at: www.indiatogether.org/2005/dec/edu-ncf2005.htm (accessed 14 November 2009).

Lancaster, Y.P. (2006) *RAMPS: A Framework for Listening to Children*. London: Daycare Trust. Available online at: www.daycaretrust.org.uk/mod/fileman/files/RAMPS.pdf (accessed 20 September 2009).

Lodge, C. (2007) Regarding Learning: Children's Drawings of Learning in the Classroom. *Learning Environment Research*, 10: 145–56.

MacNaughton, G., Hughes, P. and Smith, K. (2007) Young Children's Rights and Public Policy: Practices and Possibilities for Citizenship in the Early Years. *Children and Society*, 21: 458–69.

Macnaughton, G., Rolfe, S. and Siraj-Blatchford (eds) (2004) *Doing Early Childhood Research: International Perspectives on Theory and Practice*. Buckingham: Open University Press.

Martindale, D. (2008) *One Picture May Not Be Worth 1000 Words: Children's Drawings, Perceptions of Themselves and Their Families*. Available online at: http://business.highbeam.com/437254/article-1G1–192338114/one-picture-may-not-worth-1000-words (accessed 15 March 2011).

National Curriculum Framework (NCF) (2005) *National Council of Educational Research and Training*. Available online at: www.ncert.nic.in/html/pdf/schoolcurriculum/framework05/prelims.pdf (accessed 15 November 2009).

Punch, S. (2002) Research with Children: The Same or Different From Research with Adults? *Childhood*, 9(3): 321–41.

Rogoff, B. (2003) *The Cultural Nature of Human Development*. Oxford: Oxford University Press.

Sharma, R. (2000) Decentralisation, Professionalism and the School System in India. *Economic and Political Weekly*, 35(42): 3765–74.

United Nations Convention on the Rights of the Child (UNCRC) (1989) Available online at: www.unicef.org.uk/Documents/Publication-pdfs/crcsummary.pdf?epslanguage=en (accessed 15 January 2011).

Walker, G. (2008) *Working Together for Children: A Critical Introduction to Multi-agency Working*. London: Continuum.

Weber, S. and Mitchell, C. (1995) *'That's Funny, You Don't Look Like a Teacher': Interrogating Images and Identity in Popular Culture*. Abingdon: RoutledgeFalmer. Available online at: http://site.ebrary.com/lib/anglia/Doc?id=10058250&ppg=17 (accessed 10 February 2010).

Woodhead, M. (2005) Early Childhood Development: A Question of Rights? *International Journal of Early Childhood*, 37(3): 79–98.

Part 2

Cultures of Pedagogy

Introduction

Janet Moyles and Theodora Papatheodorou

As we have seen in Part 1, culture covers a broad spectrum in relation to children's learning. In this section, writers discuss the evolving cultures of pedagogy, considering policy initiatives and the wider national and local context. We also include the culture of home and school interactions but we begin this introduction with pedagogy which is essentially the relationship between the two concepts of learning and teaching.

In one definition offered by Stewart and Pugh, pedagogy is defined as:

> the understanding of how children learn and develop, and the practices through which we can enhance that process. It is rooted in values and beliefs about what we want for children, and supported by knowledge, theory and experience. (2007: 9)

In other words, it is rooted in the cultural norms of each particular school or setting, influenced strongly by the societal and cultural norms of the geographical context.

Alexander agrees, suggesting further:

> Pedagogy is defined as both the act of teaching and the discourse in which it is embedded. The comparative analysis of pedagogy requires that we have a viable framework for the empirical study of classroom transactions and that we locate these transactions historically and culturally at the levels of classroom, school and system. (2001: 510)

These strong links between cultural context, practitioner, child, family and community can potentially bring us into something of a collision of the social and economic cultures of early childhood education and care (ECEC). As the EFA Report asserts, 'Investment in ECEC yields very high economic returns, offsetting disadvantage and inequality …', whilst also acknowledging that 'Governments accord relatively low priority to pre-primary education in their spending' (UNESCO, 2006: 4). The same report also documents that 'The single most important determinant of ECEC quality is interaction between children and staff' – in other words, the pedagogies of practice.

Quality issues in relation to the staffing and pedagogy of nurseries, kindergartens and early years education settings have received much attention over the last few years (see, for example, Penn, 2011; Dahlberg et al., 2006). Strong support for quality practice also comes from the EFA Report which states that successful practices 'offer support to parents during the child's earliest years, integrate education activities with other services … and ease the transition to primary school' (UNESCO, 2006: 7). In their seminal study in England, Siraj-Blatchford et al. (2002) established that the main determinant of quality was the educational background of the pedagogues (practitioners) which, to a certain extent, mirrors the findings of the large US study (Bowman et al., 2001). Quality issues also emanate from the ability of practitioners to reflect deeply on their pedagogies (Moyles, 2010) and, particularly, the impact on children from multicultural backgrounds and the integration of those with identified individual needs. Such research and others stresses the need for practitioners to be researchers, theory builders, curriculum makers and public intellectuals – no mean feat!

A predominant current concern across a number of countries is highlighted in a new UNESCO Report, *Caring and Learning Together* (2010), which examines different international perspectives and practices in relation to the link between early education and care. Its recommendation is that care should be integrated with education (rather than the other way round) into one coordinated service, whilst pointing out that in a small number of countries, integration is reversed and still working reasonably successfully. This leads to a number of discussions: (1) transition and the challenges presented to children in transferring from the cultures of home, then pre-school to primary school; (2) formal versus informal (playful) pedagogies and the challenges that these present for young children; and (3) pedagogies that support multiculturalism in those countries with diverse and pluralist populations.

This latter issue is the focus of the first, very original, chapter of this section (Chapter 5) by Eva Maagerø and Birte Simonsen. The Norwegian kindergarten culture is recognised as child-centred and open-minded. In this child-centred perspective, one could believe that handling multiculturalism would be without any problem and that small children generally do not show racist attitudes. Even with integration as the nationally approved inclusion strategy in Norway, the writers show that daily practice can be very different. In their research, Eva and Birte surface different aspects of integration to illuminate the challenge to pedagogy in Norwegian kindergartens.

A very different approach is taken by Hasina Ebrahim and Mary James in Chapter 6. These writers present findings from a study exploring child–child pedagogy, research in which primary-age children acted as 'buddies' in the education of young children for whom there was no settings-based provision. Discussions in the chapter shed light on pedagogic activities which are supportive of early education through community building, affirming local cultures and the introduction of school cultures.

In the final chapter (7) of this section, Anastasia Papaprokopiou and Athina Kammenou tell of their research into transitions for young children in Greece from the culture of home through nursery care into kindergarten. In a survey of parents and teachers, the researchers asked about smooth transition and integration practices and policies. Whilst parents are clear that the role of nurseries (care settings) is that of socialisation and education, teachers, on the other hand, spoke more about the integration of children without due consideration to any substantial relationships with parents. This lack of compatibility is likely to cause cultural challenges for children as they move through the Greek ECEC system.

As the quote at the beginning indicates, we all need an open mind in order to consider the complex issues of cultures and pedagogies in different countries and the implications these have for the children who are at the heart of practice.

References 📖

Alexander, R. (2001) Border Crossings: Towards a Comparative Pedagogy. *Comparative Education*, 37(4): 507–23. *Special Number (24): Comparative Education for the Twenty-First Century: An International Response.*

Bowman, B., Donovan, M. and Burns, M. (eds) (2001) *Eager to Learn: Educating Our Preschoolers.* Committee on Early Childhood Pedagogy/National Research Council. Washington, DC: National Academies Press.

Dahlberg, G., Moss, P. and Pence, A. (2006*) Beyond Quality in Early Childhood Education and Care: Languages of Evaluation.* London: Routledge.

Moyles, J. (ed.) (2010) *Thinking About Play: Developing a Reflective Approach.* Maidenhead: Open University Press.

Penn, H. (2011) *Quality in Early Childhood Services: An International Perspective.* Maidenhead: Open University Press.

Siraj-Blatchford, I., Sylva, K., Muttock, S., Gilden, R. and Bell, D. (2002) *Researching Effective Pedagogy in the Early Years.* London: HMSO, Research Report 365.

Stewart, N. and Pugh, R. (2007) *Early Years Vision in Focus, Part 2: Exploring Pedagogy.* Shrewsbury: Shropshire County Council.

UNESCO (2006) *Education for All Global Monitoring Report: Strong Foundations.* Available online at: http://unesdoc.unesco.org/images/0014/001477/147794e.pdf (accessed 22 March 2011).

UNESCO (2010) *Caring and Learning Together. A Cross-national Study of Integration of Early Childhood Care and Education Within Education,* a report by Y. Kaga, J. Bennett and P. Moss. Paris: UNESCO.

5

Constructing an inclusive culture in kindergartens

Eva Maagerø and Birte Simonsen

Overview

The Norwegian kindergarten culture is recognised as child-centred and open-minded. Among pedagogues there is a fear of developing in a too 'schoolish' direction, since schools are looked at as more traditional and rigid. In this child-centred perspective, one could believe that handling multiculturalism would be without problem and viewed as an extra resource. It is often commented that small children are 'colour blind' (meaning without racism). If this is true, how strong is their resistance in a society where the tendency to present the world through dichotomies is overwhelming? It seems difficult to state a position without, at the same time, viewing that of others. Even if integration is the nationally approved inclusion strategy in Norway, the daily practice may differ. In this chapter, we want to surface different aspects of integration to illuminate the challenge of 'otherness' and dialogue, in general, but with a special interest and reflection directed to teacher education and everyday life in kindergartens in Norway.

A permanent inclusion debate in Norway

Immigration on a large scale started in Norway around 1970, first represented by workers from Pakistan and India and later by groups of asylum seekers and refugees from all over the world. An almost permanent debate on inclusion strategies has been taking place ever since (Maagerø and Simonsen, 2009). The official governmental standpoint during these four decades has been *integration*. Critical voices, however, have claimed that practical consequences of the policy can both lead to *assimilation* and to *segregation:* the government is concerned that kindergartens and schools seem to be fields for social reproduction, not for equal opportunities.

The question then is in what ways are the daily work and norms of kindergartens challenged by the official claim of integration? In this chapter, we seek to conceptualise these challenges by using theory that highlights problems connected to 'the other' and look at how 'othering' as an action, places people in a marginalised position. The constructed concept of 'othering' describes a process or a rhetorical device in which one group is seen as 'us' and another group as 'them' (Van Oers and Hännikäinen, 2001). We argue that, at least in western cultures, there seems to be a need to construe the world by means of dichotomies and stereotypes. If this is true, then it is not only political decisions that threaten integration; it is also a question of how each person constructs meaning in their own world and also of how they reflect on their own ways of thinking and communicating.

Our definition of integration turns back to the Latin word *integer,* which means 'whole' or 'entire' (Oxford English Reference Dictionary, 2002). This indicates that, in an integrated society, all involved groups and individuals have an equal position. To be integrated is not an upward movement from a lower and marginalised position but a description of permanent diversity within a 'whole' which is understood to include different participants.

'All children should participate in an inclusive community' (Norwegian Ministry of Education and Research, 2008–9)

The whole education system in Norway is based on offering all children, irrespective of background and abilities, equal opportunities. In the last decade, the Norwegian government, inspired by the fundamental principle of *equality*, has worked hard to realise its commitment to *Kindergarten for All*. When the Ministry of Education and Research presented its White Paper No. 41 (2008), *Quality in Kindergarten*, multiculturalism was an important issue. It stated that 'Children belonging to indigenous groups and linguistic and cultural minorities must be supported to be part of both majority and minority cultures' (p. 4). This text is a clear integrative statement describing an acceptance of diversity whilst an assimilative position would have pointed out the majority culture as the target culture.

But what consequences will follow in the everyday life of the kindergartens from this policy commitment? How can different cultures be visible at all times and not only once a year when celebrating national days or when making 'ethnic' food? How is integration reflected in the daily dialogue? When a leader of a kindergarten is asked to describe her group of children, how would that sound? Does a group of kindergarten children consist of *Norwegian* children, on the one hand, and *immigrant* children on the other? Who defines the criteria for belonging to or not belonging to the Norwegian group? Language? The children's outward appearance? Their parents' ethnic origin? Real diversity is a question of being conscious about differences and of also using this diversity as a resource; and not using these children as an easy way of sorting and classifying.

We and 'the others' – not a new phenomenon

With these questions in mind, our purpose is to strengthen knowledge and to develop more consciousness and reflection among teachers and student teachers. We have found it fruitful to deal with how the use of dichotomies influences and constructs our view of other groups and people. By raising examples from different types of literature, we want to show how easy it is to be trapped both in language and in social habits.

We start in history with the Greeks. Obviously, a similar debate as ours was taking place in those days too. The Greek philosopher, Diogenes, from the post-Socratic period around 400 BC, is well known for his special way of living – in a barrel at the marketplace in Athens! He was protesting against the Athenians' materialistic and egoistic way of living. Diogenes argued that the difference Athenians constructed between Greeks and Barbarians – people living at a distance from Athens – was strongly excluding and conflicting. A better way was to accept all people as part of the same world. In his fight for a more equal world, he is said to have been the creator of the concept 'cosmopolite', which means a citizen of the world. In Greek literature, the immigrant or the Barbarian was personalised through Anacharsis, a prince from Scythia, a country by the Black Sea. It is uncertain whether he was real or symbolic but he represented 'the stranger', an exotic man from a remote area, at least seen through Greek eyes. Some authors, like Lucian, used Anacharsis as a cover to ask critical questions about Greek society (Lucian, 1992). It was dangerous for an author to be too outspoken but speaking through others made it possible.

More than 2000 years later, Gullestad (2002), a Norwegian social anthropologist, analysed how what she calls 'the Norwegian cultural and political elite' (professors, journalists, politicians) spoke and wrote about minority groups. She found that this 'elite' expressed a growing scepticism and an oppressing attitude towards immigrants and also suffered from a lack of reflection on their own position. Since this group were the dominant meaning-formers of society, Gullestad feared that their attitudes would spread as general opinion. Perhaps we, in our time, also need strangers like Anacharsis to pose critical questions.

The 'other' is institutionalised both as an individual and as a whole society. In his work *Orientalism*, Said (1978) presented the dichotomy 'west–east'. He called for more critical and objective narratives around the West's descriptions of the Orient (East). He argues that non-orientalist writers often generalise the 'Orient' (i.e. half of the globe) as *one* culture. What is worse, he suggests an adversarial viewpoint that does not take into account the large number of smaller, culturally different regions. A ranking of immigrants, based on the distance from 'us', is the next step. We are not sure that an expression like 'Far East' is history. Said argues that using an approach that constructs other people as 'exotic' is a way of denying and giving closure to an equality dialogue.

We have found it fruitful to re-read Simone de Beauvoir (1949) who deals with another classic dichotomy – *man–woman* – presented in *The Second Sex*. She describes how women take, or are placed in, the position of 'the other'. She uses the concepts 'transcendence' (exceed borders) and 'immanence' (stand by). The transcendental is connected to the man and the immanent position is the woman's. Beauvoir claims that this situation is not caused by biological factors but by cultural norms and, since it is cultural, it is also possible to change it. Beauvoir's solution is mutual acceptance.

It is possible to transfer Beauvoir's and Diogenes's understanding of this asymmetric power into a frame of kindergarten life. If Norwegian cultures dominate, the majority of children may be placed in the Greek's or the man's role, while immigrant children take the place of Anacharsis or women. The latter group are perceived as underdogs, their culture being neither visible nor accepted in the same way.

Who decides the agenda?

Admission to intellectual development should also be debated in an integrated society. According to Freire, knowledge is a social construction whereby distribution of power in the society plays an important role: 'Knowing is a social process, whose individual dimension, however, cannot be forgotten or even devalued' (1970: 92). He demonstrated how illiterate people in Latin America, invited to be literate on the premises of the powerful class, suffered from a double oppression. They had a lack of both knowledge of letters and of the social and cultural meanings in texts. Freire's educational solution was to present systems for reading based on the experiences of the learners. The Norwegian philosopher, Skjervheim (1957), presented a similar angle in his essay on 'participants and spectators', inspired by Socrates, who used dialogue as the basis for equality of opinion. The 'other' should never be an object: when we objectivise another person, we intrude on her/his freedom. In dialogue, participants should never have control over each other; both parts should function as subjects.

Consequences

With these diverse examples, we want to demonstrate that working with integration in kindergarten needs more than sympathy, different flags and exotic food. We want to involve students and preschool teachers in theories that bring to the surface how thinking in dichotomies can marginalise individuals or groups. But the dichotomies can also be used as a basis for more professional understanding. Consciousness about the differences opens up possibilities for both teachers and children to reflect and begin a dialogue.

Perhaps our traditional concepts have lost their content and have denied us the possibility of reflecting. Do *multiculturalism* and *diversity* mean anything to teachers? Could one answer be that we need new words to create new situations? Welsch (1999) attempted that when he recommended the word 'transcultural' as a substitute to intercultural or multicultural. He argues that, in a transcultural society, the majority and the minority are challenged in equal ways. Both are 'forced' to change their meanings and adjust habituated attitudes towards each other. All are in an educational and transformational process, based on a reflection of who I am, not waiting for others to be like me. Hofstedte (1992) presents two forms of cultural meetings. First, he presents the resource perspective, where society meets different cultures as an added value and as an arena for mutual learning. Second, he warns against the problem perspective. Here, the majority is wide open for all possible conflicts, risks and added work.

In our evidence-based world, perhaps the next step could be to construct indicators of a true integrative (or transcultural) kindergarten. Then we start with visible and *wanted* diversity in cultures, language, people (both employees and children), literature, pictures and activities – and dialogue around it.

Kindergarten practice and pedagogy

The realisation of cultural equality in kindergartens is impossible to prescribe. The conscious preschool teacher can do this in a competent way. We can, however, point out some areas where cultural equality can be considered. These include:

- the kindergarten room
- language
- food
- indoor and outdoor activities
- cooperation between parents and kindergarten.

These are areas which affect the everyday life of kindergartens and where every institution more or less consciously and explicitly has defined certain practices. This is important, because it is the everyday life with all its repetitions and obviousness, which influences us the most. This also means that preschool teachers with their creativity and competence can develop these areas into arenas of equality without cultural stereotypes and prejudices and without the cultural dominance of one majority culture. In this way, the background of each and every child can be valued and every child enabled to explore cultural heterogeneous environments, broadening their knowledge of the world and increasing their respect and tolerance towards others.

The kindergarten room

In every society, there are rather stereotypical ways of organising the kindergarten room. If a photo of a kindergarten room is shown to a group of people, it will immediately be recognised as a kindergarten room. The form and the materials of the rooms, the furniture, shelves, colours, equipment and information letters at the walls tell the viewer what kind of room it is. The design is realised both through every element in the room, which can be considered as a meaning-making sign (Kress and Van Leeuwen, 2006), and through the organisation of all the elements in the room which together make overall meaning for the person entering the room or looking at a photograph of the room. When we interpret a text or a room, we build on cultural experiences and expectations. Bright colours of furniture may, for example, be associated with children's rooms. Names marked on the shelves tell us, among other things, that it is an institution and not a child's private room.

However, in this context, the question is whether the kindergarten rooms only tell of the culture of western children or of the culture of all children in the kindergarten. It is important to ask how consciously the kindergarten rooms are designed with a multicultural perspective. Is it so that the children belonging to the ethnic majority may enter familiar and safe environments in the kindergarten every day because the design of the rooms has many elements, which correspond to the children's experiences from rooms in their own houses? And is it so that children from cultural minorities have to build a bridge over gaps between the kindergarten environment and their home surroundings every day? After a while, these children will have certainly experienced that the kindergarten surroundings are safe and a part of their life too. Still, we think that it does something to the children and also to their parents if the cultural representations, in such important institutions as schools and kindergartens, recognise only the majority culture. On the other hand, a mainly culturally homogenous design of the kindergarten rooms will decrease the opportunities for all children to explore rooms recognising other cultures. It is also the case that the design of a room invites only certain activities which are considered important in a particular cultural context. In a Norwegian kindergarten, the children should have places for gatherings, places for working with colours, clay, wool and other materials but also large spaces for playing. The rooms are designed to make these activities possible. Another design gives other possibilities for activities and playing (Papatheodorou, 2011).

An interesting example was found on the walls in Storgata Kindergarten in Grimstad, Norway. The teachers told us:

> We have several world maps where we train children to find all the different countries the families come from. The parents have written 'Welcome' in their mother tongues on posters in the entrance and all the immigrant children have two flags on their name plates in the wardrobe – the Norwegian and the flag of their (or their parents') country of origin.

Language

The language of the kindergarten will, in most societies, be the language of the society's majority population. Linguistically, the dichotomy 'we' and 'they' is quite obvious, where 'we' are all the people having the majority language as the mother tongue, while 'they' are all the people having a minority language as their mother tongue. Language is used in all kinds of situations in and outside the kindergarten, sometimes constituting activities when, for example, a book is read and we talk about it, and sometimes accompanying the activities when, for example, children play football or make a drawing (Halliday and Hasan, 1989). For children with a minority language as their mother tongue, this linguistic dichotomy is a part of their daily life, and reminds them of another status in society that the majority has.

Linguists, however, emphasise the importance of exploring different languages in the early years (for example, Høigård, 2006). Two languages with different linguistic realisations of the same concept develop the mind in a fruitful way so that flexibility and nuances in ways of thinking are promoted. Instead of being seen as less experienced language users, children with two languages (or more) should be seen as a linguistic resource for all children in the kindergarten. Through the presence of competent multilinguistic children, all children are able to meet several languages if the kindergarten teachers organise daily life in a way which makes the meeting and sharing of several languages possible. Here, knowledge about the importance of linguistic diversity is crucial but also the pedagogical creativity of finding daily life situations where several languages can be used. Such situations could be anything from conversations accompanying the changing of clothing, having a meal or working with a practical task to gatherings or special events where language is the topic.

When children experience hearing and perhaps speaking a different language, it is easy to draw attention to the language itself. Developing a meta-relation for language – meaning to talk about language as language – is seen as important when children learn to read and write. In a homogeneous language society, it is rather abstract for young children to talk about language as a meaning-making system. In practice, when they recognise language diversity, it is much easier and obvious to talk about languages and to understand that it is not a one-to-one relationship between the oral and the written expression, on the one hand, and the meaning on the other.

In a research project, English was introduced to children of 3–5 years in two kindergartens in Norway (Elvin et al., 2007; Maagerø and Simonsen, 2006). The children took great pleasure in their English 'lessons' and developed a broader understanding of language in general and also a comprehension that the new language was more than Norwegian. One experience from the project is worth mentioning. In one kindergarten, we met a little boy from Pakistan. His mother tongue was Urdu and he did not use much Norwegian at home, which made him a rather lonely and quiet child in the kindergarten: he had problems of communication with other children. His parents wanted very much that he be a part of the English project and his experiences here gave him a new status in the group of children. In the project, all the children started off on the same level, including the Pakistani boy, which gave him the same possibilities to explore English as the other children. Perhaps because of his competence in Urdu and also in Norwegian (even if his Norwegian was still rather poor), he learned quite a lot of English quickly, faster than many of the other children. He was one of the competent ones and this made him motivated and much more communicative in Norwegian as well. He was not 'the other' any more but one of the proficient English users.

Again, we give an example from a teacher in Storgata Kindergarten in Grimstad, Norway:

> We say hello and count (to at least five) in a different language almost every day. In addition, the different languages have their special weeks with a special focus. It seems that all the children develop a high level of language awareness.

Food

Food is culture and food connects and separates people. This fact is easy to see when food is related to different aspects of religious life. Food is also an important issue in kindergartens. However, it seems that discussion about food in kindergartens is more related to health than to culture. Healthy food in kindergartens and schools is certainly a most important factor but this and other questions about food have, in addition, a cultural dimension. As mentioned above, food as culture seems to be a topic only in connection with so-called 'international days' in kindergarten which, in our opinion, rather emphasises the dichotomy of 'us' and 'them'. On these special days, food may be served which smells and tastes different, some-thing which makes it exotic and special and not part of people's daily life. Our question is: would it be possible to integrate food from different cul-tures in the everyday life of the kindergarten?

In the Norwegian kindergarten, the staple food is bread with cheese or salami and a drink of milk. This is easy to organise both indoors and out-doors, many children would eat it, it takes only a short time to prepare and, if the bread is brown, it is even considered to be healthy and nutri-tious. This way of eating lunch is different from even our nearest neighbours, Denmark, Sweden and Finland, where eating habits may include warm food and more vegetables. In other cultures, rice, perhaps with a sauce, is as normal for lunch as the Norwegian slice of bread. Again, it is a question of letting the majority culture be challenged by taking into account that the world has changed and that we live in a multi-cultural society. It is somehow strange that parents may visit expensive restaurants with their children where the cooking is French, Indian, Creole, Chinese and such like as something special, or cook dishes from other cultures at the weekends, but still let children with different eating habits and norms be 'the others' in the daily life of school and kindergarten. How much work would it be to let all children sample a larger variety of food from dif-ferent cultures in kindergarten? Would it be much more expensive? Would it be possible to discuss what kind of food is healthy in different cultures? Would children who meet a variety of tastes and smells be able to eat more nutritionally and healthier as adults? And will food provide positive meet-ing places across cultures?

In Storgata Kindergarten in Grimstad, they state:

> Often we have big family dinners in the kindergarten with a lot of people. The responsibility is shared by all parents and the chefs for the day choose both adult and children as assistants. The result is that the children like and respect all kinds of food, and in addition we have the social gifts.

Indoor and outdoor activities

If we take Norway as a point of departure when we talk about indoor and outdoor activities, we can perhaps, with quite a large degree of certainty, say that the mainstream opinion among kindergarten teachers is that chil-dren should play outdoors and participate in outdoor activities every day (see also Chapter 2). This has to do with important values in Norwegian society. To experience nature is considered very valuable and the relation-ship between nature and people should be strong. Another value is that outdoor activities make children healthy and strong and young children should develop their motoric competence by climbing trees and up hills and mountains. This means that children in kindergarten are outdoors in snow, heavy rain and wind. They have good clothes and boots and they also have meals outdoors in all kinds of weather. In some kindergartens, the children spend most of the day outdoors and might not have a building, but a lavvo (a kind of tent) with a small fire when they need to warm themselves. There are even kindergartens going out on the sea to an island by boat every day and their only building is the boat. All this is bound to a culture, to a Nordic culture, with strong beliefs about what is good for children.

The problem is that this way of thinking may be generalised in a way that other opinions about outdoor and indoor life are made invisible or unacknowledged. In many cultures, it seems ridiculous and also unhealthy to spend several hours outdoors if it is cold or raining. Nature is not a friendly place in such circumstances and it is not acceptable that children should walk alone in the woods or go out on the sea. From this perspective, it is not difficult to see that many parents may be anxious about their children. If kindergarten teachers do not take this into account, it is easy for the majority culture to dominate the daily life of many people. Most parents want the very best for their children. It is difficult to handle a system where somebody knows much better than you what is good and healthy for your child. The gap between cultures may be so large, especially in contexts like this, that the result is the children are taken out of kindergarten. Again, our question is, how can a great variety of activities be included in everyday life in kindergarten, activities that are representative of several cultures? Could dancing and moving to music be healthy activities in addition to outdoor activities? Could the development of a healthy body be something to discuss?

A Norwegian preschool teacher said:

> In the beginning there will be some head shaking, but very soon the parents, used to quite another climate, are happy to see their child playing outdoors in all kinds of weather.

Cooperation between home/kindergarten

Parents' participation has an important role both in schools and kindergartens in Norway. It is written in law that parents have the main responsibility for the upbringing of their children. A successful cooperation is dependent on mutual respect and understanding. Kindergarten, as an institution representing the majority culture, may put immigrant parents in an insecure position. Feeling that they have to follow a set of rules that may often be unclear, they may play a passive role that is not wanted either by the teachers in kindergarten or themselves. In the worst case, they try not to have much dialogue. The way the kindergarten copes with this challenge from the earliest encounter can turn this into a positive and developing experience. Instead of presenting the institution's expectations to the parents, it is a good start to ask what the parents think will be best for their own child. By offering the parents the role of expert on their own child, they feel welcome to represent their culture and their habits. This can be a long-lasting process, because the points of departure may greatly differ, but the gains will be worth it.

Once more, we quote a teacher in Storgata Kindergarten in Grimstad:

> We always use interpreters when we have parents' meetings to ensure that we understand each other precisely and also to give the parents a feeling of equality. And the initiatives during the meetings come from both parts.

 ## Summary

In this chapter, we have focused on the dichotomies 'we' and 'them' which, in many ways, are based in western culture (Said, 1978). The way we think and the way we do things are part of culture, and many things we just do and say without reflecting because they are so deeply grounded in our cultural context. It has been our aim to lift such unreflective attitudes and values to a level of consciousness where we can talk about them. We have done this through examples of different thinkers who we think can enable us to develop this reflection process. We will emphasise that it is a process. Thinking and habits in daily life take time to change. In this, we all are challenged, both majorities and minorities.

We have also pointed out some areas in kindergarten life which could be a starting point for practical work. We want to emphasise that these areas are examples, areas we find important because they belong to everyday life in kindergarten. The competent kindergarten and preschool teachers will perhaps see other possible ways to develop. The important thing is the willingness to rethink and renew practice to open up for the world.

 ## Questions for discussion

1. What kind of attitude to diversity is embedded in a resource perspective – and in a problem perspective?
2. What is wrong with looking at people as exotic?
3. Why should language diversity not be neglected?
4. How do you understand the double oppression described by Paolo Freire?

References and suggested further reading

Entries in bold are further reading.

Beauvoir, S. de (1949) *Le Deuxieme Sexe (The Second Sex)*. London: Vintage Books.

Elvin, P., Maagerø, E. and Simonsen, B. (2007) How do Dinosaurs Speak in England?: English in Kindergarten. *European Early Childhood Education Research Journal*, **15(1): 71–86.**

Freire, P. (1970) *Pedagogy of the Oppressed*. London: Continuum.

Gullestad, M. (2002) *Det norske sett med nye øyne [The Norwegian set of new eyes]*. Oslo: Universitetsforlaget.

Halliday, M.A.K. and Hasan. R. (1989) *Language, Context and Text: Aspects of Language in a Social-Semiotic Perspective*. London: Cambridge University Press.

Hofstedte, G. (1992) *Organisasjonerochkulturer: Om interkulturellförståelse*. Lund: Studentlitteatur.

Høigård, A. (2006) *Barns språkutvikling: muntligogskriftlig*. Oslo: Tano-Aschehoug.

Kress, G. and Van Leeuwen, T. (2006) *Reading Images: The Grammar of Visual Design.* **London and New York: Routledge.**

Lucian (1992) *Etordskifteomidrott (Anacharsis)* (translated by EilivSkard). Oslo: Det Norske Samlaget.

Maagerø, E. and Simonsen, B. (2006) *Engelsk i barnehagen [Polly put the kettle on]*. Oslo: Sebuforlag.

Maagerø, E. and Simonsen, B. (2009) *Norway: Society and Culture.* **Kristiansand: Portal forlag.**

Norwegian Ministry of Education and Research (2008–9) *Quality in Kindergarten: White Paper No. 41*. Oslo: Ministry of Education and Research.

Oxford English Reference Dictionary (2002) Oxford: Oxford University Press.

Papatheodorou, T. (2011) Creating a Positive Behaviour Environment. In J. Moyles, J. Georgeson and J. Payler (eds) *Beginning Teaching, Beginning Learning*. Maidenhead: Open University Press.

Said, E. (1978) *Orientalism*. London: Vintage Books.

Skjervheim, H. (1957) *Deltaker og tilskodar [Participant and spectator]*. Oslo: Oslo University Press.

Van Oers, B. and Hännikäinen, M. (2001) Some Thoughts About Togetherness: An Introduction. *International Journal of Early Years Education*, 9(2): 101–8.

Welsch, W. (1999) Transculturality: The Form of Cultures Today. In M. Featherstone and S. Lash (eds) *Spaces of Culture: City, Nation, World*. London: Sage.

Pedagogic activities for early education in a child-to-child programme in South Africa

Mary James and Hasina Ebrahim

Overview

This chapter presents preliminary findings from a qualitative study which explored pedagogic activities in a child-to-child programme aimed at early education. The Little Elephant Training Centre for Early Education (LETCEE) in rural KwaZulu-Natal initiated The Buddy Programme which used children between the ages of 8 and 13 years to promote early education for young children who were unable to access centre-based provision. The chapter begins with a discussion on the context for child participation. The thematic discussions shed light on pedagogic activities which are supportive of early education through community building, affirming local culture and the introduction of school culture. The value and challenges of the programme are also discussed.

In South Africa, early childhood development (ECD) refers to children from birth to 9 years. The most vulnerable children are from birth to 4 years. These children are unable to access centre-based provision. They are in home-based care with families at risk. Targeted interventions using home visiting and community outreach are emerging as ways to address vulnerabilities in the care environment of poor families (see Ebrahim et al., 2008; Rule et al., 2008). One of the key principles informing these interventions is the notion of communities as resources for ECD.

Older children are viewed as valuable human resources that can intervene in the lives of young children. The *UN Convention on the Rights of the Child*, ratified in 1995 in South Africa, was one of the key legislations enabling the use of child-to-child participation for ECD. The rural cultural context, where intervention is most needed, is highly supportive of child participation in early care and education.

Nsamenang (2008) notes that from an African perspective, sibling caretaking is part of a social network. It is not unusual for African parents to delegate the responsibility of childcare to older siblings. The author further notes that the social integration of older children into activities such as childcare helps in the development of prosocial values, socio-cognitive and production skills. Free mixing of multi-age groups is also beneficial to young children's learning and development. It could be argued that older children have more recent perspectives of early childhood than adults. They are, therefore, well placed to connect with young children.

The fertile context for child participation in South Africa has led to the development of ECD programmes in which older children serve as facilitators of young children's development and learning. The aim of this chapter is to explore the pedagogic activities in the child-to-child Buddy Programme.

Research context and methodology

The Buddy Programme was developed by LETCEE in Greytown in rural KwaZulu-Natal. It is part of a larger Family Support Programme which aims at reaching children (birth to 4 years) and families at risk. It operates in two rural communities. The buddies are boys and girls aged 8–13 who reside in the community. They mostly come from female-headed households which are poverty-stricken. Some family members are infected with HIV/AIDS.

There are two ways in which buddies are identified. Family facilitators who visit homes in the Family Support Programme identify children who are likely to provide support to young children. Information is provided to the community and some children volunteer to be part of the programme. Some children perceive the programme as a status-enhancing mechanism.

A qualitative approach was deemed most suitable for this study. This approach enabled the capturing of activities in action and discussions of experiences, perspectives, views and opinions of participants. Multiple methods were used to produce the data. Site observations were undertaken to capture the natural unfolding of pedagogic activities. These observations also provided the opportunity to scan the environment, to take note of the contents of the Buddy Programme and to hold snatching conversations with caregivers and young children. Field notes were used to capture site accounts. In order to obtain specific accounts of the programme, semi-structured interviews were held with buddies, the coordinating family facilitator, project manager and a former chief of the area. Focus group interviews were designed to deepen understanding of the programme. These were held with the buddies and the family facilitators.

Consent for the study was obtained from the community and all participants. All participation was voluntary. Confidentiality was assured. For the buddies and young children, the research activities were explained in a developmentally appropriate way by the researcher and research assistant. Respondents were encouraged to speak in the language in which they felt most comfortable. The research assistant acted as the translator as the need arose.

The data was analysed using an adaptation of the approach advocated by Miles and Huberman (1984). Each data set was read several times to identify the nature of the pedagogic activities. These were clustered into a descriptive text which informed the development of themes in the preliminary findings.

How the Buddy Programme works

The buddies receive a toy bag. The bag contains construction toys, colouring books, crayons, a ball, a skipping rope and story books both in IsiZulu and English. The buddies visit the children in the afternoons and over weekends. In winter, they visit the children mostly on weekends. For safety reasons, three buddies are allocated to groups of children from a particular geographical area closest to their homes. Buddies fetch the children from their homes and select a homestead for a session. Children between the ages of 2 and 5 years are targeted but school children aged 6–9 also join in. The session lasts for about 30 minutes. Each session begins and ends with a prayer. This practice is consistent with the religious practices of parents in the community. There is free play with toys, reading, song, dance and games.

Pedagogic activities
Building communities for early education

The notion of community creates a sense of belonging within a group (Osterman, 2000). In the Buddy Programme, this begins with the buddies building a community of practice for outreach. The buddies receive camp-style training. Once identified, they are taken to a venue in the community where they spend a week with facilitators. The first part of their training is heavily geared towards learning about themselves. They are encouraged to share their experiences through story telling. The interview of the project manager indicated that this was a culturally appropriate way to get the buddies to personally locate themselves in relation to the upcoming work. She explained that the stories are deeply emotional and help the buddies to confront their vulnerabilities, build on their strengths and connect with others that have similar experiences.

Self-esteem and leadership development are part of the training programme. Buddies are equipped with knowledge on children's rights and
responsibilities and context formation such as HIV/AIDs, risk, resilience
and factors of vulnerabilities. Practice buddies receive training on developmentally appropriate activities for young children including those who are
disabled. Once trained, buddies are supported and monitored by facilitators in the Family Support Programme.

In the Buddy Programme, the communities for learning are fluid and complex. The buddies use open-air classrooms. The sites for learning are
backyards of homes. Given the temporary nature of homes in the area, the
sites shift and change. Once the buddies go around fetching children to
form a playgroup, the surrounding homesteads become alert to pedagogic
activities. The buddies also enter backyards which are already occupied by
other activities carried out by adults and/or older children.

During site observations, it was evident that buddies have a range of
resources at their disposal. For example, upon entry into a site the buddies
met a grandmother with a 2-year-old child, two teenage boys and their
mother tilling the soil on the fringes of the backyard. The activities
attracted a teenage mother with a toddler and a nearby neighbour.
Together with the children in the playgroup, all community members
remained for the full duration of the activities. Some took an active role as
participants in activities.

The buddies together with the community members developed a sense of
shared work and commonality of purpose. Balaban (2003) states that this
togetherness is an important element for community building. For example,
once the activities were underway, the grandmother participated as an
observer and then as an instructor. She directed the buddies on how to facilitate a transition from a reading activity to Zulu dancing. Once this was in
progress, she noted that the buddies were not cheering on the children. She
encouraged and praised the children and the buddies joined in. During the
dancing, a teenage boy became an extra resource to demonstrate dance movements to the children. They also showed children how to complete activities
when buddies were occupied. Other adults took on onlooker roles which pre-
sumably would shape their thinking about young children's learning.

It was evident that the context in the Buddy Programme favoured multi-
age and generational participation for early education. These informal
clusters served as important platforms to expose young children to learning as a social experience. The older children and adults used their
competence and experience to support the buddies. The open-air classroom provided a flexible environment for learning.

Adults, either through active participation or onlooker roles, also bene-
fited. In an interview, a grandmother indicated that the buddies were

providing her with ways in which to work with young children. An interview with a family facilitator revealed how buddies were playing an important role in helping the community understand activities suitable for young children. This was especially important in a context where adults experience high levels of stress and trauma which affects the nature of adult–child relations.

Affirming the culture of the community

The spirit of community building described above is in keeping with the notion of *ubuntu* which encourages people to live in connected ways (Nussbaum, 2003). When *ubuntu* is the driving force, the responsibility for children does not only reside with biological parents but also with others that inhabit the community. This collectivist way of early education is affirmed in the Buddy Programme. It develops older children's skills to be responsive to the needs of the community and serves as an important way to bring people together to intervene in the lives of young children.

The Buddy Programme plays an important role in facilitating social integration. In a focus group interview with family facilitators, it was noted that boys aged 10–13 are most likely to take to drugs and alcohol. Girls fall pregnant at an early age. The Buddy Programme creates an alternative which helps the children to see themselves as worthwhile beings who can make a difference in the lives of people in the community. They intervene in the lives of young children and strengthen relationships in the community for early education. In a description of how buddies are contributing to the community, a former chief of the area noted that they were learning respect for themselves and teaching it to others around them.

From a cultural perspective, the Buddy Programme used the local ways of knowing as a strong resource to shape early education. The mother tongue was used as the language of teaching and learning. This served as an important tool for the buddies to help young children to name things, make connections and talk about what they were learning. Some story books were in IsiZulu. Some books had illustrations which were relevant to the rural context in which the children lived. This presented images that young children could easily identify with.

Zulu dancing, songs, counting and rhymes were used to affirm cultural experiences and to create fun and enjoyment. In site observations, this part of the programme was enjoyable for young children as they attempted to repeat words and imitate the body movements of buddies and other community members who joined in. The children were exposed to perspectives in body movements. The buddies tended to be extremely agile and the older members had difficulty keeping up with movements. This made young children laugh.

Introducing school culture

One of the critical problems experienced in reception year classes (5–6 years) in the South African context is the lack of school preparedness of children making direct transitions from home to school. Poor socio-economic circumstances mean that parents, especially those in rural areas, are unable to access centre-based early education. The Buddy Programme socializes children into a school culture.

One of the first ways in which the buddies introduce a school culture is through redefining the backyard space. The moment the buddies arrive with their toy bags, the backyard becomes a place and space where young children encounter the world of books, toys, routines, transitions and activities. They are exposed to a new world to meet their developmental, literacy and numeracy needs. In one site observation, the buddies trans-formed the existing space by placing a grass mat on the floor and arranging the toys and equipment on one side. This was the buddies' attempt to cre-ate an inviting learning environment.

The buddies used timetables in a flexible way to introduce the children to a structured environment. In site observations, the buddies used their own judgements, the interests of the children, changes in the weather and reac-tions from community members to shape activities with the children. They attempted to include children in both individual and group activities. In order to alert children to transitions, they used verbal cues, songs and clap-ping. For younger children, the change was difficult. These children integrated into the new activities once they began. The joining in of com-munity members, the activity around the backyard and the sounds of animals did create some disruptions in the learning programme.

One of the ways in which the buddies encouraged learning was through modelling. This teaching technique helps young children to learn by copying the behaviour of others, either in totality or in part (Gordon and Browne, 2004). For example, in the colouring book session, the buddies sat next to the children. The children were taught how to grip the crayons and colour. Verbal descriptions and actions were used. For those that experienced difficulty, the buddies held their hands to guide fine motor movements. The children were encouraged to talk about their pictures. Some buddies used sentence starters such as 'I see ...' to assist the children.

Reading was approached in an age-appropriate way. For younger children, the buddies sat next to the children and told them a story through picture reading. Sometimes the children would identify the pictures before the buddy could continue with the story. The buddy responded and carried on. During this session, children got distracted and this led to a change in activity. School-aged children who joined the programme were encouraged to read to the buddies, either in IsiZulu or English, whilst young children listened for short durations or played with toys. During this time, there was code switching from IsiZulu to English. This was one of the ways in which young children received exposure to English.

The value of the Buddy Programme

Training and notions of raised self-esteem helped buddies to play a valuable role not only in early education but also in supporting households. The project manager noted how buddies were becoming active in repairing homes, fetching medication from clinics, checking up on children and fetching water from communal taps to assist the elderly. They were also taking on the role of peer messengers. In visiting homes, they were able to identify situations of risk and reported them to peers and their project coordinators.

In interviews with the buddies, they spoke about how the programme was helping them to become better people in the community. They spoke about how the programme had assisted them to learn about themselves, how to work with young children and people in the community. They were grateful for being given the opportunity to be teachers and to show respect to other children. They also spoke about how their work as buddies brought relief from the responsibilities they are normally tasked with in their homes.

The children under the care of the buddies had positive things to say about them. In conversation with the young children, they spoke about enjoying activities with the buddies. They wanted the buddies to remain with them or to come back quickly. The school-aged children enjoyed the play activities with the buddies and the opportunities to develop their reading skills and learn new things.

Family facilitators in a focus group interview noted that the Buddy Programme was creating new images of children in the community. The buddies were viewed as people doing good work for the communities. Families were happy that the children were gainfully occupied. One family facilitator explained how sibling conflict created negative images of brothers and sisters in families. She noted that the Buddy Programme equipped children with skills for relationship building which provided them with alternatives on how to relate to siblings in the family.

Challenges experienced

The buddies explained that whilst they liked the work they did, it did cut across other competing priorities. This related to demands that the school made on their time. They had to juggle buddy activities and school work on the same day. During the winter months, the days were short and it was difficult for the buddies to reach the families. During these months, sessions were reduced to weekends.

Whilst there were mostly positive images of the buddies, some did have negative experiences. They were stigmatised for playing with young children. This social group lacks status and work with them is, therefore, perceived as unimportant. The task of home visiting was not viewed as valuable although this was changing.

Both the communities in the Buddy Programme lived in sparse settlements. This meant that buddies had to walk long distances to reach the children. This was tiring for them. The family facilitators and the buddies proposed the use of bicycles for quick access to the children.

The family facilitators noted the need for stakeholders to be brought in to talk to buddies aged 11–14 years. They felt that the buddies needed more guidance in managing their sexual behaviour. The buddies leave the programme by age 14. In order to ensure that they expand their knowledge and skills, there needs to be a follow-up programme and a youth programme is now being developed.

In some quarters, children's participation in early intervention programmes is perceived as child labour. In this programme, the community context is highly supportive of older children positioning themselves as early educators and caregivers. The buddies learn life skills and become agents for community building and social cohesiveness. They do not receive monetary gains but are rewarded by broadening their scope for being contributing members of their community. This perspective of child participation needs greater exposure in order to change perceptions on children's roles in intervention programmes.

 Summary

The Buddy Programme, as an example of child-to-child participation, presents a way of reaching young children who are unable to access centre-based early education. It shows potential for how older children in a poor community can be used as resources in young children's lives. The buddies play a modest part in helping expand the developmental potential and opportunities for optimal learning for young children. They form an extra helping hand in a larger programme aimed at supporting the development of socio-cultural capital for early education in a vulnerable context.

Questions for discussion

1. Why do we need alternatives to centre-based provision for early childhood education in the developing world context?

2. How can older children/adolescents be used as resources for early childhood education for poor and vulnerable children?

3. What is the value of generational participation in early childhood education in the context of rurality and poverty?

References and suggested further reading

Entries in bold are further reading.

Balaban, N. (2003) Creating a Caring, Democratic Classroom Community for and with Young Children. In J. Silin and C. Lippman (eds) *Putting the Children First: The Changing Face of Newark's Public Schools*. New York: Teachers College Press.

Ebrahim, H.B., Killian, B. and Rule, P. (2008) *Report on Practice, Principles, Methodologies, Core Interventions, Networking, Stakeholder Analysis, Outcomes and Benefits* – Lesedi Family Support and Community Development Programme – Free State. Unpublished research report, UNICEF.

Gordon, A.M. and Browne, K.W. (2004) *Beginnings and Beyond: Foundations in Early Childhood Education*. New York: Thomson Delmar Learning.

Gracia, M., Pence, A. and Evan, J.L. (eds) *Africa's Future, Africa's Challenge*. Washington, DC: World Bank.

Hawes, H., Bailey, D. and Bonati, G. (eds) *Child to Child Resource Book*. Available online at: http://www.child-child.org/resources/index.html.

Miles, M. and Huberman, M.A. (1984) *Qualitative Data Analysis*. Beverly Hills, CA: Sage.

Nsamenang, B. (2008) (Mis)Understanding ECD in Africa: The Force of Local and Global Motives. In M. Gracia, A. Pence and J.L. Evans (eds) *Africa's Future, Africa's Challenge*. Washington, DC: World Bank.

Nussbaum, B. (2003) Ubuntu: Reflections of a South African On Our Common Humanity. *Reflections*, 4(4): 21–6.

Osterman, K. (2000) Students' Need for Belongingness in the School Community. *Review of Educational Research*, 70(3): 323–67.

Rule, P., Ebrahim, H.B. and Killian, B. (2008) *Report on the Practice, Principles, Cost Drivers, Interventions, Methodologies and Stakeholder Analysis of the Project Based on the Concept of ECD Programmes as Resources for the Care and Support of Poor and Vulnerable Young Children – LETCEE: Siyabathanda Abantwana and Sikhulakahle Interventions*. Unpublished research report, UNICEF.

UNICEF and SIDA (2006) *Child and Youth Participation Resource Guide*. Available online at: http://www.unicef.org/adolescence/cypguide/files/child_and_youth_participation_guide(1).pdf

Transition to preschool education in Greece: attitudes of parents and educators

Anastasia Papaprokopiou and Athina Kammenou

Overview

From its establishment until now, Greek social policy has been differentiating the needs of children in education and care/welfare. This policy has led to two different types of institutions for early years provision: kindergarten and daycare centres, respectively. Even though in many European countries education and care have been integrated to establish a framework for integrated services, in Greece the two types of provision continue to co-exist and operate under different operational frameworks which inform practice. The induction of young children into daycare, the focus of this chapter, is one of the issues guided by the requirements of the relevant policy frameworks. This chapter reports on the preliminary findings of a study conducted among parents and teachers to examine their attitudes and practices with regard to the induction of young children into daycare settings. The findings indicate that induction procedures and processes for children are mainly informal. Parents appear satisfied with the services they receive, making no suggestions for change.

Studies at international level highlight and demonstrate the social and educational benefits of early years institutions for young children and draw attention to the importance of the smooth transition of children from family to these institutions (Brooker, 2008). Many researchers have particularly emphasised the significant role which parents play in their children's adjustment and participation in early years institutions and their period of transition (Bosse-Platière et al., 1995; Moss and Pence, 1994). Children's transition from home to early years settings is seen as a natural continuation in their lives rather than as an unavoidable necessity and, for this reason, many researchers and teachers have focused their interest on exploring children's transition from one setting to another (Dunlop and Fabian, 2006; Rayna and Brougère, 2005; Pirard and Thirion, 1998; Rayna et al., 1996; CRESAS, 1983).

In Greece, however, parents' roles and involvement in the transition of children from family to daycare centres is less explicitly acknowledged. This chapter presents the findings of a study which examined the attitudes of parents and early years practitioners towards transition practices. But, first, we provide background information about early years provision in Greece by considering historical and policy issues influencing the current situation.

Early years provision in Greece

From its inception until now, social policy in Greece has differentiated the needs of children in relation to education and care/welfare. This model of social policy has been instrumental in the development of two types of early years institutions: the kindergartens (νηπιαγωγείο – nipiagogeio) which focus on children's education, and daycare centres (παιδικός σταθμός – paidikos stathmos) which concentrate on children's care and welfare. Traditionally, the first were, and still are, regulated by the Ministry of Education, while the latter were controlled by the Ministry of Health and Welfare (Iatridis, 1980) and, currently, by local government.

Attempts by the state in Greece to validate early years provision were first made in 1896, leading to the establishment of the first public kindergarten and state daycare centres in 1922 and 1926 respectively. Later on, especially during 1941–1960, state daycare centres were established for large minority groups mainly in border and rural regions of Greece in order to support language and literacy skills among the population of these regions. In the following decades, the State continued to establish and operate daycare centres in these regions, ignoring the changing demographics of the country which experienced rapid urbanisation and saw the rise of women's employment. This led to the unequal distribution of daycare centres throughout the country, demonstrating that the choices made by the State did not coincide with the contemporary needs of the Greek urban family (Papaprokopiou, 1988; Papathanasiou, 2000).

In many European countries, childcare institutions have now evolved into integrated education and care regimes (Oberhuemer et al., 2010; Plaisance, 1977). However, until recently in Greece the two types of institutions coexisted. Kindergartens were providing education and care for children aged 4–6, while daycare centres were available for children aged 2 years 6 months to 5 years 6 months. The current situation with regard to early years provision in Greece has been marked by a series of measures taken by the State to respond to the needs of both young children and their families. During the last decade, national policies and laws, and directives from the European Union, have created demands and new challenges which have decisively influenced and determined the structure and operation of preschool institutions (Papaprokopiou, 2003). These measures concern:

- the establishment of 'all-day public kindergartens' in order to address the needs of working parents. The 'all-day kindergartens' operate extended hours (from 08.00 to 16.00) and are under the jurisdiction of the Greek Ministry of Education, Lifelong Learning and Religious Affairs (Public Law 2525/97)

- the introduction of compulsory early years education for all children from the age of 4 years (Public Law 3687/2008)

- the changeover of the supervisory body of state daycare centres from the Ministry of Health and Welfare to the local government, and attempts to address operational matters (Public Law 2218/94, Article 42). Municipalities and communities undertook the administration of the childcare centres and integrated them into their own structures and internal operating regulations, creating opportunities for decision making and local arrangements.

Today, educational provision in kindergarten is offered free of charge to all 4- to 6-year-olds (from 08.00 to 12.00) with extended hours for a number of children attending all-day kindergartens (from 08.00 to 16.00). State daycare is only available to families in which both parents are in employment and have low incomes. This separation decisively contributed to taking 4–6-year-olds out of daycare centres. However, a large number of 4-year-olds still remain in daycare centres, thus depriving younger children of free places. In Greece in 2010, only a small number of nursery schools accepted children under 2 years, and mainly in large urban centres, while the percentage of children under 1 remains extremely low.[1] In effect, in the past, the state policy mainly encouraged private initiatives.

The operation of daycare centres

Since their establishment, daycare centres have been operating with specialised staff holding a relevant professional qualification. Initially, all positions were filled by staff with a graduate qualification from the wider field of welfare (e.g. βρεφονηπιοκόμος – vrefonipiokomos; nursery teacher – νηπιαγωγός). Over the years, many changes have taken place with regard to the employment and working conditions of staff in daycare centres. However, these were mainly based on the government's negotiations with teachers about work conditions rather than an in-depth analysis of the operation of the daycare centres. The child–teacher ratio continues to be high, while specific administrative responsibilities and boundaries with regard to the roles of personnel are not clearly defined (Papaprokopiou, 1988).

It was not until 1988 that daycare centres adopted explicitly child-centred educational curricular activities. Childcare and welfare remained as the primary functions of nursery provision, given that the law did not clearly define the requirements in order to formulate educational curricula (Government Gazette FEK 546/1988). Daycare centres were strictly childcare and not educational centres.

Previous studies converge in their conclusions concerning three main issues related to the operation and function of daycare institutions in Greece (Papaprokopiou, 1988; Papathanasiou, 2000). These are: the structure and operation of daycare classes; children's everyday life in nursery schools; and the role of parents.

The structure and operation of daycare classes

Most public daycare centres are housed in rented properties and often in old detached houses, apartments or shops. The areas where children mainly spend their time include the playroom, the dining hall, the bedrooms and the yard, if one is available.[2] The typical layout seems to be repeated across all nursery schools with tables and chairs for each child and the areas of interest and learning often being poorly equipped. Educational materials are usually found on the highest shelves because the majority of teachers believe that the materials may be destroyed due to the children's inability to respect or handle them properly.

The walls are either decorated with posters or with unvarying patterns and filled-in outlines. The windows are covered with multi-coloured curtains that seal off the natural light. According to a study by Papaprokopiou (1989), these arrangements reflect specific educational beliefs which are designed to restrict the movement of children in an effort to preserve a kind of calmness. This, however, hides systematic efforts of coercion by staff on children.

The curriculum is followed almost exclusively only when the children are seated in chairs and at desk-based activities, with limited freedom for children to choose either materials or friends. Restricting the movement of children is also taken into account when choosing areas in general, the larger rooms being used as bedrooms, while the smaller areas are used as playrooms (Papathanasiou, 2000). The outdoor areas are rarely designed in a purposeful way that would help children to organise their own activities and games, and the outdoor equipment is often unsuitable or poorly maintained. Interestingly, even daycare centres which are housed in contemporary buildings constructed more recently, have maintained the model outlined above. As a result, the areas basically available for activities involving all the children are still restricted.

Children's everyday life in daycare centres

Everyday life in public daycare centres faithfully follows the specifications of the legal framework and the approach that governs their operation (Government Gazette FEK 546/1988). Eating time, nap time and tidying-up time take up most of the day and are well organised. During those times, the staff are present and activities are well coordinated within the given timetable. The rest is free time which is not systematically organised around educational goals. When the opportunity arises to implement curriculum activities, these include a short, specific and structured group task of colouring in photocopied sheets, doing some handicraft usually based on a current celebratory theme or reading a story. The aim of these routine activities and lack of playful activity is to calm the children (Sidiropoulou and Tsaoula, 2008; Papathanasiou, 2000; Papaprokopiou, 1988).

The role of parents

By studying the laws and decrees referring to preschool education, it is evident that the government believes a child's learning comes exclusively from teachers. Nowhere is it stated that there should be communication or collaboration with other bodies or individuals whose presence will be linked to learning activities within the nursery school. Parents in particular do not have the opportunity to express their view formally, as staff seem to believe that daycare conveniences them sufficiently; it does them a 'favour' and 'cares' for their child when they cannot do so at home. In addition, staff also appear to believe that parents who, in the majority, belong to lower socio-economic strata, are uninterested in these relationships (Papaprokopiou, 1989). As a result, loneliness and seclusion traps teachers in a daily routine which does not allow them to add value to their relationships with parents.

Formal meetings usually take place at the beginning of the school year (perhaps to elect a parent representative) or around holidays including (and mainly) Christmas. The informal daily contact between parents and staff usually concerns questions of everyday matters, such as whether the child has eaten or not and other such mundane or routine issues. The absence of parents from their children's daily activities and events in the daycare setting follows the complete and abrupt transition of the child into the new environment. Despite the fact that the induction of children is considered the most significant criterion for the quality of provision (Brooker, 2008; Dunlop and Fabian, 2006; Lazaridou, 1985), current regulations and guidance do not require any specific arrangements for children's transition to their first environment outside the family.

Administrative autonomy – opportunity for innovation and change

Within this overall situation, the Athens Municipal Crèche (AMC), which has adopted a contemporary operational framework, is an exception. The administrative autonomy which the daycare centres have enjoyed with the changeover of supervisory authority and the political choices of those in charge of the AMC to give priority to children of working mothers, are the main factors for change (Papaprokopiou, 1988). Other factors include the representation of external interested partners in the administration of the AMC and the emergence of a dynamic educational movement which developed during its founding. This movement managed to promote contemporary educational provision and innovations and include many of them in an internal operating regulation.[3]

The introduction of ideas from contemporary educational models has positively influenced the restructuring of areas that have been problematic in the past (such as inappropriate accommodation or lack of outdoor space). The creativity of teachers and the support offered on the part of administrators have brought about changes such as setting up play areas, introducing borrowing libraries and recycling corners and the creation of areas to be used exclusively by the infants of the crèche departments or for specialised workshops.

By instituting the presence of parents and restructuring the curriculum, the Athens Municipal Crèche gave teachers an opportunity to prepare for the adjustment of new children by introducing staggered induction, with the parents being present inside the classroom often over a number of days (Grammeni, 2001). This contact helped parents build a positive relationship with the teachers and the rest of the staff who actively participate in the life of the daycare centre at all levels, for example from bringing in materials and contributing financially to having a say in the educational curriculum as well as participating in the life of the centre. Although the relationships with parents differ, depending on the policy followed by the centre, the majority of head teachers make strenuous efforts to improve their relationships with parents. They strongly believe that, in order to address the personal needs of children, they have to support daily contact with parents to share information. This approach demonstrates the potential for a quality relationship between parents, their children and the staff of the daycare centre.

Interaction with external partners also creates a momentum in relationships and attitudes, which constantly make teachers question their educational practices. Over the last few years, an intrinsic investigative educational approach is starting to emerge and, with the support of other bodies (such as the European Institute for the Development of the Potential of All Children [IEDPE], the Society for the Development and Creative Occupation of Children [EADAP], the University of Patras and the Melina

Merkouri Foundation), it creates new conditions for evaluating and propagating innovative actions. The contribution of the Synergy Educational Programme (EADAP, 2003) in promoting innovations and especially in fostering the relationship between parents and teachers has been significant (Papaprokopiou and Papadakou, 2004).

This analysis demonstrates that when the internal operating regulations adopt contemporary stances for preschool education, they can affect positively the relationships between those involved, the views they hold and the educational climate that prevails in daycare centres. It also demonstrates that the integration of the two functions of childcare and education can work effectively. However, the specific regulations apply only to the Athens Municipal Crèche; the majority of childcare institutions continue to focus on childcare, whereas education, in principle, remains an exclusive privilege of kindergartens.

Investigating parents and teachers' attitudes towards children's induction practices

Within this overall context, it was considered important to examine the attitudes and expectations of both parents and teachers towards induction practices for young children entering daycare centres. We report only on the findings of the initial stage of an ongoing study which has been conducted in the prefectures of Attica and Fokida, Greece. The study participants were 150 teachers and 213 parents, whose children attend public daycare centres (Kammenou, 2009). They completed a questionnaire anonymously which included both open and closed responses. The questions concerned:

- the structure of the first meeting with the new parents and the meeting process
- the child her/himself and any possible innovative practices to facilitate her/his smooth transition and integration into the daycare setting.

Some questions were common for both groups of participants.

The key findings of this study supported the results of previous studies with regard to the relationship between the policy of the childcare centre and the way teachers approach the induction of new children.

Teachers' attitudes and practices

The vast majority of teachers reported that initial contact was made with the head of the daycare centre mainly for exchange of information, for instance for parents to 'fill out the paperwork' and the head teacher to 'give them information about the timescale and hours, what the children should bring with them – clothes, water bottle, etc.'. Parents' first contact with the daycare centre is usually made informally as 'most of them learn about the nursery school because they live in the neighbourhood ... they usually see me [the head teacher] out on the street'. This first meeting with the parents may last from a few minutes to half an hour.

The teachers, however, meet the parents for the first time on the day they bring their children to the daycare centre. On this first day, the parents may stay for a short while, usually outside the classroom. Only a small number of teachers welcome parents into the classroom and some of them, with the agreement of staff, may stay for a few hours and/or over a period of 3–4 days. What mainly concerns teachers is getting to know the parents but not for the parents to get to know the daycare centre, its staff and curriculum (see Figure 7.1). Teachers, however, are aware that parents want to know and be informed about the curriculum, the daily pace of life and how the teachers meet their child's needs (see Figure 7.2). They are also aware that parents' requests go beyond what teachers consider to be the priorities.

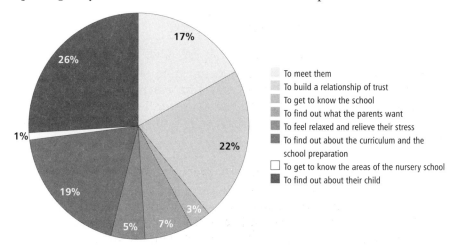

Figure 7.1 What concerns teachers?

When children are accompanied by their parents for the first time, the techniques of induction are mainly substituted by parents' love, pleasant dispositions and calmness. Only a small percentage of accompanied children deal with someone other than their own parents. Teachers follow different approaches to parents' presence and children's responses. Some state that 'when they (parents) come, I tell them to sit for a while and then leave mainly because the child is crying, and the more it sees them, the worse it is'. Others invite parents to 'sit in a corner and observe for as long as they like. If a child cries, then they leave with her/him'.

Only a very few teachers suggested some type of formal induction practices (11 per cent). These practices included having individual questionnaires to be filled in by parents on the first meeting and shared copies of them to facilitate conversations.

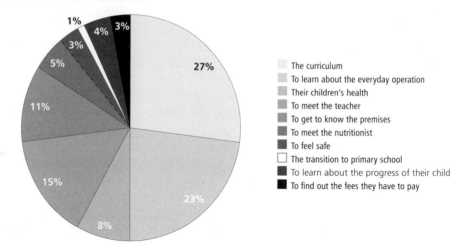

Figure 7.2 How do teachers meet children's needs?

Parents' attitudes and expectations

The parents confirmed the teachers' responses with regard to how long they stayed at the daycare setting and the time rarely exceeded half an hour. The parents explained that 'they [the teachers] told me to leave because the other way would have been worse' or 'I was sitting on a bench across from the daycare centre and waited just in case they called me and told me to pick up my child'.

Parents' expectations about teachers' practices were clear and mainly focused on recreation rather than childcare. About 48 per cent of parents preferred for the staff to occupy their child with recreational activities, while 18 per cent said they would like staff to assist their child in expressing her/himself and learning to be self-sufficient. Some parents (15 per cent) expressed an expectation that teachers would educate their child so that s/he would 'become sociable', 'play with other children' and 'not become egocentric'.

With regard to the first days of integration, more than half of the new children stayed at the daycare centre for 3–4 hours without the parent being present. It is important to note that, although parents seemed satisfied with the daycare centre, they were not always happy to leave their child. Their dissatisfaction, however, mainly concerned their own feelings of guilt, stress and sense of loss rather than concern about the daycare practices (see Figure 7.3).

This also explains why most families do not want to change anything with regard to their association with the nursery school (80 per cent). The changes they suggested primarily concerned the way the children were occupied (20 per cent). For example, they wanted the child to 'be more creative' and to be informed 'about how their child is kept occupied'. A very small percentage of participants (2 per cent) made suggestions that concerned the institutional framework and raised issues such as child–teacher ratios or their longer stay at the daycare centre during their children's induction there.

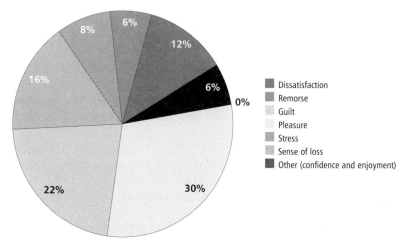

Figure 7.3 Parents' views on daycare practices

☐ Summary

From the preliminary findings of the initial stage of this study, it is evident that informality and teachers' own attitudes and judgements guide how young children are inducted and integrated into the daycare setting when they first arrive; there are no formal procedures and practices nor is there any formal relationship with parents. Formal requirements are restricted to information exchange by filling out forms. Only a small percentage of teachers consider the parents' presence a constraint for the smooth adjustment of their children.

Parents, on the other hand, appear satisfied with the induction strategies. Their concerns are mainly about the way children are occupied in the daycare setting. They have a clear picture of the role of the daycare settings as places for children's socialisation and recreation. As a result, the majority of them made no suggestions for change with regard to their relationship and collaboration with the teachers, and the educational curriculum.

Teachers and parents' attitudes and expectations, however, require further investigation to understand them within the existing policy framework and the cultural underpinning of Greek society.

Questions for discussion

1. What kind of framework/strategy could ensure a qualitative induction in daycare centres?
2. Should a framework/strategy of induction be universal or flexible and adapted to each setting?
3. Could the adoption of practices in the family setting by the day-care centre improve the children's livelihoods there?

Notes

1 The data comes from lists made available by the practicum committee of the Athens Technological Education Institute, Preschool Education Department.
2 This term refers to the layout of the classroom based on old school beliefs, whereby the main element is the absence of respect for the personal needs of the children. See Frangos (1999).
3 The operating regulation for the Institute's nursery schools was approved by committee decision 12915–60/81.

References and suggested further reading

Entries in bold are further reading.

Bosse-Platière, S., Dethier, A., Fleury, C. and Loutre-Du Pasquier, N. (1995) *Accueillir le jeune enfant: quelle professionnalisation? [Welcoming the Young Child: What is Professionalism?]* Ramonville: ERES.
Brooker, L. (2008) *Supporting Transitions in the Early Years.* Maidenhead: Open University Press.
CRESAS (1983) Ecole en transformation: zones prioritaires et autres quartiers, *[School in Transformation, Priority Zones and Other Areas]*. 1. Paris: L'Harmattan INRP.
Dunlop, A.W. and Fabian, H. (2006) *Informing Transitions in the Early Years: Research, Policy and Practice.* Maidenhead: Open University Press.
EADAP The Society for Development and Creative Occupation of Children (2003) *Towards Co-operative and Participative Training in Preschool Education.* Athens: Typothito Press.
Frangos, H. (1999) *Psychopedagogiki.* Athens: Gutenberg.
Grammeni, F. (2001) Organisation and action research for the gradual entry and adjustment of children to nursery schools. Proposal at the 3rd annual convention of the methodology and educational programmes unit entitled The Teacher as a Researcher. University of Patras.
Iatridis, D. (1980) *Social Planning and Policy Alternatives in Greece.* Athens: National Center of Social Research.
Kammenou, A. (2009) Parents' Points of View About the Role of Nursery Schools. In M. Paramythiotou and C. Angelaki (eds) *OMEP European*

Regional and Conference 2009 Conference Proceedings – Current Issues in Preschool Education in Europe: Sharing the Future (pp. 195–201). Available online at: www.omep.gr/texts/Conference_proceedings_Syros.zip

Lazaridou, L. (1985) Integration and adjustment. In *Nursery Schools: Educational and Preventive Issues*. Material 2 of the Preschool Education Seminar. Thessaloniki: Psychological Health Centre.

Moss, P. and Pence, A. (eds) (1994) *Valuing Quality in Early Childhood Services: New Approaches to Defining Quality*. London: Paul Chapman.

Oberhuemer, P., Schreyer, I. and Neuman, M.J. (2010) *Professionals in Early Childhood Education and Care Systems: European Profiles and Systems*. Opladen and Farmington Hills, MI: Verlag Barbara Budrich.

Papaprokopiou, N. (1988) *Les structures d'accueil pour les enfants de moins de trois ans en Grèce: Réflexions critiques et perpectives d'avenir. [Daycare Centres for Children under Three in Greece. Critical Reflections and Future Prospects.]* Doctorat du 3ème cycle. Paris: Université Paris V Sorbonne.

Papaprokopiou, N. (1989) Social Interactions in Preschool Education. *Syghroni Ekpaidefsi*, 48: 66–72.

Papaprokopiou, N. (2003) Daycare Centers, Yesterday, Now and Tomorrow. In EADAP (ed.) (2003) *Towards Cooperative and Participative Training in Preschool Education*. Athens: Typothito Press/Giorgos Dardanos.

Papaprokopiou, N. and Papadakou, E. (2004) *10 Years of Synergy*. Athens: EADAP.

Papathanasiou, A. (2000) *Curricula and Activities in State Nursery Schools of the Ministry of Health and Welfare*. Athens: Typothito Press/Giorgos Dardanos.

Pirard, F. and Thirion, A.M. (1998) Une formation-action-recherche qui favorise le développement de nouvelles compétences professionnelles d'encadrement des lieux d'accueil de la petite enfance. In Impulser, accompagner, coordonner: une formation européenne à l'encadrement des professionnels de la petite enfance. [Training-action-research that promotes the development of new professional competences and frameworks for early childhood. Promote, assist, coordinate: a European training framework for professionals in early childhood. Report IEDPE. Construction of a methodology for the support and training of professionals of preschool education.] Rapport IEDPE dans le cadre du Programme Leonardo da Vinci de la CCE. Paris: IEDPE.

Plaisance, E. (1977) *L'Ecole maternelle aujourd'hui. [Nursery School Today.]* Paris: Fernand Nathan.

Rayna, S., Laevers, S. and Deleau, M. (1996) *L'éducation préscolaire: quels objectifs pédagogiques? [Early childhood education: pedagogical objectives?]* Paris: Nathan Pédagogie, INRP.

Rayna, S. and Brougère, G. (2005) *Accueillir et éduquer la petite enfance: les relations entre parents et professionnels. [Welcoming and educating young children: relationships between parents and professionals.]* Lyon: INRP.

Sidiropoulou, T. and Tsaoula, K. (2008) *The Daycare Centers and the Research*. Athens: Ypsilon.

Part 3

Cultural Perspectives on Curricula

Introduction

Janet Moyles and Theodora Papatheodorou

In this section, we turn to issues related to the early childhood curricular experiences of children and teachers with three further chapters which explore measurement, literacy and observation and assessment. In a majority of countries, the curriculum is prescribed by a central or regional government who will use national and community cultures to determine what – and sometimes how – children should learn and be taught. But the greater socio-cultural and economic issue is concerned with the purposes of education and, relatedly, curriculum content and processes. Some societies, such as the Scandinavian countries, value early childhood as a period in its own right, whereas others see this phase as developing children for later formal education and work. If the content and methods prescribed by policy makers appear inappropriate or irrelevant to children's needs, this can create real conflict for teachers and other practitioners as they try to balance curricular demands against socio-cultural perspectives of children and childhood, classroom cultures and their own beliefs and values. As Ruddock and Flutter (2000) remind us, schools in particular have changed less in their deep structures in the last 20–30 years than children have changed. Whilst new curriculum policies appear to be developing all the time, they are often predicated on very traditional – and often formal – education practices. Specific tensions arise from these social developments and the particular curriculum, content, pedagogy and assessment practices which have evolved as a result of specific national cultures.

Early education internationally is 'clearly intended to be the dominant means of the intergenerational transmission of culture' (Moyles and Hargreaves, 1998: 5) and, as UNESCO has shown, a majority of countries are now financing early childhood education and care (ECEC) with this and economic determinants in mind (UNESCO, *Education for All*, 2006). High up on any curriculum content list is literacy and numeracy, without which it is known that children cannot progress satisfactorily in the school context, but how this content is determined and implemented in practice is open to much debate, especially in the early years (Taylor and Pearson, 2002). At all stages in education, however, there are different facets of a curriculum to be considered, for example the official (or government regulated) content element, the schools', settings' and teachers' planned curriculum, the 'delivered' curriculum (what actually happens in classrooms and settings, often influenced by observation and assessment) and the curriculum as it is received by children. Each of these is culturally influenced and it is not difficult to see how complex the interplay between each of these elements is likely to be. Moreover, in the early years, we must consider children's overall development, well-being, health, socialisation and such like, adding to the complexity.

Bertram and Pascal produced a résumé of international early years practices and drew several conclusions:

• virtually all participating countries had defined curriculum guidelines for children over the age of 3 (not under 3) but they varied in detail and prescription

- most curriculum guidelines for those over 3 years of age included: social and emotional; cultural; aesthetic and creative; physical; environmental; language and literacy; and numeracy

- many countries emphasised cultural traditions and aimed to enhance social cohesiveness.

Interestingly, only three countries (England, Ireland and the Netherlands) emphasised early literacy and numeracy within the early childhood curriculum (2002, adapted from p. ii).

In terms of assessment, Bertram and Pascal found that some countries had (summative) 'assessment on entry to compulsory schooling, primarily a developmental checklist for identifying special needs' and that 'most countries used assessment as a diagnostic ... tool in developing their curriculum programmes' (2002: iii). This contrasts with many Scandinavian countries – and particularly the *Reggio Emilia* settings in Italy – which all use formative assessment based on observation and analysis to respond to individual children's learning and development needs.

Contributors to this section essentially examine the link between the core values embedded in the curriculum and its implementation. The issue of numeracy – and in particular children's understanding of linear measurement – is the focus of Chapter 8, in which Ronit Alin reports on her investigation in Israel into young children's understanding of the concept of linear measurement. She found that a structured study programme has the capability of long-term enhancement of mathematical knowledge in young children. She also revealed the crucial importance of positive teacher attitude, subject knowledge, pedagogy and knowledge of child cognitive and social development in effective teaching, thus linking with earlier sections of this book.

Literacy, in the form of children's books, is the focus of Chapter 9, the context for which is the USA. Pat Kostell stresses her belief that the narratives in children's books, whether fiction or non-fiction, enable the child to create an understanding of diverse cultures. Pat found in her research that, as they tell and retell stories, whether orally or in writing, children can be seen to construct their own knowledge of a culture and land other than their own.

From numeracy and literacy, we turn finally to observation and assessment. Paulette Luff uses examples from European contexts to explore the concept of policy-determined 'learning outcomes' (as in England) as the antithesis of the more open and responsive practices of our European neighbours. Paulette contrasts the clear guiding philosophies and cultural ideals of these countries with the prescriptive, statutory framework of the English Early Years Foundation Stage (DCSF, 2007) and the challenges and dilemmas that this presents to practitioners. However, she follows this up by suggesting how a middle way can be found, in which systems of observation, assessment and planning required by prescriptive curricula such as the EYFS can be used effectively to promote children's care and enrich their learning.

No doubt international arguments will continue to rage over what young children should learn but, returning to the opening quote, whatever is taught needs to lead learners to their own understandings and to the threshold of their minds, if they are all to achieve at the highest possible level.

References

Bertram, T. and Pascal, C. (2002) *Early Years Education: An International Perspective.* Birmingham: Centre for Research in Early Childhood/London: QCA. Available online at: www.inca.org.uk/pdf/early_years.pdf (accessed 15 March 2011).

Department for Children, Schools and Families (DCFS) (2007) *Early Years Foundation Stage.* London: DfES.

Moyles, J. and Hargreaves, L. (1998) *The Primary Curriculum: Learning from International Perspectives.* London: Routledge.

Ruddock, J. and Flutter, J. (2000) Pupil Participation and Pupil Perspective: Carving a New Order of Experience. *Cambridge Journal of Education,* 30(1): 75–89.

Taylor, B.M. and Pearson, P.D. (eds) (2002) *Teaching Reading: Effective Schools, Accomplished Teachers.* Mahwah, NJ: Lawrence Erlbaum Associates.

United Nations Educational, Scientific and Cultural Organisation (UNESCO) (2006) *Education for All – Global Monitoring Report: Strong Foundations.* Available online at: http://unesdoc.unesco.org/images/0014/001477/147794e.pdf (accessed 14 March 2011).

Teaching linear measurement in the Israeli kindergarten curriculum

Ronit Alin

Overview

This research investigated the influence of the implementation of a linear measurement concepts programme in a kindergarten in Israel. The research aimed to create a new understanding of existing theories on the development of mathematical concepts in kindergarten children and to define issues that would help kindergarten educators to develop a programme to support these concepts. The findings indicated that the designed programme enhanced the children's understanding and that their linear achievement level was markedly higher than that of a control group, even after a period of seven months. This suggests that a structured study programme has the capability of long-term enhancement of mathematical knowledge in young children and that they can learn beyond their cognitive stage, subject to appropriate learning conditions. The findings also revealed the crucial importance of positive teacher attitude, subject knowledge, pedagogy and knowledge of a child's cognitive and social development in effective teaching.

In Israel, for many years, young children in kindergarten were not engaged with subjects considered to be beyond their cognitive development stage. The philosophy was that 'kindergarten is not school' and that teaching

115

and learning in the kindergarten should deal with general subjects that concern children and relate to their everyday routines. The daily programme in kindergartens often varied as some teachers put emphasis on language, reading and writing, while others emphasized creative activities or nature and science subjects.

In my work as a maths instructor, I realized that few kindergarten teachers underscored maths education. There was no official mathematics work plan and even the curriculum gave only a broad outline that was not always implemented. Although in most kindergartens there were maths games and, occasionally, a corner with numbers and quantities, little was being done apart from simple counting. Most kindergarten teachers did not know how to teach mathematics in general and linear measurement specifically to the children with whom they worked.

In 2003, a kindergarten teacher challenged me to teach linear measurement in her kindergarten, when she stated: 'I know that linear measurement is in the curriculum, but I don't know what and how to teach it'. Moreover, she was not the only one; other kindergarten teachers made the same statement. This statement and the teacher's confusion brought me to plan a programme for teaching the subject of linear measurement to kindergarten children.

The study programme was based on three themes: (1) the subject of linear measurement focusing on concepts of linear measurement, approaches to teaching the subject and the requirements of the Israeli curriculum; (2) developmental psychology related to the cognitive and social development of 5–6-year-old children; and (3) the kindergarten ethos with particular emphasis on peer interaction and teacher–child interactions.

What do we know already?

Most of the research into teaching mathematical concepts is based on the work of Piaget who argued that young children have limited understanding of concepts of measurement due to their lack of general understanding of quantity (Piaget et al., 1960). While some researchers supported his view (Bladen et al., 2000; Kamii and Clark, 1997), others showed that young children can learn the subject when the tasks are simple enough and they receive appropriate support (Stephan et al., 2003; Hiebert, 1984, 1981; Bryant and Trabasso, 1971). Vygotsky's (1978) work, especially his concept of the 'zone of proximal development' (ZPD), is supportive of the view that these concepts can be taught with appropriate support and considering children's experience in their social environment. My assumption is that for a better understanding of how children develop linear measurement concepts, we must take into account the training techniques we use, the child's cognitive and social development and the social context of the kindergarten setting.

Research set within both Piagetian and Vygotskyan frameworks indicates that collaboration with both adults and peers can have positive effects on children's cognitive development in the course of collaboration. Ellis and Rogoff's (1982) and Gauvain and Rogoff's (1989) results indicate that working with adults in pairs has benefits: other researchers such as Azmitia (1988), Roazzi and Bryant (1998), Verba (1998) and Johnson-Pynn and Nisbet (2002) suggest that working with an 'expert' child in pairs advances the novice child's cognitive skills.

The premise that the teacher's behaviour has an effect on the children's behaviour has been examined by theoreticians and researchers, for example Cohen (1981) and Birch and Ladd (1998). Although these theoreticians and researchers came from different schools of thought, they all agreed that positive teacher–child relationships have an important role in shaping children's behaviour and, as a result, influence their perceptions of the ability to learn.

The programme to teach linear measurement

Although Vygotsky's theory (1978) did not deal with linear measurement directly, it influenced the planning of my programme. My assumption was that for a better understanding of how children develop linear measurement concepts, we must take into account the child's cognitive and social development and the social context of the kindergarten setting in our teaching practices. Following Stephan et al. (2003), I planned an intervention programme that focused on five study stages: direct comparison, direct comparison and seriation, indirect comparison, measuring length with non-standard devices and measuring length with a non-standard ruler. In the course of the programme, the use of linear measurement vocabulary and terms and the concepts of linear measurement were developed.

The programme consisted of 18 sessions (as outlined in Table 8.1) and was conducted in one kindergarten in Israel, with 12 children with an age range of 4:11–5:11 years (the average being 5:2 years). The work was undertaken once a week for seven months. In most of the sessions, the children were divided into three groups. Each session was for a period of 20–30 minutes with a similar structure. I followed Kazemi's (1998) and Steele's (1998) models of teacher–children interaction during the structured learning experience. The sessions usually started with posing a problem that the children had to solve (Kirova and Bhargava, 2002) and used open-ended questions such as 'I wonder what would happen if …?' to expand thinking and draw the children's attention to new ways of thinking and interacting. This was followed by an activity in which the children worked alone or with a partner using materials arranged on the table. Most of the materials and objects used were kindergarten toys, such as Domino blocks and building blocks.

Then we had a discussion and each child or pair presented their solutions while the other children commented. The session ended with conclusions and a summary of what had been learned in the lesson; sometimes a new problem (based on a previous study) was posed and the children had to solve it, using the same materials, in the whole area of the kindergarten.

Although the programme was basically structured (the study stages, concepts, terms and vocabulary), only some of the activities were planned ahead. It remained flexible and allowed for the everyday social life in the kindergarten to influence it by changing or revising the activities. For example, the activity *teaching young children to measure lengths by using non-standard devices* (session 7), was not planned ahead and the ideas came from the children themselves. The children in the 'younger group', who did not participate in the programme, were curious and interested in what the older children were doing. They gathered in the study corner and followed the older group in the playground and tried to copy their actions. On the other hand, the children who participated in the research also wanted to share their learning with their younger friends. They liked to show them the material and how to compare length. They even wanted to teach them what they had learned in the subject of linear measurement. The idea of teaching the younger children came from the research group, as Josef explained: '*B (a young child) hasn't learned how to work with the circles. Can I teach him?*' The children were seated in pairs, a research group child with a younger child, and the research children taught the younger ones how to measure length with non-standard devices. Both groups enjoyed the activity. The benefit to the research group of this interaction was twofold: on the one hand, they revised their learning and, on the other hand, the 'teaching' gave them confidence in their actions and especially helped the shy and less confident children in gaining self-confidence and believing in their ability to learn and understand the subject of linear measurement.

Another example relates to the activity *creating identical bracelets by comparing a ribbon strip with a same-length stick* (session 3). The idea for this activity arose from observing the children creating bracelets for their hands. For the created ruler, it was the children's suggestion to use the 10cm block as a measuring device.

Evaluating the linear measurement programme

For the evaluation of the programme, the following tools were used:

1. Tests: To assess the children's progress in the study of linear measurement, I used a pre-test at the beginning of the study; a post-test at the

Table 8.1 The programme design

Topics	Concepts	Terms and Vocabulary	Materials
Pre-test			
1 **Direct comparison** Compare the lengths of two strips	Unit iteration	'common starting line', longer/shorter than	Two strips: 10cm and 11cm.
2 **Direct comparison** Compare the lengths of objects to the stick's length	Unit iteration	'common starting line', longer/shorter than, longest, shortest	15cm stick, boxes, dolls, big cubes, pencils etc.
3 **Direct comparison** Create a ribbon strip with the same length as the stick	Unit iteration *Transitivity*[1]	'common starting line', longer/shorter than, longest, shortest	15cm stick, roll of ribbon, scissors.
Assessment tasks			
4 **Comparison using a single mediator**	Unit iteration Transitivity	'common starting line', longer/shorter than, longest, shortest	Picture of two lines of equal length (one horizontal and the other at an angle) materials from the kindergarten: pencils, paper strips, sticks.
5 **Measuring with non-standard devices**	Unit iteration *Accumulation of distance*	'common starting line', straight line, 'attached end to end'	The same picture from lesson 4. Domino tablets, small cubes, small circles, sticks.
6 **Measuring with non-standard devices** Measuring furniture and big objects	Unit iteration Accumulation of distance	'common starting line', straight line, 'attached end to end'	Domino tablets, small cubes, small circles, sticks. … Books, bench and tables.
7 **Measuring with non-standard devices** Peer interaction and teaching the young children	Unit iteration Accumulation of distance	'common starting line', straight line, 'attached end to end'	Domino tablets, small cubes, big cubes, small circles, sticks. Books, bench and tables.
8 **Measuring with non-standard devices** The need to measure with the same device	Unit iteration Accumulation of distance	'common starting line', straight line, 'attached end to end'	Pictures of animals, Domino tablets, small cubes, small blocks, small circles, paper clips.
9 **Thoughts about arranging a 'Linear Measurement Corner'**			Collective discussion.
10 **Constructing a 'Linear Measurement Contract'**			Paper, glue and material from the 'Handiwork corner'.
11 **Designing the 'Linear Measurement Corner'**			Collective discussion.
12 **Measuring with non-standard devices** Measuring large objects	Unit iteration Accumulation of distance	'common starting line', straight line, 'attached end to end'	Rug, table.
13 **Measuring with non-standard devices** Measuring with two types of device	Unit iteration Accumulation of distance *Relation between number and measurement*	'common starting line', straight line, 'attached end to end'	Picture of two lines (see lesson 4). 5cm blocks and 10cm blocks.
14 **The need to create a ruler**			Collective discussion.
15 **Creating rulers and measuring with the same length or shorter objects**	Unit iteration Accumulation of distance	'common starting line', straight line, 'attached end to end'	60cm paper strips, 10cm blocks, pencils. Objects from the kindergarten: boxes, books etc.
16 **Measuring with the ruler** Combine rulers to measure furniture	Unit iteration Accumulation of distance	'common starting line', 'straight line', 'attached end to end'	The children's rulers, tables, bench, chest.
17 **Measuring with the ruler** Combine rulers to measure objects in the kindergarten yard	Unit iteration Accumulation of distance	'common starting line', straight line, 'attached end to end'	Objects from the kindergarten yard: sandbox, ladder, etc.
Post-test			
18 **Peer learning**	Length conservation Relation between number and measurement		Box with 1cm blocks to 10cm blocks.

[1] The concept that was learned for the first time is emphasised with italic.

end of the programme; and a post-post test six months later after the completion of the programme. The post-post test was also given to a control group that included children attending other kindergartens.

The test provided information about cognitive and behavioural aspects of children's learning. The tasks in the tests examined the study stages, the concepts of linear measurement and children's understanding of specific terms. Some of the tasks were the same ones given in the pre-test, while the other tasks examined concepts, terms and vocabulary that were learned during the programme: some of them were also given in the assessment tasks. In addition, sitting individually with children during these tests helped me to know what each child really understood about the subject of linear measurement, how s/he coped with the given task and whether s/he used correct vocabulary – issues not always clear while working in a group.

2. Observation: During the sessions, I used video observation and took field notes. The observations and documentation helped me to assess the children's understanding and make decisions as to whether to go on with the planned programme, to revise or add more activities.

3. Children's work: Samples of children's work were examined to give me an idea of what the children had learned during the programme. Samples included worksheets, where the children designed, created and drew what they thought important to exhibit in the 'linear measurement corner'. The children worked on these sheets individually without directed instructions. Therefore, those worksheets were another way of assessing the children's understanding of the concepts and which they found to be the most important.

What we know now

Changes in children's understanding of linear measurement concepts

The data gathered from all tests (pre-test, assessment tasks, post-test and post-post test) was analysed. The tasks in the tests examined the study stages, the concepts of linear measurement and children's understanding of specific terms. Some of the tasks were the same ones given in the pre-test, while the other tasks examined concepts, terms and vocabulary that were learned during the programme: some of them were also given in the assessment tasks.

The study stages tasks dealt with the children's ability to compare lengths, to arrange objects according to their length and to measure lengths with non-standard devices and non-standard ruler. The test results show that there was a marked improvement in the children's achievements in four study stages of linear measurement (direct comparison, direct comparison and seriation, indirect comparison and measuring length with non-standard devices). The fifth study stage, measuring length with a non-standard ruler, was not assessed at the pre-test stage.

There was no marked difference between the achievements of the research group and those of the control group in the first and second study stages. However, a marked difference between the achievements of the two groups was evident in the third, fourth and fifth study stages (see Figure 8.1).

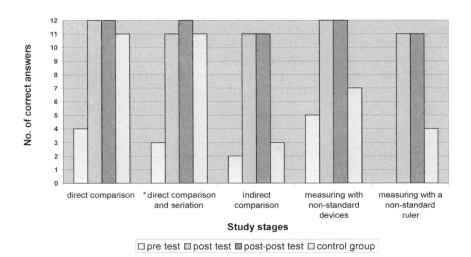

Figure 8.1 Level of success in the tests according to the study stages of linear measurement

As can be seen from the test results, in only two study stages – those of direct comparison and direct comparison and seriation – were there minimal differences between the research group and control group. It would seem that progress in children's understanding in these stages is the result of their natural process of cognitive development and not necessarily a result of the study programme. Support for these findings and assumptions can be found in the work of Halford (1982, 1993) and Baroody and Coslick (1998).

The differences between the groups indicate that improvement in the three study stages (indirect comparison, measure with non-standard devices and ruler) is due to the study programme and compatible with the Informational Processing Approach (Hiebert, 1984); by using meaningful activities and giving assistance, children were capable of understanding how to compare objects by using indirect comparison, how to measure by using non-standard devices and a ruler, why they have to do so and what it means.

Most of the concepts were understood and practised during the fourth and fifth study stages (measure with non-standard devices and ruler). The concepts – unit iteration, accumulation of distance and partitioning – were assessed in the pre-test while others – transitivity, conservation and relation between number and measurement – were assessed during the learning period in the assessment tasks. All the concepts were assessed in the post-test and in the post-post test. The results of the tests indicate that there was an increase in the children's achievements in all linear measurement concepts, although not all the concepts were understood to the same degree (see Figure 8.2). The concepts of unit iteration and transitivity were understood by all children, while in others (the concepts of conservation and relation between number and measurement) only some of the children showed understanding. In all concepts, however, the research-group children achieved higher scores than the control group. This progress in the ability to understand the concepts was mainly due to the study programme. Support for this assumption appears in the work of Sophian (2002) and Castle and Needham (2007).

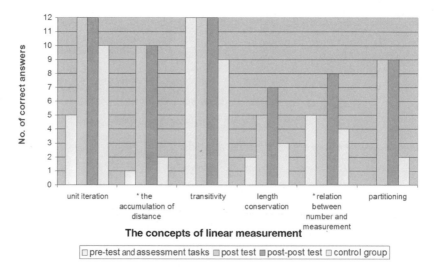

Figure 8.2 Level of success in the tests according to the understanding of the concepts of linear measurement

Concept development through peer interaction

The programme was based on both types of learning interactions, that is, with peers and with the teacher. I found that both had an equally crucial role in learning and in developing cognitive abilities in the subject of linear measurement. According to Piaget (1932), discussion between children has an effect on cognitive development since it prompts children to give up old conceptions and structures and build new ones.

The findings from video-recordings and field notes showed that when the children were presented with solutions which conflicted with their own, they re-examined their own responses leading them to reconstruct their ideas. It was also found that in situations where the children worked in asymmetric peer pairs, the less advanced child learned from a peer. Additionally, three different ways of learning from peers were observed: verbal and non-verbal explanation, demonstration, and observation. This is exemplified in the excerpt below, where the children were shown two identical lines, one was measured with yellow blocks and the other with orange ones:

R: So what do you think? Which line is longer?

David: The line with the yellow (smaller) blocks because there are more yellow blocks than orange blocks.

Rebecca: [*referring to David's answer*] No, the line's length is the same, because the yellow blocks are smaller than the orange ones.

R: I see that we have a disagreement here about which line is longer. What do you think? Which line is longer?

Eva: [*bursting in*] I have an idea!

R: Yes? What is your idea?

Eva: Let's put them attached. [*Eva moves the orange blocks and attaches them to the yellow blocks.*]

R: OK, the blocks are attached. What have we found?

David: They are the same length.

Rebecca: I knew it … [*looks at her friends*] I told you before …

R: So which line is longer?

David: [*smiles embarrassedly*] Both … They are the same length.

An example of learning through demonstration is when Adam tried to measure a table in the kindergarten area with non-standard devices. He laid his circles on the table's length without noticing the edge of the table where he should have started laying them. Rachel came near him, shook her head as 'no' and rearranged the circles so that the first circle was laid on the edge of the table. Later, when Adam tried to measure another object's length, at first he made the same mistake but after laying some of the circles, he stopped for a moment, looked at his work again and rearranged the circles correctly.

Another way of learning is by observing peers and learning new strategies from them. For example, after the children had laid their measurement devices (10cm blocks) on the carpet, they were asked to count how many blocks each one of them used to cover the carpet's length. Lea started to count but had trouble with her counting. The blocks moved as she touched them and caused mistakes in her counting. She looked around and noticed that Rebecca was using another strategy for counting the blocks. Instead of just touching the blocks while counting, Rebecca collected the blocks one after the other and put them in a heap while counting. Lea returned to her blocks and, by using Rebecca's strategy, managed to count correctly. Later on, in another task, I found Lea counting by using the adopted strategy.

Developing mathematical vocabulary

Mathematical language is an essential part of mathematics education. It is a way of sharing ideas and clarifying understanding. Using mathematics vocabulary and terminology is important since it allows the child to express mathematical ideas precisely. Listening to explanations by others gives children opportunities to develop their own understandings. On the other hand, when children struggled to express ideas clearly, they developed a better understanding of their own thinking (metacognition).

Teaching the subject of linear measurement in the kindergarten included using a specific vocabulary such as: long, short, longer than, shorter than, length, measurement and the terms: 'common starting line' and 'attached, end to end'. During the pre-test and the first lesson, most of the children did not use the correct vocabulary: they used 'big and small' instead of 'long and short', 'size' instead of 'length' and only a few of them used the word 'measurement' or 'to measure'. In the first session, the children were asked to sort sticks according to their length. In the discussion, the children explained their sorting: 'This one is big and that one is "smaller"'; 'Both are the same size'; 'This one is short and the other one is bigger'.

In order to enhance the learning of the correct vocabulary and terms, several teaching strategies were used: linear measurement vocabulary and terms were presented in a meaningful context during their activities and, eventually, most children internalized the terms and used them in their explanations without assistance. Another strategy was to use correct words in my talks with the children and to repeat their answers using the correct vocabulary. By doing so, I found that the children started to use the correct vocabulary. I found this strategy helpful and noticed in the recorded sessions that the children themselves occasionally corrected their friends' words during discussions in lessons. For example, in session 6 the children measured the length of objects by using non-standard devices. Rachel counted the number of devices she used in measuring two objects.

Rachel: They are the same size.

Eva: [correcting Rachel] The same *length*.

By analysing children's oral answers in the test's tasks, the data gathered from the video-recordings of discussions during the sessions and from the kindergarten teacher's notes, it was found that, at the beginning of the programme, most children gave simple answers without explaining their strategies and actions and preferred to demonstrate their work by using concrete materials. Using the correct language in discussions, correcting the children's language, providing opportunities to discuss and explain thoughts and work, and by asking clarifying questions that helped them to express themselves clearly, I had an influence on the children's ability to acquire the specific linear measurement vocabulary and terminology, and to explain their strategies.

The results of the last tests and the video transcripts of the sessions indicated that there was an improvement in children's ability to use appropriate vocabulary and terms and to express themselves. At the end of the programme, most children used the specific vocabulary and terms and explained their strategies and actions (using verbal and non-verbal explanations) without being asked to do so.

Teacher–child interactions

The study programme also emphasized the mutual influence of teacher/researcher and child social and behavioural interactions on the learning and structure of the study programme. The findings indicated that the teacher has a crucial role in helping the child to develop an understanding of mathematical concepts. This is more likely to happen when interactions between teacher and child are positive. I influenced the children's motivation to learn and cooperate with their peers by using two kinds of positive feedback: verbal and non-verbal. The verbal feedback consisted of either praise for and responses to their work or clarifying questions that emphasised the thinking and problem solving that constituted their process. The non-verbal feedback (body language) included eye contact, smiles, sitting on a small chair next to the children and focusing on their work and words. The children felt free to express themselves and shared their feelings with me, and their behaviour during the programme reflected their level of interest in the subject of linear measurement, as well as the difficulties and successes they had experienced while working on the tasks.

As with the teacher's behaviour, the child's behaviour also included verbal feedback and body language. The children's behaviour also had an influence on my decision to revise the programme's structure and on my strategy of teaching, by creating more activities, reviewing subjects that were difficult for the children and changing the session's duration.

Teachers' subject and pedagogical knowledge

The issues of what children in kindergarten know and how they learn have been discussed at length in the past several decades. According to Piaget's stage theory, children need to be at a certain age/stage to learn certain mathematical ideas. Others argue that children often do not act as though they belong at a particular stage. The results of this study programme are compatible with Vygotsky's ZDP theory (1978) and show that the development of the kindergarten child's cognitive ability is not always related to his age or stage but to his/her learning. This study shows that children's learning depends on how the teacher teaches and the children's receptivity to learning.

There is no doubt that, in order to enhance the children's understanding in subject knowledge, teachers must know the subject content in detail and from a more advanced perspective than they teach. Their role is not only to help children to connect between their experience and the specific language: teachers themselves must use the correct vocabulary and terminology in discussion, correct the children's language, provide the children with opportunities to discuss and explain their thoughts and work, and ask clarifying questions to help children express themselves in a clear way. Teachers must also be familiar with child development in both cognitive and social aspects. Since development is not an inevitable process in which one waits until the child is cognitively 'ready' to learn a specific subject, the teacher has a critical role in directing the course of study, structuring activities and supporting learning attempts.

The teacher should have a pedagogic stance which emphasizes effective pedagogical practices, materials and curriculum principles and which also takes into account learning mechanisms and ways to improve teaching effectiveness. The importance of listening to and thinking about how children learn and how they see the subject content is very significant to teachers who should assist/enable rather than direct/guide. The teacher can enhance learning by creating kindergarten environments that include child-initiated learning. This environment should emphasize the importance of the child as an active learner, interacting with others, and also as reviewer and documenter.

The teacher's behaviour influences the children's motivation to learn and helps in building self-confidence. One aspect of positive teacher attitude is the importance of maths and its relationship to daily life. The teacher should create a supportive learning environment built on trust, understanding and acceptance which allows the children to express themselves freely – a truly relational pedagogy (see Papatheodorou and Moyles, 2008).

Summary

This research highlights the importance of starting the study of mathematics in the kindergarten. It emphasises the role of children's active engagement in developing mathematical knowledge and the teacher's mediating role in this development through subject/mathematics pedagogical knowledge. Teachers should have a wide knowledge of maths, initiate appropriate learning activities and create a learning environment which provides children with opportunities to gain knowledge.

The importance of the training of the kindergarten teacher in the fields of mathematical knowledge, pedagogy, developmental psychology and kindergarten ethos cannot be emphasized too strongly. Within the Israeli context, the new curriculum stresses the importance of the role of the teacher in enhancing the children's mathematical knowledge. But how can we assist the teachers in the implementation of the curriculum?

Questions for discussion

Do you agree with my conclusions that:

a. Teacher trainees need:

- to acquire thorough mathematical knowledge by means of specific courses?
- to acquire a variety of pedagogical and assessment strategies and a basic knowledge of developmental psychology?

b. Practising teachers need enhancement and refreshment of:

- mathematical knowledge by means of specific courses?
- pedagogical and assessment strategies and developmental psychology in regular regional study meetings?

References and suggested further reading

Entries in bold are further reading.

Azmitia, M. (1988) Peer Interaction and Problem Solving: When Are Two Heads Better Than One? *Child Development*, 59: 87–96.

Baroody, A.J. and Coslick, R.T. (1998) Sizing Up Things: Measurement and Measurement Formulas. In A.J. Baroody (with R.T. Coslick) *Fostering Children's Mathematical Power: An Investigative Approach to K-8 Mathematics Instruction.* Mahwah, N.J: Lawence Erlbaum Associates.

Birch, S.H. and Ladd, G.W. (1998) Children's Interpersonal Behaviors and the Teacher-child Relationship. *Developmental Psychology,* 34(5): 934–46.

Bladen E., Wildish K. and Cox J.A. (2000) The Development of Linear Measurement in Elementary School Children: An Empirical Study. *The Genetic Epistemologist,* 28(3): 2–12.

Bryant, P. and Trabasso, T. (1971) Transitive Inferences and Memory in Young Children. *Nature,* 232: 456–8.

Castle, K. and Needham, J. (2007) First Graders' Understanding of Measurement. *Early Childhood Education Journal,* 35: 215–21.

Cohen, L. (1981) *Perspectives on Classrooms and Schools.* New York: Holt, Rinehart and Winston.

Ellis, S. and Rogoff, B. (1982) The Strategies and Efficacy of Child Versus Adult Teachers. *Child Development,* 53: 730–5.

Gauvain, M. and Rogoff, B. (1989) Collaborative Problem Solving and Children's Planning Skills. *Development Psychology,* 25(1): 139–51.

Halford, G.S. (1982) Transitivity, Seriation and Classification. In G.S. Halford (ed.) *The Development of Thought.* Hillsdale, NJ: Lawrence Erlbaum Associates.

Halford, G.S. (1993) *Children's Understanding: The Development of Mental Models.* Hillsdale, NJ: Lawrence Erlbaum Associates.

Hiebert, J. (1981) Cognitive Development and Learning Linear Measurement. *Journal for Research in Mathematics Education,* 12(3): 197–211.

Hiebert, J. (1984) Why Do Some Children Have Trouble Learning Measurement Concepts? *Arithmetic Teacher,* 31(7): 19–24.

Johnson-Pynn, J.S. and Nisbet, V.S. (2002) Preschoolers Effectively Tutor Novice Classmates in a Block Construction Task. *Child Study Journal,* 32(4): 241–56.

Kamii, C. and Clark F.B. (1997) Measurement of Length: The Need for a Better Approach to Teaching. *School Science and Mathematics,* 97(3): 116–21.

Kazemi, E. (1998) Discourse That Promotes Conceptual Understanding. *Teaching Children Mathematics,* 4(7): 410–14.

Kirova, A. and Bhargava, A. (2002) Learning to Guide Preschool Children's Mathematical Understanding: A Teacher's Professional Growth. *Early Childhood Research and Practice,* 4(1). Available online at: www.ecrp.uiuc. edu/v4n1/ kirova.html (accessed 10 October 2010).

Papatheodorou, T. and Moyles, J. (eds) (2008) *Learning Together in the Early Years.* London: Routledge.

Piaget, J. (1932) *The Moral Judgment of the Child.* London: Routledge and Kegan Paul.

Piaget, J., Inhelder, B. and Szeminska, A. (1960) *The Child's Conception of Geometry* (E.A. Lunzer, trans.). London: Routledge and Kegan Paul. (Original work published 1948.)

Roazzi, A. and Bryant, P. (1998) The Effects of Symmetrical and Asymmetrical Social Interaction on Children's Logical Inferences. *British Journal of Developmental Psychology,* 16(2): 175–83.

Sophian, C. (2002) Learning About What Fits: Preschool Children's Reasoning About Effects of Object Size. *Journal for Research in Mathematics Education,* 33(4): 290–302.

Steele, D.F. (1998) Look Who's Talking: Discourse in a Fourth Grade Class. *Teaching Children Mathematics,* 4(5): 86–292.

Stephan, M., Bowers, J., Cobb, P. and Gravemeijer, K. (2003) Supporting Students'

Development of Measuring Conceptions: Analyzing Students' Learning in Social Context. *Journal for Research in Mathematics Education, Monograph No. 12*. Reston VA: The National Council of Teachers of Mathematics (NCTM).

Verba, M. (1998) Tutoring Interactions between Young Children: How Symmetry can Modify Asymmetrical Interactions. *International Journal of Behavioral Development*, 22(1): 195–216.

Vygotsky, L.S. (1978) *Mind in Society: The Development of Higher Psychological Processes* (M. Cole, V. John-Stiener, S. Scribner and E. Souberman, eds). Cambridge, MA and London: Harvard University Press.

How children's books create a scaffold to understanding diversity

Patricia H. Kostell

Overview

Beginning with Bruner's (2002) theory of 'self-making narratives', the author believes that, for the young learner, telling, retelling and engagement activities cultivate the construction of knowledge for the learner. Similarly, self-making narratives help to create a sense of one's self: the narratives in children's books, whether fiction or non-fiction, enable the child to create an understanding of diverse cultures based on what they know about their own culture. It is through hearing, seeing and imagery from the books that children move to telling and retelling. The project, discussed in this chapter, supports the view that literature, in the form of children's books, creates a scaffold in understanding diversity; as the children tell and retell stories, whether orally or in writing, they start constructing their own knowledge of a culture and land other than their own. Children begin to understand others' beliefs, customs and feelings.

This chapter focuses on the use of literature and communication as the basis for a multi-modal and meaningful approach to learning (Kress, 2003) and outlines how the use of children's books can create a scaffold in understanding diversity. Beginning with Bruner's theory of 'self-making narratives', I show through my own study that for the young learner telling, retelling and engagement with activities cultivate the construction of knowledge. Similarly, self-made narratives help to create a sense of one's self; the narratives in children's books, whether fiction or non-fiction, enable the child to create an understanding of diverse cultures based on what they know about their own culture. It is through hearing, seeing and imagery from the books that children move to telling and retelling stories. As they tell and retell, whether orally or in writing, they are constructing their own knowledge of a culture and land other than their own. They begin to understand others' beliefs, customs and feelings.

Why books are important for children

The study discussed in this chapter comes from my experience of using real story books within educational settings for various ages of children in the USA. There is a major thrust, with much research yet to be accomplished, on the topic of *Read Alouds* which consist of the teacher reading to the students, usually from picture books (which themselves can also be called *Read Alouds*). In many US preschools, elementary and middle schools, there are special rooms called literacy rooms. These are areas of the school separate from the library or media centre, where the books are stored and organized into reading levels. Often within this room, there is a large section of picture books, or *Read Alouds*, to be used by the teacher for this purpose.

Laminack (2006) – a well-known proponent of a pedagogic strategy called *Read Alouds* – and I have worked within the same schools in the USA in different capacities. Laminack was working to promote children's writing and I was working to improve learning in specific curriculum areas (primarily reading, writing and social studies). *Read Alouds* are most often used by teachers to create experiences for children, helping them to visualize events and promote a love of reading.

Bruner (2002) refers to the fact that, as adults, we may sometimes not trust books entirely and that this stops us from making the leap from intuition to explicit understanding. I believe that after the teacher has established credibility as well as trust, children, at the age of 6–7 years, are able to make this leap and begin constructing an understanding of diverse cultures.

In teaching, we need to remember that the mind of each individual does not work the same as anyone else's, no matter what the age difference or similarity. In order to compensate for this, it is necessary to allow the child to talk about their learning, to talk with other children and to talk with the teacher. During this talk, the teacher can assess the level of learning and, at times when needed, ask a question of the child to help clarify the thinking of the child or the understanding of the teacher. Content written by peers that is different from the child's writing may have been presented in the story, but the child may not have focused on this or have been able to make a connection to it. However, hearing it from a peer may have provided more understanding for the child.

Learning from this standpoint is holistic, referring to individual goals and guidelines and to the whole picture, perhaps even the relationship the child has in connecting this new culture to the culture in which he or she resides. Laevers (2005) is careful to point out that this holistic learning is very important in teachers' assessment of learning. At the same time, such assessment should serve to help the child construct a clearer view of their own knowledge and how it is acquired. If it is the teacher's intention to analyse and break down the information acquired from the children and the *Read Aloud* processes for the purposes of assessment, it is paramount that she takes a holistic approach; that is to examine how things relate to one another, not just miniscule facts (Laevers, 2005).

Paley (2005) reminds us that children love stories and that they learn to play from stories. These stories are used as the first step in beginning to create the play. Retelling the stories encourages the child to internalize some of the facts learned. The teacher's role is to support the children, scaffolding their learning, as described by Vygotsky (1978).

Using *Read Alouds* to diversify the curriculum

Drawing upon these ideas, the goal of the study discussed in the next sections was to use *Read Alouds* to create a foundation and the beginning of a diversified curriculum (Sanchez, 1998; Hernandez, 1989; Kosmoski, 1989). More specifically, the aims were to:

1. help children recognize and understand the values and experiences of their own ethnic/cultural heritage

2. promote sensitivity to diverse ethnicities/cultures through exposure to other cultural perspectives

3. develop awareness and respect for the similarities and differences among diverse groups

4. identify challenges and discrimination in behavior, textbooks and other instructional materials.

The setting for the practice-based study was a rural school in the USA, in the state of South Carolina. The participants were 6- and 7-year-olds from low socio-economic backgrounds and diverse cultures, including Hispanic, Black and Caucasian, with the majority being Hispanic and Black. The topics chosen were the continent of Africa and the country of Iceland, of which it was unlikely that the children would have had previous experience.

Learning about Africa

The continent of Africa was chosen first for this scaffolding process, preparing children for the fact that they could gain a great deal of information about other countries and occasionally about families, all from reading books. After the children sat in a semi-circle on the floor around the reader and found Africa on the globe, they discussed the position of the equator and what they already knew about the climate around the equator as well as what they knew about Africa. A book called *Hot Hippo* (Hadithi and Kennaway, 1992) was shared. It contained factual material about hippopotami, the climate and the terrain of Africa. After listening to the text, the children shared a few facts they had learned from the book. After returning to their desks, arranged in groups of four, they individually wrote the facts they had learned on a graphic organizer – a visual drawing to organize thoughts or facts. Whether this visual is a jotting, drawing or a representation in some way of a concept or a concrete pattern, it is an aid to retelling and organizing thoughts.

The specific graphic organizer used assisted children in retelling orally and in writing the story in sequential order. Each child then read to their group what they had written. They began to see similarities and differences between their culture and the new culture in Africa. They did not voice these findings as similarities or differences but their questions and statements led me to make that deduction. At the same time, it was evident that they were internalizing the content and reflecting on new ideas and information. An example of this is the set of questions that came from the children as they were internalizing what they were hearing in the story. Samuelsson and Johansson so aptly say that, at this point, the children were 'perceiving and experiencing different aspects of their world' (2009: 79).

The 'Aha' moment was evident with many of the students after their own verbalizations and as they listened to others. They began to know something about Africa and about hippos. The 'talk' became more adult, as if they were becoming experts on the subject. There was a feeling of ownership of the talk. They were confident in their own engagement and this was deduced both from the talk and the body language exhibited.

Learning about Iceland

A few days later, Iceland was the topic and children were eager to learn about this country as they saw the globe carried to the circle setting. Again, I started with the geographical location on the globe and the position of the equator, and found that the initial assumption, that the children didn't know anything about Iceland, was true. When they saw its proximity to the North Pole as well as the distance from the equator, they did deduce that it was cold, using their prior knowledge of Santa Claus and his workshop in the North Pole.

The book, *Going Fishing* (McMillan, 2005), was introduced. It is non-fiction and featured photographs of a young boy and his two grandfathers, both fishermen in Iceland. Two different types of boats, two different cities that each grandfather called home, and two very different types of fish were introduced and pictured within the book. Simple examples of everyday life for the little boy were also pictured and written about, like going to the post office to mail letters to his grandfather, remembering to wear the hat that his grandmother made for him and walking through town with his father. These all provided a glimpse of the boy's culture. Children used a graphic organizer before reading and again after reading the book.

Before reading, but after taking a 'picture walk' (turning several pages slowly while allowing the children to see the pictures), the children wrote some of their 'wonderings'. 'Wonderings' used in this way represented questions that came to their mind while taking the picture walk or after completing the picture walk. The questions were then written on the graphic organizer. This graphic organizer was one that they had used many times before to promote their own questions about what they were hearing in the story. The children listed some ideas about which they hoped to find more information to give them a better visual of life within that country.

After listening to the text, they returned to their desks and wrote down some of their thoughts, which in some cases included finding answers to their 'wonderings'. Each child then read to their group what they had written. They discussed afterward what they heard that was the same or different from their own writing. At the same time, they were internalizing content (written by them) and reflecting on new content (written by their peers).

In this study, it became possible for the children to question each other about the two countries (the USA and Iceland). Their questions were very obviously based on their own experiences within their own country. They wondered whether the children from the other country had the same experiences, for example what they watched at the movies, what they liked to eat and, for the girls, what their favourite colour of nail polish was! When they heard that their movie likes were the same and that their toys and their nail polish colours, including sparkles, were the same, they were surprised and happy.

These 'facts' then automatically became points of similarities and differences with the children. They realized, without my questioning, that some things were different, just as rules were very different at school. One culture had very specific rules and another had a great deal of freedom. Their classrooms also looked very different, reflecting the culture with the freedom in the schools having lots of space and large motor toys, whereas the culture with the stricter rules showed a direct orderliness in the classroom arrangement and exhibited a lack of play materials. Some things were very much the same, like family structures. All children referred to mothers and grandparents either directly or by questioning that came from them.

Discussion and implications for practice

After reading the writings of the children and reflecting on them, it became evident that the approach of using *Read Alouds*, the globe, graphic organizers and discussion accomplished several meaningful scaffolds for the child's learning.

First, the books provided new information on the exact geographical locations and details on the families who lived there. The illustrations in the books provided a visual image to aid in clarifying the children's understanding of facts. Some of the clarification was relevant to the words that had direct roots in the foreign language. Other clarification that the books provided was a sense that, although all of this looks very different, it has meaning and is acceptable. The books were written in a comforting style and just the fact that the teacher was reading was calming. The reading was certainly a more settling approach than reading a list of facts and then asking questions orally or in writing.

Second, the globe aided in their initial understanding of the spatial concept of place and distance of countries, as well as general information about the climate. Consistently using the globe when talking of other cultures provided the children with a chance for constructing knowledge of geography in a meaningful way. As children are exposed to more cultures and countries, there will be connections that they will be able to make. Several of these connections are part of their social studies curriculum at this age and will serve as a foundation for learning for many years.

Graphic organizers, a third scaffold, provided a drawn or printed organizational visual tool to consolidate and categorize information. Used before reading and after reading, it provided a sense of organization and sorting that is comforting and reassuring to most children. Often the question, 'Where do I start?', is a road block in their minds that stops or muddles their thinking and is truly overwhelming. The graphic organizer provided the children with a sorted list of facts or questions and produced a sense of 'I can do it', or 'Wow, look what I *do* know'. The graphic organizer as a visual tool provides an image that can be the link to remembering facts or questions. Using jottings or drawings here may also promote their ability to remember facts or questions.

The fourth scaffold, the children's talk with each other after reading their own writings, began in a tentative manner. They were unsure of whether what they wrote was going to please the teacher. They were not certain if their writing was correct and they were worried what others would think of their writing. These were children who had been writing proficiently for their age and sharing their writing with their peers for more than six months. However, their writing was primarily for entertainment and story telling, not factual nor containing questions relating to understanding geography or families. As each child in the group of four shared and the talk continued, they became more at ease and some became quite confident in what they reported.

The use of books with the visuals and words, the globe with the concrete and directional aid, the graphic organizer for order and focus and the talk for clarification and internalization together provided the scaffolding that aided the children's understanding of diversity. The use of books, concrete objects, graphic organizers and talk can help in many instances where concepts are difficult for the child to grasp.

As Van Oers defines narrative competence so, too, do I agree that it is:

> the ability and disposition to (re)construct and use textual representations for the purpose of clarifying meaning to oneself or others in the context of some socio-cultural activity (social practice). (2007: 304)

Thus, it was observed that children demonstrated ease and confidence with what they had accomplished. However, the learners with English as a second language were less confident and significantly less proficient in their writing and discussion. There were very few words and, what there were, were expressed in phrases not sentences when the children joined in the discussion. These children exhibited pleasure and understanding in listening to the others' readings and explanations and seemed comfortable within the discussion. This same level of participation and confidence is described by Soderman and Oshio (2008) when they write about their experiences with children of a similar age acquiring a second language.

A great deal of emphasis on talk relies on how much time the teacher is able to give by engaging in the talk with the child and also how much time she is able to give reflecting on the talk. Underlying both of those premises, however, is how much the teacher values this time. Is this important? Does the teacher see this as a possibility to extend the child's thinking? Fumoto and Robson (2006) and I question the idea of how much time the teacher perceives she has to spend with the child. And how much of this time is spent in observation and assessment?

Without direct instruction, young children may create a sense of other's cultures with the use of books. Scaffolding (use of graphic organizers), mediation (support or assistance by the teacher) and assisted learning (adult modelling and coaching with the writing and discussing stages) are all part of Vygotsky's (1978) idea of the adult's participation or role in the learning of diverse cultures.

The point of reading what they wrote and then discussing what each of them wrote within the small group of four children is a time for collaboration, clarification and extended learning. Communication or dialogue between teacher and children literally becomes a means for helping children 'scaffold'.

There are always many ways to change and enhance teaching approaches and pedagogies and the needs of the children guide the teacher in necessary changes to accommodate the academic needs and learning styles of the children. Observing children in telling and retelling adds a reflective component that helps the teacher in assessing the children's learning. However, children witnessing other children, telling and retelling, are experiencing what the actual construction of knowledge may sound or look like. The process of constructing knowledge then becomes known to the student very indirectly but it is easier for children to then use some of the same talk and during the course of the talk witness their own thinking (metacognition) as they vocalize it. In a natural and non-testing format, the children then are assessing what it is they have learned – not in an assessment of what is right and what is wrong but in an initial awareness of what the child has learned.

Summary

As a result of the reading of *Read Alouds*, social engagement (reporting and discussing), writing (graphic organizer and summarizing) and intrinsic motivation to learn more about others, this method of using books, the globe, graphic organizers, writing and discussion is highly encouraged to help young children to learn about diverse cultures. For these children did indeed start on a meaningful foundation of understanding diversity. In the USA, we must admit that very few programmes require any courses focusing on children whose families do not speak English and too small a number of programmes require a course in working with racially and ethnically diverse children (Karp, 2005).

If we look in the USA at the number of teachers who have entered the field before 2005, we know that the training of the current teachers in the workforce did not prepare them for today's diversity. The method of using *Read Alouds* with children can help these teachers immensely. We know that lack of preparation is now being remediated with courses and real-life practicums. These must be expanded to the experience and study of various suggested pedagogical strategies to meet the diversity that is current in today's world. These must be made available to current education students and to very recent graduates in the field. Pairing the use of books with various ways of telling, retelling and questioning is an authentic teaching strategy that will provide educators with a continual analysis based on experiences with many children as well as many cultures. This method also serves as a practical scaffold for teachers currently faced with daily issues of diversity.

Questions for discussion

1. In thinking of the many academic needs and learning styles of children, how might you modify the approach described in this chapter?

2. Vivian Paley, a veteran kindergarten and nursery school teacher and distinguished author, has encouraged us to have children tell their stories and then act them out to make sense of their worlds (as cited in Carr, 2005). Do you believe it is important enough to allow the children time to retell and act out the stories?

3. How might you use storybooks with your children in your country to enhance their understanding of other people and other cultures?

References and suggested further reading

Entries in bold are further reading.

Bruner, J. (2002) *Making Stories: Law, Literature and Life*. Cambridge, MA: Harvard University Press.

Carr, M. (2005) The Leading Edge of Learning: Recognizing Children's Self-making Narratives. *European Early Childhood Education Research Journal*, 13(2): 41–50.

Fumoto, H. and Robson, S. (2006) Early Childhood Professional's Experience of Time to Facilitate Children's Thinking. *European Early Childhood Education Research Journal*, 14(2): 97–111.

Hadithi, M. and Kennaway, A. (1992) *Hot Hippo*. Sevenoaks, Kent: Hodder Children's Books.

Hernandez, H. (1989) *Multicultural Education*. Columbus, Ohio: Merrill.

Karp, N. (2005) Building A New Early Childhood Professional Development System Based on the Three Rs: Research, Rigor, and Respect. *Journal of Early Childhood Teacher Education*, 26(2): 171–8.

Kosmoski, G.J. (1989) *Multicultural Education*. Chicago, IL: Third World Press.

Kress, G. (2003) *Literacy in the New Media Age*. London: Routledge.

Laevers, F. (2005) The Curriculum as Means to Raise the Quality of Early Childhood Education: Implications for Policy. *European Early Childhood Education Research Journal*, 13(1): 17–29.

Laminack, R. (2006) *Reading Aloud Across the Curriculum*. Portsmouth, NH: Heinemann.

McMillan, B. (2005) *Going Fishing*. Boston, MA: Houghton Mifflin Company.

Paley, V. (2005) *A Child's Work: The Importance of Fantasy Play*. Chicago, IL: University of Chicago Press.

Samuelsson, I.P. and Johansson, E. (2009) Why Do Children Involve Teachers in Their Play and Learning? *European Early Childhood Education Research Journal*, 17(1): 77–94.

Sanchez, T. (1998) Multiculturalism: Practical Considerations for Curricular

Change. In C. Cauley, F. Linder and J. McMillan (eds) *Annual Editions of Educational Psychology.* Guilford, CT: Dushkin McGraw Hill.

Soderman, A.K. and Oshio, T. (2008) The Social and Cultural Contexts of Second Language Acquisition in Young Children. *European Early Childhood Education Research Journal*, 15(3): 299–312.

Van Oers, B. (2007) Helping Young Children to Become Literate: The Relevance of Narrative Competence for Developmental Education. *European Early Childhood Education Research Journal*, 15(3): 299–312.

Vygotsky, L.S. (1978) *Mind and Society: The Development of Higher Psychological Processes.* Cambridge, MA: Harvard University Press.

10

Challenging assessment

Paulette Luff

Overview

Critics of the English Early Years Foundation Stage (EYFS) curriculum suggest that it places too much emphasis upon children achieving specified learning outcomes at a young age. In contrast, early childhood care and education in the Nordic countries, in New Zealand, and in the pre-schools of *Reggio Emilia* in Northern Italy, is seen as more open and responsive to community concerns and children's interests. From an outsider's perspective, what these admired international models have in common are clear guiding philosophies, with consistent aims, that are worked out in practice in early childhood settings. In this chapter, I argue that this link between core values and implementation of the curriculum is less clear in England. On the one hand, the EYFS advocates a holistic approach, promoting and supporting young children's developing skills through the provision of enabling environments within which they can thrive. On the other hand, the statutory framework is prescriptive with each child's growth tracked and practitioners held accountable for children's progress in six areas of learning. These contradictions are evident when practitioners are faced with the challenges of observational assessment. Here, illustrations, drawn from practice in early years settings, show that formal observation conforms to a process of mapping each individual child's progress towards developmental milestones and identification of targets to be met. Informally, though, observant practice is a shared endeavour which celebrates children's experience and supports their well-being.

The aim of this chapter is to highlight and discuss some of the challenges posed by the English Early Years Foundation Stage (EYFS) curriculum framework (currently under review), particularly in relation to observation and assessment. It is my intention to draw attention to potential and actual difficulties, in order to find ways of working with and overcoming these for the benefit of young children and their families. The approach taken in this chapter is to summarise, from an outsider's perspective, the consistency between aims and assessment in two exemplary approaches to early childhood curricula, *Reggio Emilia* and *Te Whāriki*. These are then contrasted with aspects of the EYFS, with reference to the published statutory curriculum (DCSF, 2008) and *Foundation Stage Profile* (QCA, 2008) documents. I argue that there is a contradiction between following children's individual interests and also ensuring that every child makes progress towards the same prescribed outcomes in six areas of learning. Case study material, based upon participant observations of practice within early childhood settings, is used to illustrate how some early years practitioners experience and cope with these inherent tensions. Throughout the chapter, positive examples are offered from settings where incongruities are resolved successfully. I conclude by raising questions to foster reflection upon positive ways forward for current practices internationally.

Reggio Emilia

The curriculum philosophy underpinning the *Reggio Emilia* approach emphasises communication, participation and democracy, with deep commitment to and from parents and the wider community (Rinaldi, 2006; Edwards et al., 1998). The child is seen as an active, capable protagonist in the educational process:

> The search for the meaning of life and of the self in life is born with the child and desired by the child. This is why we talk about a child who is competent and strong – a child who has the right to hope and the right to be valued, not a predefined child seen as fragile, needy, incapable. (Rinaldi, 2006: 64)

The teacher's role is to guide, facilitate and encourage children in their learning. Their task is to focus on the development of knowledge, through a collaborative partnership and relationship between children and adults. These principles of community-based, relational, learning and teaching translate into research-like approaches to observing and assessing which form part of a 'pedagogy of listening' in which evidence is recorded and interpreted with meanings attributed (Rinaldi, 2005, 2006).

Teachers in *Reggio Emilia* act as researchers and record evidence of the learning process as it occurs. This takes the form of detailed pedagogical documentation that includes photographs, children's drawing and other artwork, together with transcribed records of children's conversations. All these together provide evidence for the teachers to reflect upon and consider possible next steps and new possibilities for the children's learning. The documentation is a way of capturing and celebrating something of the 'hundred languages of children' and 'making learning visible' (Giudici et al., 2001) so that it can be discussed with the children, atelierista (a trained artist who works in the school to support the children's creative expression) and pedagogista (who consults with and acts as a mentor for the teachers), as well as parents and the wider community.

There are examples where insights from *Reggio Emilia* have been used effectively in a UK context (e.g. Holmes, 2007; Beels, 2004). The *5x5x5=Creativity* scheme (Fawcett, 2009; Bancroft et al., 2008) featured both children and adults working together on arts-based projects via the preparation and discussion of documentation. These, and similar initiatives, are admired and enrich the curriculum but are not always fully integrated within it. The processes of documentation in *Reggio* are difficult for English practitioners to understand, particularly the focus upon the project group, rather than the individual child and the valuing of subjectivity, characterised by uncertainty and enquiry, rather than upon objective measurement. The focus of the assessment is different, too, as processes are seen as more significant than outcomes. The distinctiveness of the 'progettazione' approach, and the reason that it is difficult to replicate, is that it is imbued with the values of shared knowledge construction and the underpinning principles are reflected in all aspects of the pedagogical practice, including observation and documentation (Rinaldi, 2005).

Te Whāriki

The *Reggio Emilia* approach is a regional one, embraced by municipal early childhood settings within a particular locality. To make a more accurate comparison with the EYFS, the transfer of values to early childhood assessment within another national curriculum has to be the focus of attention. I will, therefore, now consider the *Te Whāriki* bi-cultural early childhood curriculum of New Zealand (NZ Ministry of Education, 1996). Like the *Reggio Emilia* approach, *Te Whāriki* has attracted worldwide interest, respect and admiration. It is also characterised by a strong consistency between foundation principles (Empowerment, Holistic development, Family and community and Relationships), strands of the curriculum (Well-being, Belonging, Contribution, Communication and Exploration) and the Learning Stories mode of assessment (Carr, 2001).

The *Te Whāriki* curriculum is founded on aspirations for all children: 'to grow up as competent and confident learners and communicators, healthy in mind, body, and spirit, secure in their sense of belonging and in the knowledge that they make a valued contribution to society' (NZ Ministry of Education, 1996: 9). In line with these aims, Learning Stories are important for documenting young children's achievements and also for constructing their identities as learners: 'Assessments don't just describe learning; they also construct and foster it' (NZ Ministry of Education, 2004: 3). Learning Stories vary in style and format but typically include a description of what the child has achieved, either written by the teacher or dictated in the child's own words, often accompanied by a drawing or photograph, with contributions from the child and parents. There is also space for a brief analysis of the learning and identification of possible next steps. The Learning Stories are collected together in a portfolio or folder that becomes a special record of their early childhood education (Carr, 2001; Peters, 2009). Educators are supported in this assessment work with 20 booklets, *Kei Tua o te Pae*, containing published exemplars of assessment for learning in early childhood education that illustrate the significance of noticing, recognising and responding to children's learning and of developing narratives with children and families (Peters, 2009; NZ Ministry of Education, 2004).

There are ongoing dialogues between academics and educators in New Zealand and England, with exchange of ideas between the two countries. The interest in fostering dispositions for learning, for example, is shared (e.g. Claxton and Carr, 2004; Carr and Claxton, 2002); and Carr (2001) and Drummond (2003) write positively about one another's understandings of assessment in early education. The Learning Journeys (National Strategies, 2010) used by many early years settings in England as a way of recording children's learning in the EYFS, are adapted from the Learning Stories method. Just as adopting *Reggio Emilia* style pedagogical documentation presents difficulties in an English context, so, too, does a Learning Story/Journey approach. The community focus of *Te Whāriki* means that Learning Stories become relevant narratives created by and for teachers, children and families. With the focus always on what children can do, they facilitate the development of positive identities and foster dispositions towards learning (Cowie and Carr, 2009; Peters, 2009; Carr, 2001). Although there is a commitment to parental involvement in the assessment processes of the EYFS (National Assessment Agency, 2008), this is not always achieved (QCDA, 2010). The reasons why this is difficult in the English context form an element of the discussion in the next part of this chapter.

The challenge for English early years educators

The *Reggio Emilia* and *Te Whāriki* approaches (and many more, which could be detailed in a longer chapter, e.g. localised approaches, such as the Basic Development Curriculum in the Netherlands, or national curricula in Nordic countries) use methods of assessment which challenge educators in positive ways. They have to look closely at what children are seeing, saying, doing and knowing in order to understand, celebrate and elaborate learning. The assessment then leads to new levels of challenge for children as they are offered worthwhile activities which are engaging and offer and extend opportunities for holistic growth. Policy makers and early childhood educators in England also aspire to provide these 'powerful learning experiences' (Dubiel, 2010: 11) but may be hampered by an attempt to achieve both instrumental and more progressive aims. The EYFS can be characterised as progressive in the sense that it aims to offer a high quality of inclusive care and education to all young children and particularly to those who are growing up in the most socially and economically deprived circumstances. On the other hand, there is an emphasis on demonstrable progress towards certain standards and the measuring of each unique child, at the age of 5 years, against the same set of 13 assessment scales, each with nine points, relating to six areas of learning (a total of 117 elements). These include three assessment scales for both literacy and numeracy. The highest attainment on this *Foundation Stage Profile* is only possible for 'children who have significant abilities' (QCA, 2008: 26).

The *Starting Strong II* report contrasts two curricular traditions: *Readiness for School* and *The Nordic Tradition* (OECD, 2006: 141). The emphasis on audit and accountability and assessment of the attainment of learning goals, within the Foundation Stage, aligns the English curriculum with the school-readiness approach (Ellyatt, 2009). Other studies, comparing world views of early childhood curricula, praise the child- and community-centred curricula of *Reggio Emilia* and *Te Whāriki* but see the Foundation Stage as prioritising skills, standards and preparation for future school and work (e.g. Papatheodorou, 2008; Soler and Miller, 2003). In my experience, this is not how the EYFS is perceived by many practitioners, who see it positively as a document which supports a holistic play-based approach to early childhood education and care.

The EYFS: progressive and play based

The theme and principles underpinning the EYFS (DCSF, 2008) have some similarities with those of the *Te Whāriki* curriculum. The 'Unique Child' is seen as a capable, competent and confident learner, growing from a base of loving 'Positive Relationships', within supportive 'Enabling Environments' that play a role in extending 'Learning and Development' in important, interconnected areas. The value-based and child-centred statements within the curriculum are welcomed by practitioners, as they resonate with their beliefs in play-based pedagogy underpinned by liberal aims that focus on the potential of each individual child and stress equality and access. Similarly, the emphasis upon child-initiated activity within well-resourced provision is: 'the sort of approach that's almost second nature to most early years childcare providers' (DCSF, 2008: 3).

The strand of the EYFS framework for observation and assessment is located under the 'Enabling Environments' theme. There is an emphasis upon understanding each child's interests and then planning open-ended learning opportunities in response to these. This practice accords with the examples set by the pioneer educators, Maria Montessori (1912) and also, in an English context, Margaret McMillan (1919) and Susan Isaacs (1929), whose work placed importance upon understanding children's lives through careful watching, in order to develop educative opportunities and experiences. When visiting early years settings, both informally and for research, I have seen practitioners observantly 'tuning in' to children and working responsively to support their learning. The examples in the following paragraphs are typical.

> Day nursery practitioners, Laila and Diane, take a small group of 2- and 3-year-old children to the library and support them in paying attention to the 'Elmer' elephant story that the children's librarian reads, sitting them on their laps when needed and whispering encouragement and prompts. In another nursery, Donna plays a sound lotto game with a group of 3-years-olds, giving small clues where needed to help the children identify the noises or notice whether they have the corresponding picture on their card. In school, Hayley organises a printing activity in which the children create designs by covering marbles in paint and rolling them on drawing paper placed in the base of a cardboard tray. The children come to do the activity individually or in pairs and Hayley responds either by allowing the children to complete the activity independently or, when needed, structuring the task step-by-step, demonstrating or reminding children of the technique.

In addition to these daily undocumented observations, since the introduction of the Foundation Stage curriculum practitioners have been creating and using different types of observational records as a basis for noting and planning for learning. These include home/setting diaries, in which parents and key persons exchange information; digital records, including both photographs and video; and various other formats for capturing a child's engagement with an activity and using this for mapping future possibilities to extend the experience (for examples, see Collins et al., 2010). Wall displays, similarly, offer a means of creating a record of events or experiences that can form the basis for continuing learning dialogues. Two positive examples include: a developing account, using photographs and drawings, of planting different fruit pips and stones and nurturing the growing plants; and a pictorial account of a visit to a local mosque that stimulated some very rich discussions, and complex questions, from children, staff, parents and visitors.

Overall, observations of children are viewed as an important means of developing close working relationships with parents, in order to foster children's well-being, learning and development; and successful implementation of the EYFS requires an exchange of information concerning each child, including parental involvement in record keeping (National Strategies, 2010; Wheeler and Conner, 2009; DCSF, 2008; QCA, 2008). Positive equal partnerships with parents are sometimes difficult to achieve as, unlike in the *Reggio Emilia* and *Te Whāriki* curricula where learning is open-ended, in the EYFS the balance of power is influenced by the educators' knowledge and awareness of the specific learning outcomes that children must achieve.

The English EYFS: prescriptive and performative?

Whilst there is coherence between the principles of the EYFS and the child-centred methods of observation and assessment discussed above, there is another dimension to recording progress within this curriculum framework. Despite describing the 'Unique Child', and acknowledging that children may learn in different ways and at varying rates, there are universal targets to be achieved by the end of the final year of the Foundation Stage. In England, the EYFS is the first stage of a centralised curriculum with an associated national assessment regime and a high degree of audit and accountability for schools and settings. In line with a 'school-readiness' approach (OECD, 2006; see above), there is great emphasis on tracking individuals' progress within different domains of development and 'laying a sure foundation for learning' (DCSF, 2008: 6).

The requirement to show that all children are developing knowledge and skills, in relation to the six areas of learning and associated development matters and early learning goals, means that child observations are carefully documented. Brief written observations, often jotted down on labels or Post-it notes during children's play, are filed in children's portfolios as sources of evidence to indicate, to inspectors, that progress is being made. Some nurseries and schools use target-tracking tools, such as software for recording assessments that can then be printed in the form of summary charts. For example, teachers assess children against each of the 13 9-point scales of the Foundation Stage Profile at entry to reception class and update this judgment each half-term or term and can display this as a spider-web style chart for each child that gives a visual overview of where progress is being made. It is also possible to create charts to summarise the progress, in one or all of the EYFS areas of learning, of all children in a class group.

It is this measurement and labelling of children against universal standards that has drawn criticism. Papatheodorou (2008: 8) suggests that it links with a concept of the 'child as becoming'; and is about much more than each child realising her/his potential, as the future prosperity of the nation is also invested in her/his achievement. This instrumental view of curriculum, emphasising the production of citizens to benefit society and the preparation of young children for the future worlds of school and work, has been described by Moss (2008) as technocratic. He characterises the prescriptive curriculum as a manual, linked to a regime within which observation becomes a conformist activity of evidencing skills and identifying next steps to ensure improvement. He contrasts centralised early years policies in England with more progressive and community-centred approaches that emphasise participatory practice and open up exciting and creative possibilities for learning (Moss, 2008).

In the nursery and school settings mentioned above, I have witnessed the staff very carefully documenting learning for children's records. In the nursery where Diane and Laila work, portfolios are maintained for every child by their key person and, Hayley, in a school reception class, is tasked with collecting observations as evidence to support Foundation Stage Profile judgements. Gemma who works with 3-year-olds in a day nursery, alongside Donna (above), describes their practice:

> The observations we have here, we have tick charts for each of the children. So you might have something like, say if they're very young, 'is able to express themselves verbally' and you'd tick yes if they were able to do that. We have a tick chart and it covers all the different areas of developmental needs. We have observations where if you notice them doing something you jot it down, you know: 'Ally was playing and they were able to say to their friends, "Look there's one, two, three of us"'. So you tick able to count, knows how to count a group, or practising counting, and that's ongoing. And then with each key child, say every three to six months you update their tick chart to see how they're going along. We do have our own key children but obviously if you notice something from someone else's key child you might write down notes and say to the person 'Oh I've noticed them doing this'. Or they might do an activity with them, say colours and say 'So and so knows all their colours'. Or you could set up an activity and do an observation then.

One thing that is evident from Gemma's account is the way in which particular developmental outcomes may dictate what is attended to and recorded. There is a risk that policies which stress the achievement of targets limit opportunities for educators' observations to inform broader learning processes (Broadhead, 2006). Ellyatt (2009) suggests that, even where choices are available to children, non-verbal signals from adults will indicate to children what is valued and targets and outcomes may take priority over community and creativity. Laing also strongly criticises this form of assessment:

> a setting can only sometimes 'see' what they are looking for. And with a greater understanding of government policy comes the realisation that what staff and settings are being encouraged to look for are the learning goals, a very narrow framework of targets that I believe are anything but a focus on the 'unique' child. (2009, no page number)

Laing's contribution highlights another danger of outcomes-based assessment: that parents may feel alienated from the process. It was her experience of receiving a report about her child's progress at nursery, in England, that prompted her, as a journalist, to record her arguments and experiences in a blog (Laing, 2009) and to apply for her child to be exempted from the compulsory learning and development requirements of the EYFS.

Summary

In this chapter, I have outlined how educational aims translate into worthwhile assessment practices in the early childhood communities of *Reggio Emilia* and *Te Whāriki*. I have also highlighted a tension, in an English context, between centring upon the child and focusing on charting progress. Such discrepancies and dichotomies are not new for English early years educators, nor did they arrive with the introduction of a national curriculum for early years. The respected pioneers of early childhood education, mentioned above, also expressed apparently contradictory views. Margaret McMillan (1919) saw the value of education as both an individual process and as preparation for participation in society; Susan Isaacs (1929) adhered to the significance of quantifiable developmental norms and corresponded enthusiastically with Piaget, whilst sustaining a commitment to understanding the inaccessible world of the child's unconscious mind. The challenge for English educators in the 21st century is to go beyond monitoring and assessing what each child can or cannot do and to use insights from observations to provide meaningful, educative experiences for every child.

 ## Questions for discussion

1. Educational philosopher Nel Noddings considers an insistence upon testing children and measuring their attainment, even when they are very young, as 'largely a product of separation and lack of trust' (Noddings, 2005: no page number). Do you agree?

2. Can a balance be achieved between knowing and responding to the unique child and charting his or her progress towards universal learning goals?

3. What positive examples of observation and assessment for learning have you witnessed in early years practice?

References and suggested further reading

Entries in bold are further reading.

Bancroft, S., Fawcett, M. and Hay, P. (2008) *Researching Children Researching the World: 5x5x5=Creativity*. Stoke-on-Trent: Trentham.

Beels, P. (2004) All About Documentation. *Nursery World*, 5th February. Available online at: www.nurseryworld.co.uk/news/713096/share-documentation/ (accessed 3rd January 2009).

Broadhead, P. (2006) Developing an Understanding of Young Children's Learning through Play: The Place of Observation, Interaction and Reflection. *British Educational Research Journal*, 32(2): 191–207.

Carr, M. (2001) *Assessment in Early Childhood Settings: Learning Stories.* London: Paul Chapman Publishing.

Carr, M. and Claxton, G. (2002) Tracking the Development of Learning Dispositions. *Assessment in Education*, 9(1): 9–38.

Claxton, G. and Carr, M. (2004) A Framework for Teaching Thinking: The Dynamics of Disposition. *Early Years*, 24(1): 87–97.

Collins, S., Gibbs, J., Luff, P., Thomas, L. and Sprawling, M. (2010) Thinking Through the Uses of Observation and Documentation. In J. Moyles (ed.) *Thinking About Play: Developing a Reflective Approach.* Maidenhead: Open University Press.

Cowie, B. and Carr, M. (2009) The Consequences of Socio-Cultural Assessment. In A. Anning, J. Cullen and M. Fleer, (eds.) *Early Childhood Education, Society and Culture* (2nd edn). London, Thousand Oaks and New Delhi: Sage.

Department for Children Schools and Families (DCSF) (2008) *Statutory Framework for the Early Years Foundation Stage*. Available online at: http://nationalstrategies. standards.dcsf.gov.uk/node/151379 (accessed 5 February 2011).

Drummond, M.J. (2003) *Assessing Children's Learning* (2nd edn). London: David Fulton.

Dubiel, J. (2010) Assessment Priorities. Early Years 2010 London: Early Years Priorities and International Perspectives on Children's Learning, 30th January. Conference Review Analysis and Interviews. *Early Years Educator*, 11(12): 11–12.

Edwards, C.P., Gandini L. and Forman G.E. (eds) (1998) *The Hundred Languages of Children: The Reggio Emilia Approach – Advanced Reflections* (2nd edn). Westport, CT: Ablex Publishing Corporation.

Ellyatt, W. (2009) Learning and Development: Outcomes – Own Goals, *Nursery World,* 15th July. Available online at: www.nurseryworld.co.uk/inDepth/ 920092/Learning—Development-Outcomes—-Own-goals/ (accessed 28 November 2009).

Fawcett, M. (2009) *Learning Through Child Observation* (2nd edn). London: Jessica Kingsley.

Giudici, C., Rinaldi, C. and Krechevsky, M. (2001) *Making Learning Visible*. Project Zero/Reggio Emilia: Reggio Children.

Holmes, C. (2007) Playful Beginnings, Creativity in the Early Years: An Evaluation. Available online at: www.sightlinesinitiative.com/fileadmin/users/files/Sightlines/ Projects_and_Reports/Playful_Beginnings.pdf (accessed 5 February 2011).

Isaacs, S. (1929) *The Nursery Years*. London: Routledge and Kegan Paul.

Laing, F. (2009) Parents' Guide to the Early Years Foundation Stage (blog). Available online at: http://parentsguidetoeyfs.wordpress.com/2009/08/ (accessed 5 February 2011).

McMillan, M. (1919) *The Nursery School*. London: Dent.

Montessori, M. (1912) *The Montessori Method* (A.E. George, trans.) New York: Frederick A. Stokes Company. Available online at: http://web.archive.org/ web/20050207205651/www.moteaco.com/method/method.html (accessed 5 February 2011).

Moss, P. (2008) Foreword. In A. Paige-Smith and A. Craft, *Developing Reflective Practice in the Early Years*. Maidenhead: Open University Press.

National Assessment Agency (2008) *Engaging Parents and Children in Foundation Stage Profile Assessment*. Available online at: http://testsandexams.qcda.gov.uk/libraryAssets/media/Engaging_parents_and_children_in_EYFS_profile_assessme nt.pdf (accessed 5 February 2011).

National Strategies (2010) Early Years Foundation Stage: Template for Learning Journeys. Available online at: http://nationalstrategies.standards.dcsf. gov.uk/node/84404 (accessed 24 November 2010).

New Zealand Ministry of Education (1996) *Te Whāriki: He Whāriki Mātauranga mō ngā Mokopuna o Aotearoa – Early Childhood Curriculum*. Wellington: Learning Media. Available online at: www.educate.ece.govt.nz/learning/curriculumAndLearning/ TeWhariki.aspx (accessed 5 February 2011).

New Zealand Ministry of Education (2004) *Kei Tua o te Pae/Assessment for Learning: Early Childhood Exemplars*. Wellington: Learning Media. Available online at: www. educate.ece.govt.nz/learning/curriculumAndLearning/Assessmentforlearning/ KeiTuaotePae.aspx (accessed 5 February 2011).

Noddings, N. (2005) Caring in Education. In *The Encyclopedia of Informal Education*. Available online at: www.infed.org/biblio/noddings_caring_in_education.htm (accessed 5 February 2011).

Organisation for Economic Cooperation and Development (OECD) (2006) *Starting Strong II: Early Childhood Education and Care, Volume 2*. Paris: OECD Publishing.

Papatheodorou, T. (2008) *Some Worldviews of Early Childhood in Contemporary Curricula*. Inaugural professorial lecture presented at Anglia Ruskin University, Chelmsford, 20th October.

Peters, S. (2009) Responsive Reciprocal Relationships: The Heart of the Te Whāriki Curriculum. In T. Papatheodorou and J. Moyles (eds) *Learning Together in the Early Years: Relational Pedagogy*. London: Routledge.

Qualifications and Curriculum Authority (QCA) (2008) *Early Years Foundation Stage Profile Handbook*. Available online at: http://nationalstrategies.standards. dcsf.gov.uk/node/113520?uc=force_uj (accessed 5 February 2011).

Qualifications and Curriculum Development Authority (QCDA) (2010) *Implementation and Moderation of the Early Years Foundation Stage Profile 2009/10*. Annual Monitoring Report, December. QCDA/10/5411. Available online at: http://orderline.qcda.gov.uk/GEMPDF/1445950294/QCDA-10-5411-p_Implementation_and_moderation_of_the_early_years_foundation_stage_prof ile_2009–10.pdf (accessed 5 February 2011).

Rinaldi, C. (2005) Documentation and Assessment: What is the Relationship? In A. Clark, A.T. Kjørholt and Moss, P. (eds) *Beyond Listening*. Bristol: The Policy Press.

Rinaldi, C. (2006) *In Dialogue with Reggio Emilia: Listening, Researching and Learning*. London: RoutledgeFalmer.

Soler, J. and Miller, L. (2003) The Struggle for Early Childhood Curricula: A Comparison of the English Foundation Stage Curriculum, Te Whāriki and Reggio Emilia. *International Journal of Early Years Education*, 11(1): 57–68.

Wheeler, H. and Conner, J. (2009) *Parents, Early Years and Learning: Parents as Partners in the Early Years Foundation Stage; Principles into Practice*. London: National Children's Bureau.

Part 4

Cultures of Professional Development

Introduction

Janet Moyles and Theodora Papatheodorou

In this final section, we have five chapters all related to the professional development of teachers and other early years practitioners. Schools and settings vary significantly, both nationally and internationally, in the provision of professional development experiences for staff but we know this to be a crucial element in ensuring the highest quality practitioners and, hence, learning and teaching opportunities for children (Thompson and Thompson, 2008). It is you as a person and a professional – your own cultural background, beliefs about ECEC, knowledge, skills, capabilities and insights – who will significantly affect young children's learning through your own developed pedagogies. As we learn more about our roles and the children whose learning we stimulate, we recognise that there is more we *need* to – and must – learn! As Paulo Freire reminded us over 40 years ago (1970), we need to think in terms of a teacher who learns and a learner who teaches as the basic roles of classroom participation.

As professionals, early years practitioners have a broad pedagogic role, as we have seen in Part 2. Their roles and own learning are both best served by them seeking to become action researchers, theory builders, curriculum makers and public intellectuals. It means entering the political domain and analysing and evaluating the most effective ways, for example, of integrating policy requirements with practices which are known to be appropriate for the children in their settings, bearing in mind the family and community cultures of those children. In this way, practitioners will find their own voices and, in the process, generate new knowledge and new discourses through articulating their well-considered beliefs and finding appropriate ways of putting these into effective practice.

Part of professional development is sharing with others. We can learn much from international ECEC exchanges and comparisons – one intention of this book! However, in England (and the UK as a whole), there has been a surge to emulate practices from the *Reggio Emilia* and New Zealand *Te Whāriki* curricula. These ideals are culturally determined and culturally specific and cannot be transported wholesale into an English culture. Much thought and flexibility is needed by practitioners to capture the core of the principles, ideals and philosophies of such curricula while remaining true to the underpinning cultures of one's own setting and even nation.

One challenge within early years has been the slow, and sometimes hard-fought, professionalisation of the workforce (Miller and Cable, 2008). In a majority of countries, early years workers have had a traditionally low status and accordingly low salary. However, once legislated curricula prevail in the early years (as has happened in England) then the issue of higher quality, higher status workers has inevitably surfaced. Alongside this, the findings from several research projects (as we've seen earlier) have shown the relationship between high quality ECEC practices and more highly qualified practitioners, especially qualified teachers. Issues such as the need for degree-trained practitioners, the most appropriate models of professional development and the range of benefits to societies in higher quality staffing, are currently influencing early years thinking across the world. These issues are reflected in the chapters that follow.

The story of their work as teacher educators and curriculum developers in New Brunswick, Canada is told by Anne Hunt and Pam Nason in Chapter 11. They tangentially raise the issue of professionalism, considering whether teachers and other practitioners are technicians or intellectuals. They suggest that a government focus on these contradictory discourses creates tensions in the lives of childcare educators and poses a threat to their already fragile and fragmented professional identities. In the chapter, Anne and Pam explore ways of enabling educators to claim their voices and generate new knowledge and discourses.

Growing professionalism is the focus of Jill Sach's Chapter 12. Against the backdrop of South African policies on early childhood development, Jill explores three case studies in the form of personal stories and testimonies showing the significance and impact of a particular South African Early Years Teacher Training Course which emphasises personal development, knowledge building and skills attainment and motivates individual teachers to become inspirations in their classes and communities.

International academic exchange programmes for practitioners between three higher education institutions in Europe and three higher education institutions in Canada are the focus of Carolyn Silberfeld's Chapter 13. Fieldwork was a compulsory component of the exchange programme and the participants all worked in early years settings. For most participants of this research, their practical experiences in early years settings contributed to their developing knowledge about childhood and children's learning. The experience challenged the practitioners' own beliefs and led to articulation of those beliefs and of the benefits of practising in a different country and culture.

In Chapter 15, Christine Such and her colleagues review changing policies in early years provision and practice in England and how these are linked to the professionalisation of the workforce. Effective pedagogical practice is now part of the discourse promoting professional development using the Early Years Professional Status (EYPS) role as the focus of this inquiry. Chris and colleagues explore models of professional development and provide examples from their own practice to identify networks of support through the use of an online forum which encourages shared learning and the promotion of professional dialogue and identity.

Finally, Hazel Wright, in Chapter 15 presents research evidence revealing how, in the UK, training and working in the early years may be undertaken for personal reasons but can generate a range of unanticipated benefits for society. In exploring the unplanned social payback, Hazel reminds policy makers that educational second chances and diversity matter and are worth conserving. She argues for a more sensitive approach to changing professional status that recognises human values, especially in the field of ECEC where many practitioners without formal, recognised qualifications work with young children.

Following this final section, the book concludes with a closing chapter from Lilian Katz, a world-renowned early years expert from the USA, who rounds up our book by taking a forward-looking perspective on the various aspects we have explored, that is: children's learning cultures, the culture of pedagogy, cultural perspectives on early years curricula and the cultures of professional development.

References

Freire, P. (1970) *Pedagogy of the Oppressed*. New York: Continuum.

Miller, L. and Cable, C. (2008) *Professionalism in the Early Years*. London: Hodder.

Thompson, S. and Thompson, N. (2008) *The Critically Reflective Practitioner*. Basingstoke: Palgrave MacMillan.

11

Colliding discourses: negotiating spaces to enact pedagogy as an ethical encounter

Anne Hunt and Pam Nason

Overview

This is the story of our work as teacher educators and curriculum developers. Although our story is local and particular, it raises questions of common interest regarding, on the one hand, a discourse which encourages the production of the child as developmental subject and educators as technicians and a counter discourse which frames educators as action researchers, theory builders, curriculum makers and public intellectuals. We focus on the ways in which these contradictory discourses – both of which have been authorized by the New Brunswick provincial government (GNB) – create tensions in the lives of childcare educators, positioning them in untenable situations and posing threats to their already fragile and fragmented professional identities. Through our deepening relationship with these educators, we explore ways of opening up a space between these colliding discourses, a productive hybrid cultural space, where educators may claim their voices and generate new knowledge and new discourses.

1991 was an important year in Canada. This was the year we ratified the *United Nations Convention on the Rights of the Child*. It was also the year a national survey of wages and working conditions in childcare settings came out. In our own province of New Brunswick, two important and related events contributed to a feeling of hopefulness for educators, children and their families as we looked forward to a new century. The Commission on Excellence in Education was established to report on the public school system in New Brunswick and full day kindergarten was implemented for all 5-year-olds (Government of New Brunswick, 1992).

The Commission's Report, *Schools for a New Century* (1992), was the result of a highly consultative process. This process was initiated by the publication of an issues paper distributed throughout the province. The Report states:

> More than one hundred meetings were held by the commissioners either together or individually, around the province with groups and individuals who so requested. More than four hundred briefs were received in response to the Commission's invitation. (1992: 7)[1]

The voices of students, parents and educators were heard and considered. Recommendations included additional resources, partnerships with universities involved in teacher training and, more significantly, partnerships with students, parents and communities. Through performance-based tests and establishing a collective of businesses in the private sector to encourage participation in the public school system and the general mandate of fostering excellence in education, training and human resource development have, in the two decades since the report, done serious damage to the image of teacher as professional and marginalized many parents and children.

However, at the time, the early childhood sector moved forward with a sense of optimism. The implementation of kindergarten in the public school system was long overdue. Work had been ongoing since the 1975 Task Force Report, *Learning in a Play Environment*, was released (Government of New Brunswick, 1975). Controversy over which governmental department (Education or Social Development) would have jurisdiction, full-day versus half-day, staff qualifications, funding and availability of space all contributed to this delay. However, curriculum development proceeded during this time with contributions from the many educators working in private kindergartens around the province. They and their children and families were an integral part of *Young Children Learning: A Teacher's Guide to Kindergarten*, the curriculum document that was implemented provincially in 1991 (Government of New Brunswick, 1991). The kindergarten program was not compulsory. However, 95% of the province's eligible children attended.

The document spoke to the teacher in an empowering, collegial tone. It explicitly 'made some assumptions' about teachers:

> We assume that you are intelligent and resourceful, that you have had some teaching experience and that, through your experience and education, you have gained an understanding of the importance of play and direct experience for young children. (GNB, 1991: 1)

It also made assumptions about children:

We are assuming, too, that the children bring to school with them a curriculum of their own, contained in their curiosity about themselves, each other and the world around them, contained in their eager energy to explore, be active and seek friendships; in short, the curriculum of growth. (GNB, 1991: 1)

Families, too, were acknowledged and upheld as 'the prime factors in most children's lives'. It went on to say that they have:

their own value systems, which we must respect. To downgrade or undermine the values which individual children bring to kindergarten through our attitudes to their appearance or behavior is destructive to the positive development we should be nourishing. (GNB, 1991: 35)

Neo-liberal discourse dominates

This optimistic time was short lived. By 1997, as a result of the *Report on the Early Years Initiative 1993–94,* and work done by the Atlantic Provinces Education Foundation to develop a set of curriculum outcomes standardizing the curricula of four separate provinces, a Kindergarten Curriculum Development Advisory Committee was formed and tasked with revising the existing curriculum (Government of New Brunswick, 1994). By 1999, the New Brunswick Kindergarten Curriculum was revised to meet those Atlantic Provinces standards and match the format of other Atlantic curriculum documents (Government of New Brunswick, 1999). Overlapping areas or domains (physical, social and intellectual), with subsets such as investigation, creative problem solving, communication and representation, which had been expressed as active verbs (speaking, listening, reading, writing, representing pictorially, dramatizing), were replaced by a curriculum expressed in terms of outcomes by subject and subsets of that subject. Outcomes were listed as isolated skills and stated in strong, directive language. 'Students will be expected to begin to develop strategies for prewriting, drafting, revising, editing and presenting' (New Brunswick Kindergarten Curriculum, E-12, 2008). No longer does the curriculum refer to *children:* they have become *students.* These students are on a life-long learning track, defined by grade-specific outcomes which are further combined into key stage outcomes, testable at grades 3, 6, 9 and 12 and culminating in outcomes known as Essential Graduation Learnings. The human resource development referred to in 1991 is well under way.

Other shifts of note included making kindergarten mandatory in 1998, and later establishing the Early Years Evaluation: Direct Assessment (EYE-DA, undated) administered to all children in January and February of the year they enter kindergarten, ironically not by their prospective teachers but by assessors with whom the children have had, and will have, no subsequent relationship. Although the Department of Education does not have official jurisdiction over children before their entry into school, there is no wording in the communication to parents that indicates this, and most families believe preschool testing to be mandatory. The instrument assesses children's learning in five domains of early learning and sorts children into three categories – 'appropriate development', 'experiencing some difficulty' and 'evidence of significant difficulty'. Each category is represented by a coloured square – green for appropriate development, yellow for experiencing some difficulty and red for evidence of significant difficulty. This traffic light metaphor appears to be intentional as children who receive a red square are certainly stopped before they even start school, while the green square indicates 'good to go'. After taking the EYE-DA, families are sent a *Report to Parents* which can be found in *Support Surveillance That Informs Prevention* (Willms, 2009a) coding their child with green, yellow and red 'lights' which, on the basis of this approximately 30-minute screening, indicates whether they are in need of intervention prior to school. Programs are available in June for those children needing 'intensive intervention', *i.e.* those scoring in the 'evidence of significant difficulty' category. What parent would not be desirous of all green lights for their children, even those who might otherwise contest the construction of 4-year-old children as schoolified subjects, already 'students' progressing (or not) along a narrowly defined path of 'lifelong learning' towards an already envisioned future? And the downward pressure for an even earlier start is on.

Local reflects global

This New Brunswick story reflects a global climate in which a neo-liberal discourse of *human capital development* aligns slickly with the dominant discourse of *child development* to construct the existence of young children in a normative–performative mould. Quality control is an essential component of policy agendas that cast young children as the hope for a brighter future, and position early childhood services as sites for the production of children as subjects who will conform to the social and economic demands of globalized economies (Cannella and Bloch, 2006; Duhn, 2006; Osgood, 2005, 2009) and are 'programmed to become a solution to certain problems arising from highly competitive market capitalism' (Moss, 2006: 128), the future solution to our current problems (Dahlberg and Moss, 2005: vii) .

Such neo-liberal rhetoric is proliferated globally through the World Bank and through the practice of 'policy borrowing' (Kuehn, 2008: 56). In Britain, HM Treasury asserts that: '*Investment in children* to ensure that they have opportunities and capabilities to contribute in positive ways throughout their lives *is money well spent* and it will reduce the costs of social failure' (italics added) … and 'Investment in learning in the 21st century is the equivalent of investment in the machinery and technical innovation that was essential in the first great industrial revolution'. Osgood also refers to the English Department for Education and Employment (DfEE) acknowledgment in the *Excellence in Schools* document, that in the past 'it was physical capital; *now it is human capital* …' (1997: 24, italics added).

Billed as human capital in futures investment, children must be constantly monitored to ensure the promised high rate of return. An externally pre-scribed curriculum aligned to closely prescribed assessment criteria works to 'guarantee' the investment, so long as the workforce can be relied upon to produce the pre-determined curriculum outcomes. Educators are seen as technicians, regulators of and regulated by children's progress along pre-determined paths.

When discourses collide: our local story continues

In 2005, after Canadian federal funding was allocated to the provinces for work in the early years, the government of New Brunswick initiated the production of an official curriculum for children from birth to 5, to be implemented in early learning and childcare settings (New Brunswick Dept of Social Development, 2008). It is interesting to note that at about this same time, various school districts throughout the province began piloting school readiness testing.

We, at the Early Childhood Centre, University of New Brunswick, were invited to submit a proposal to write the curriculum and implement a related program of professional learning for the approximately 1350 child-care educators in New Brunswick's English childcare sector. Aware of the powerful potential of official curricula for the regulation and surveillance of children and teachers, it was with some trepidation that we accepted (Nason and Hunt, 2011).

The questions that structured our work reflect our sense of being caught between contradictory discourses and a heightened concern about 'school-ification'. We wondered whether and how we could produce an official curriculum document and an associated program of professional learning that resisted the dominant developmental discourse in early childhood education and destabilized the audit culture? How, in the presence of nor-mative/performative agendas, might we celebrate diversity and encourage difference amongst children and professionals (see also Chapter 10)? How/could we honour polyphony, make educators' work and words visi-ble and foreground their agency as researchers and public intellectuals? How (and could) this work be enacted and understood within an ethic of care and an ethic of an encounter that emphasized responsiveness, listen-ing carefully with a sense of open-ended responsibility and obligation, and respect for the alterity (otherness) of the 'other'?

Five years into the project, we have managed to produce a curriculum framework and support documents that resist normative–performative constructions of children and childcare educators.[2] A process of ongoing consultation, co-construction of curricular documents and co-presenta-tions at workshops and conferences, has given voice to diverse experiences and perspectives of childcare educators (Ashton et al., 2009, 2008).

Whose discourse is this anyway?

Yet we continue to be plagued by questions relating to educators as public intellectuals, and how we enact and understand our own work within an ethic of an encounter. We are acutely aware of the privilege of our position and of our obligation to the educators involved in this undertaking. We have visited them at work and worked alongside them, establishing relationships of respect and growing in our awareness of the challenges that face them. Many of them work long hours and are poorly paid. Materials and equipment are often inadequate. Some feel isolated and unsupported. Many have no formal training. Current standards require that only one in four educators at a given centre have credentials in early childhood. Considering these circumstances, it is not surprising that many educators had not thought about themselves as curriculum makers, action researchers and theory builders. They, in fact, often felt quite powerless, and, in some cases, may have been resigned to or even comfortable with deferring power and the responsibility it entails.

Educators in the collision zone

Changing or, for that matter adopting, a professional image is always accompanied by some degree of discomfort and is made even more difficult when it is mandated, as is the case in the province of New Brunswick. As one educator said in her evaluation of the program, 'We had no choice in the matter'. Not only did they have no choice, but accepting this contract, as per Dahlberg and Moss (2005: 60), '... placed us in [an] uncomfortable and responsible position' of having asked the educators to accept a particular professional image. Previously, their identities may have been framed as a mother substitute and, more recently, in the school readiness discourse, as technician. There was, in fact, no legal obligation to enact either of these identities. Now, ironically, there is no choice but to adopt the New Brunswick Curriculum Framework for Early Learning and Child Care (GNB, undated) – one that encrypts the image of the 'good teacher' as curriculum maker, theory builder and action researcher. Compliance is backed by legislation, regulation and surveillance. At the same time, the downward press for school readiness is on, emanating from a school system completely immersed in the audit culture. Colliding discourses – both authorized by the same government.

The tensions educators experience in negotiating these contradictory discourses are alluded to in their written responses to the program of professional learning, such as: 'Parents are considering pulling their children from licensed to non-licensed preschools because of curriculum and preschool preparation.' 'Children who have been in childcare for years have had a difficult time with not as much directed activities.' 'As a preschool we didn't like being roped in with daycare. We are preparing kids for school and parents' expectations are different than daycare.'

Opening spaces between discourses

Here, we saw our role as opening spaces for ongoing professional conversations, providing support for educators to articulate their views and returning them to the values upon which the curriculum framework is based. As we worked alongside these educators, we sensed their growing awareness of the power of professional discretion. Their words on the evaluation form they returned at the end of the professional learning program supported our observations. 'Every facility is now "on the same page", but still having the flexibility to pick and choose [their] own aspects of the program.' 'Regulations – we have gotten keen on getting around them in a safe way.' 'Used own words to get used to [the new curriculum because it was] sometimes too wordy.' 'Reflection pieces [as written in the framework] are not enough. Staff are now using own reflections and emotions more often.'

This sense of the curriculum framework as both forming and being formed by professional identities is also evident in the co-construction with educators of 'professional support documents [that] further elaborate the framework in practice'. Through this work, we have been able to more deeply explore the interactive and improvisational potential of the child-care centre as 'contact zone' – a place in which transculturation can take place with the construction of new hybrid texts (Pratt, 1992). We found our ideas quickly appropriated and transformed.

Shifting images of both educator and child

Work, presented by educators to their colleagues in the support documents and in institute sessions, gave substance to theory for educators and had a sense of credibility that was enabling. They were able to see the children with whom they worked in a new perspective, and to express their shifting image of the child. 'The work the children have been doing is more documented and parents are getting to see a lot more of their children's work with the explanations of how it happened, why it happened and all the fun stuff in between the beginning and the end.' 'We take more pictures, we listen more to what the children are saying.' 'More of a learning process for educators than the children.' 'Loved seeing my daughter's name in the binder – her words were quoted.'

Finding a professional voice

As they began to document learning, educators found their public voices as professionals. 'We are more conscious of our responsibility in making parents aware of what their child is doing at preschool/daycare.' 'Community drops in to ask about our program.' 'The Elders (this being a First Nations site) are more interested in our curriculum.' 'Effective, but not enough time at meetings to share with other front line workers. One of the best ways of helping to learn new things is discussion among peers.' 'Got to brainstorm and learn from other centres' work – i.e. ideas, situations and solutions.' Voices of dissent were also heard: one educator was explicit in her refusal to bring any of her documentation to professional meetings – she was concerned that it would be interpreted as a sign that she subscribed to the values and goals of the curriculum when in fact she did not.

When asked what support they might need to continue moving forward, they wrote about the need for more staff, less paperwork and primarily about positive reinforcement or direction from colleagues and directors and staying connected: 'I think even the idea of a daycare newsletter filled with stories, comments and ideas from daycares as well as some upcoming community events, being delivered to all daycares would be a great way for all daycares in the areas to see what's happening and it would be a great way to stay connected!'

They also asked for 'a school information session for teachers' that would introduce the curriculum framework and help them explain the contextual learning that is taking place in their programs. Even the most confident educators who are firmly committed to the values and social pedagogical approach that underpin the curriculum framework feel challenged by the growing perception that school readiness is the raison d'être for early childhood education, and that all children must be made 'ready' for school by performing well within the norms determined by the EYE-DA that is now administered to all 4-year-old children prior to their entering kindergarten.

One educator's story encapsulates her critique of this battery of preschool assessments in her school district, referred to euphemistically in the invitation to parents and children as *The Teddy Bear's Picnic*.

> This Teddy Bears' Picnic, I can tell you, it's no picnic! The children were taken into a gym where testing stations were set up all around the room. They were separated from their parents. The parents were taken into another room. The children had never been in this gym before and had never met the people who were running the testing stations. Some children were really upset and didn't want to leave their mothers, but eventually were separated from them. When one child couldn't do the task, he was made to stay at one station for 30 min, practising how to write his name. We could have told them he couldn't write his name. He is a child with special needs. His mother was really upset. (Director, NB Childcare Centre)

It is remarkable that more than two years after this educator first told this story, and even though she has since left the field of early childhood education, she still speaks as passionately about this event, and offers more stories – of a child who was obliged to practise 'the correct' way to hold a pencil, a child who was so traumatized by the experience ... She feels sure things must have improved since then.

But, in fact, her stories resonate strongly with those told by educators and parents more recently: a child who can read fluently but was 'red lighted' on a phonics item; a child who could name what police, firefighters, garbage collectors do, but was flummoxed by the 'schoolish' term 'community helpers'; a child who incorrectly named rhyming pictures as 'race' and 'face' when he should apparently have said 'run' and 'fun' (in spite of the fact that the pictures illustrated runners wearing numbered race aprons lined up at a starting line, and a smiling face – an item that has since been changed to an equally ambiguous rhyming pictures pair of a single man running and grinning children on a trampoline).

What ties parents' and educators' stories together is a deep concern for children's ethical treatment. Intertwining themes in their story are: the validity of the test and children's right to fair assessment practices. Educators now accustomed to writing Learning Stories are becoming critical of the idea that knowledge can be separated from relationship, or emotions from intellect; that children's individual strengths are less important than what appear to be fragmented and relatively trivial skills; that the yardstick for judging learning, growth and development should be an age-related norm. Where children with already identified disabilities are concerned, the sense of injustice is heightened.

The individual assessment (EYE-DA) is billed as 'part of an important partnership between you (the parent) and your child's new school … [that] provides information to encourage a positive transition to school' (EYE-DA, *Report to Parents*, in Willms, 2009b). Written out of this partnership and the transition to school is the early childhood educator who may have participated in the education and care of the child from 6 months of age. Many childcare educators feel that 'We could have told them that …'. But they were not asked. Not only did their assessments go unsolicited, but in some cases – where parents have brought their children's portfolios and Learning Stories to the preschool assessment session, or where early childhood educators have offered input – they were perfunctorily dismissed. Such systematic exclusions speak both to the way in which childcare educators' professional judgment and moral engagement is devalued in the audit culture of school, and to the chasm between the discursive practices.

Implicit in the sharing of stories is the sense that we will act in solidarity with educators and parents, a sense that we are able to act where they are not, in ways that are inaccessible to them, either in terms of preserving anonymity – mindful of children's and families vulnerability – or in terms of the circles in which we move. We are perhaps perceived to have a more powerful voice in influencing policy, able to make social injustices visible and responsible for dealing with the fallout from colliding discourses.

Indeed, we have accepted that responsibility, making our critique of marginalizing discourses explicit in professional, academic and bureaucratic venues, aware that education is always political. Yet these efforts can seem academic, far removed from the actual experience of childcare educators struggling to negotiate colliding discourses in their daily practice.

Being in between

Early in this project, we designed a diagram for the curriculum framework which has, on one side, the New Brunswick K-12 Curriculum Outcomes Framework: Essential Graduation Learnings, and, on the other, the four Broad-based Goals of the Early Learning and Child Care English Curriculum Framework. Lines crossing the space between them connect related elements. The lines were intended to tie us together in some way other than one-to-one correspondence of subjects and skills. Presently, that space in between continues to be a 'no man's land' – a space where 'dangerous discourses' collide. Throughout this chapter, we have focused on the ways in which contradictory discourses authorized by the GNB create tensions in the lives of childcare educators, positioning them in untenable situations and posing threats to their already fragile and fragmented professional identities. However, it is not our intent to construct childcare educators as victims simply caught between colliding discourses, but as active agents, engaged in the complex process of negotiating discourses as they construct professional identities through the performance of their daily work.

As Bhabba notes (quoted in Moje), being 'in between several different funds of knowledge and discourse can be both productive and constraining in terms of one's literate, social and cultural practices, and ultimately one's identity development' (2004: 42). They go on to assert that: 'The third space ... becomes a productive hybrid cultural space, rather than a fragmented and angst-ridden psychological space only if teachers and students incorporate divergent texts in the hope of generating new knowledges and discourses' (2004: 43). This prompts us to wonder how we might work with educators to construct collision as potentially dynamic and productive, and the space between discourses as a 'third space' full of possibility.

Summary

This is our summary but not our ending. We understand the threat of human capital development to the moral landscape of education and care, and we will not balk at 'challeng[ing] the political order of the state in the name of our ethical responsibility to the other' (Levinas and Kearney, 1986: 30). Yet at the heart of our practice is a commitment to dialogue, a celebration of polyphony and an openness to new possibilities. Our ongoing responsibility lies in the maintenance of a conversational space where it is safe to speak and listening is practised quite simply in response to the other's humanity, a discursive space where 'even the same signs can be appropriated, translated, rehistoricized and read anew' (Bhabha, cited in Moje, 1994: 46). For us, it is in this space that the hope for the future resides.

Questions for discussion

1. How/could we honour polyphony, make educators' work and words visible and foreground their agency as researchers and public intellectuals?
2. How might we work with educators to construct collision as potentially dynamic and productive, and the space between discourses as a 'third space' full of possibility?

Notes

1 Note that the population of the province is only 750,000 and it is scattered over an area approximately the size of Scotland. Initially referred to as a training program, this is one instance of our changing the language to *Program of professional learning* in a bid to construct early childhood educators and education in a professional image. There is a parallel project for the French sector, but none specifically designated for the First Nations. See Moss (2006) for a discussion on the need for continuous and rigorous critique to ensure that the 'powerful potential' of a shared orientation and values does not result in stronger regulation and governing of children. See the *New Brunswick Curriculum Framework for Early Learning and Child Care – English*, available at the NB Department of Social Development website: www.gnb.ca/0017/Promos/0003/curriculum-e.asp

2 In fact, this item appears to be on the complementary EYE-TA that is administered by teachers after kindergarten entry (Willms and Beswick, 2008).

References and suggested further reading

Entries in bold are further reading.

Ashton, E., Hunt, A. and White, L. (2008) *Well Being*. Support Document Series for New Brunswick Early Learning and Child Care Curriculum Framework (English). In P. Whitty and P. Nason (series eds). Fredericton, NB.

Ashton, E., Stewart, K., Hunt, A., Nason, P. and Scheffel, T. (2009) *Play and Playfulness*. Fredericton, NB.

Cannella, G.S. and Bloch, M.N. (2006) Social Policy, Education and Childhood in Dangerous Times: Revolutionary Actions or Global Complicity. *International Journal of Educational Policy, Research and Practice: Reconceptualising Childhood Studies*, 7: 5–19.

Dahlberg, G. and Moss, P. (2005) *Ethics and Politics in Early Childhood Education*. New York: Routledge.

DfEE (1997) *Excellence in Schools*. London: The Stationery Office.

Duhn, I. (2006) The Making of Global Citizens: Traces of Cosmopolitanism in the New Zealand Early Childhood Curriculum: Te Whāriki. *Contemporary Issues in Early Childhood*, 7(3): 191–202.

Early Years Evaluation: Direct Assessment (EYE-DA) (undated) KSI Research International Inc. Available online at: http://earlyyearsevaluation.com/EN/images/EYEDA_Overview_v5_03012011.pdfhttps://www.ksiresearch.com/eye/project_pt2.php (accessed 27 March 2011).

Government of New Brunswick (GNB) (1975) *Learning in a Play Environment.* Report of the Kindergarten Task Force. Fredericton, NB: GNB.

Government of New Brunswick (1991) *Young Children Learning: A Teacher's Guide to Kindergarten.* Fredericton, NB: GNB.

Government of New Brunswick (1992) *Schools for a New Century: Report of the Commission on Excellence in Education.* Fredericton, NB: GNB.

Government of New Brunswick (1994) *An Independent Report: Early Years Initiative, 1993–94.* Frederickton, NB: GNB.

Government of New Brunswick (1999) *New Brunswick Kindergarten Curriculum.* Fredericton, NB: GNB.

Government of New Brunswick (undated) *The New Brunswick Curriculum for Early Learning and Child Care.* Available online at: www.unbf.ca/education/ecc/childcareCurriculum/Framework.pdf (accessed 27 March 2010).

Kuehn, L. (2008) The Education World is not Flat: Neoliberalisms Global Project and Teacher Unions' Transnational Resistance. In M. Compton and L. Weiner (eds) The Global Assault on Teaching, Teachers and their Unions. New York: Palgrave Macmillan.

Levinas, E. and Kearney, R. (1986) Dialogue with Emmanuel Levinas. In R.A Cohen (ed.) *Face to Face with Levinas.* Albany, NY: State University Press of New York.

Moje, E. (2004) Working Toward Third Space in Context Area Literacy: An Examination of Everyday Funds of Knowledge and Discourse. *Reading Research Quarterly*, 30(1): 38–70.

Moss, P. (2006) Early Childhood Institutions as Loci of Ethical and Political Practice. *International Journal of Educational Policy, Research and Practice: Reconceptualizing Childhood Studies*, 7: 127–37.

Nason, P. and Hunt, A. (2011) Pedagogy as an Ethical Encounter: How Does it Look in our Professional Practice? In A. Campbell and P. Broadhead (eds) *New International Studies in Applied Ethics, Vol. 5, Working with Children and Young People: Ethical Debates and Practices Across Disciplines and Continents.* Oxford: Peter Lang.

New Brunswick Department of Social Development (2008) *New Brunswick Curriculum Framework for Early Learning and Care (English).* Fredericton, NB: Early Childhood Research and Development Centre, University of New Brunswick.

Osgood, J. (2005) Who Cares? The Classed Nature of Childcare. *Gender and Education*, 17(3): 289–303.

Osgood, J. (2009) Childcare Workforce Reform in England and 'The Early Years Professional': A Critical Discourse Analysis. *Journal of Educational Policy*, 24(6): 733–51.

Pratt, M.L. (1992) *Imperial Eyes: Travel Writing and Transculturation.* London: Routledge.

Willms, J.D. (2009a) Pre-school Benefit from New Skills Assessments. *Education Canada*, 9(5): 36–9.

Willms, J.D. (2009b) *Support Surveillance That Informs Prevention.* Available online at: www.mcgill.ca/files/ihsp/May12009DougWillms_Presentation.pdf

12

The individual as inspiration: a model for early years teacher transformation

Jill Sachs

> ## Overview
>
> Against the backdrop of South African policies on early childhood development (ECD), this chapter explores three case studies in the form of personal stories and testimonies showing the significance and the impact of the Caversham Early Years Teacher Training Course. Caversham Education Institute has adopted the mission statement: *Inspiration in the Individual and the Individual as Inspiration.* The pedagogical model developed by Caversham has three clear strands: Personal Development, Knowledge Building and Skills Attainment. The methodology used incorporates the Caversham *Hourglass Process©* of Reflection, Dialogue and *CreACTion™* leading to Ownership and is proving effective in inspiring individual teachers to become inspirations in their classes and communities.

First-year students sit around a table with the rays of the warm, African sun streaming through the windows and lighting their faces. Their looks are serious, concentrated, intense and empathetic. One after another, they speak of their early experiences during the difficult times of South Africa's apartheid era. As they listen, others' stories trigger long-buried memories and emotions and they catch glimpses of the experiences of others and find that theirs were not unique. Others had similarly suffered. They realise that they, too, could rise above the legacy of their past and achieve their dreams. Read the stories of three of these amazing women through their journals and watch them grow to become teachers.

South Africa is a land wounded by its past. While the country is moving forward into the 21st century, its peoples carry a legacy of injustice and discrimination (Christie, 2008). Young women striving to start their careers carry within them the hurts and pains of their childhood. Nowhere is this more evident than in the students who embark on the road to becoming teachers of young children. Early childhood development (ECD) has always been the Cinderella of the teaching profession, often poorly funded and deemed unimportant. Those who strive towards a career in ECD face a battle for recognition, adequate training and recompense. Many of its teachers come from rural areas, many have received a less than adequate education but all have a passion to teach young children. Training such a cadre of teachers needs to take cognisance of the individual, who she is and where she wants to go, so that she, in turn, can care for and nurture each young life in her charge.

This chapter aims to provide evidence of the value of including a personal development component in teacher training programmes. The content gives a perspective on one model for teacher education and provides a bridge for dialogue with academia. It explores one teacher training programme from the Caversham Education Institute through the eyes of three students: Sheri, Suzy and Khani (not their real names), tracking their growth using excerpts from their journals. Meet them:

> **Sheri** is in her thirties, has a BA degree and lives with her husband and young daughter in a suburb outside Pietermaritzburg, the capital of the province of KwaZulu-Natal. She offers part-time classes in crafts and creativity to young children.
>
> I am good at: *drawing, cooking, gymnastics, listening, being a friend, loyalty*
>
> I'm passionate about: *animal rights, counselling, environmental awareness, relationships*
>
> I really dislike: *disloyalty, people who abuse animals and children, fussiness*

> **Suzy** is in her forties and teaches at a special needs school in the city of Durban. She is the single mother of a 21-year-old daughter. She grew up in a middle-class environment, leaving school after 11 years.
>
> I am good at: *anything crafty, beadwork, sewing, scrap-booking, decoupage, sketching*
>
> I'm passionate about: *my work and about being the best teacher I can be*
>
> I really dislike: *people who disrespect others, unpunctuality (I suppose it's disrespect again) – maybe I'm just grumpy!*

Khani is in her twenties and teaches at a small village pre-primary school in Zululand. She has a 7-year-old son and a baby daughter. She grew up in rural KwaZulu-Natal, walking long distances to a poorly resourced school, became pregnant and left school at 18.

I am good at: *working with a team*

I'm passionate about: *helping people*

I really dislike: *disrespect*

The South African education context

Before Apartheid ended, South Africa's black majority received a deliberately structured, inferior education to meet the needs of menial labour. The racial policies of the Apartheid government resulted in separate Departments of Education, Welfare and Health for each racial group. Funding and resources were disproportionately allocated with the majority being directed to white departments; black departments received the least. The results meant first-world facilities for whites and third-world facilities for blacks. Classrooms in black schools were hopelessly overcrowded, often with more than 100 pupils in a class; teachers were inadequately trained and resources were minimal (Chapman and Chisholm, 2004).

The school experiences of the three case study participants reveal this disparity:

Sheri: *I attended private schooling; it was expensive but there were small classes and good teachers prepared to go the extra mile. Many extra-curricular activities were offered. The teachers put a lot of effort into assisting with presentations, symposia, etc. In the late 1970s my 'whites only' school began admitting black girls, Indians and coloureds. They remained in the minority right up to my matric year but we all mixed well, learning about our different backgrounds.*

Suzy: *When I went to school, I loved it. We lived a 15-minute walk away and I walked to school with other children who lived on our road. My books and stationery were provided by the school. Doing this exercise [writing in a journal as part of the course] made me go back to my school photographs. To my absolute shock I realised that in the 11 years I went to school there was not one person of colour (African) in any of my school photos.*

Khani: *I was young, not knowing what was going on and confused. I was beat up at school from arriving late. No questioning the teacher if I didn't understand, always yes. Lots of rote learning.*

The South African ECD context

While great strides have been made since the first democratic elections in 1994, problems of poverty, inequality, HIV and Aids, crime and violence are still prevalent. Prior to 1994, ECD was a low priority on the political agenda and consequently little funding was expended. It was also regarded as unimportant women's work for which little or no training was necessary. There were huge disparities in provision between urban and rural communities and between different racial groups. Subsidies targeted middle- to upper-class preschools where teachers received a salary, while centres catering for children from poor and working-class families received little or no subsidy. ECD services range from sophisticated preschools and reception year classes at well-resourced primary schools, to learning experiences offered in homes, garages and church halls. Over the past 16 years, however, confronted with the high repetition and failure rates in the first year of formal schooling, recognition of the importance of the early years has grown.

The South African Government has embarked on a number of ECD initiatives to redress the disparities (Department of Education, 2001a, 2001b, 2001c). Structures have been set up, qualifications articulated, curricula designed in line with national imperatives (Ministry of Education, 2003) and a compulsory reception year for 5–6-year-old children is being phased in.

Qualifications and training for ECD teachers

Divisions of the past are still seen in the type and quality of teacher qualifications and training available to early years teachers in South Africa. Depending on education access, the range of training extends from minimum short courses in basic 'educare' to post-graduate degrees. The parameters provided by the National Qualifications Framework (NQF), supported by the South African Qualification Authority (SAQA) (Office of the President, 1995) and the setting up of the Education, Training and Development Practices Sector Education Training Authority (ETDP SETA, undated) provide guidelines and accreditation for qualifications and service providers. In 1997 the NQF drafted the first set of Core and Elective Unit Standards for ECD. This began the process of establishing structures and systems for providing a career path for caregivers/teachers of young children from level 1 (at the end of Grade 9) through to degree level.

Teacher training initiatives

South African teacher training institutions are being challenged to inspire teachers to become agents for transformation – in their own lives, the lives of the children they teach, their families, their communities and, ultimately, South Africa. This is where the Caversham Education Institute is playing an important role.

Accredited in 2006, the Institute is the teacher training component of Caversham Centre, an arts-based organisation found in the beautiful mid-lands of KwaZulu-Natal. Its vision is: *Inspiration in the Individual and the Individual as Inspiration.* Caversham's logo is the hourglass symbolising the individual as 'container' and 'conduit'. It stresses the need to receive in order to be able to contribute but also the need to take responsibility to 'turn one's own hourglass'.

Caversham's values speak to the importance of honouring the individual:

- **Significance** in one's own life – as individuals, we need meaning, pur-pose, relevance, to grow our self-esteem and to make a difference
- **Ownership** – taking responsibility for ourselves and others by recognis-ing our past, being rooted in the present, moving forward confidently into the future
- **Legacy** – understanding that our legacy is present through all our choices/deeds and is not only important after our death
- **Collaboration** – building together, taking shared responsibility and ris-ing above competition
- **Empowerment** – through acquiring knowledge, skills, self-confidence, self-management and contributing to others
- **Excellence** in all things – our potential, our courage in facing chal-lenges, our perseverance, our achievement
- **Innovation** – fostering critical, creative thinking and leadership skills and finding more effective ways of being and doing.

The Caversham *Hourglass Process*© evolved from working with artists, writ-ers, teachers, community women, youth and children and is now used as the underpinning methodology for its early years teacher training. The *Hourglass Process*© encompasses:

- **Reflection** – purposefully taking the time to pause and explore oneself to gain a deeper understanding
- **Dialogue** – listening, talking, sharing, debating to test, confirm or change one's thinking/perceptions/beliefs
- **CreACTion™** – taking creative action – using learning from reflection and dialogue to bring about changes in one's own life and the lives of others
- **Ownership** – taking responsibility for the future whilst living in the present and recognising the past.

An alternative model of teacher training

This chapter focuses on Caversham's Higher Certificate in ECD, a two-year part-time programme at NQF level 5. It targets a range of teachers from varied backgrounds offering them flexibility by combining studying with employment. It encompasses three key elements: Personal Development, Knowledge Enhancement and Skills Development and is structured to meet the following Exit Level Outcomes:

- Explain and apply consistent theories of child development within the national curriculum framework
- Demonstrate the ability to implement a comprehensive safety and health policy in a holistic, inclusive and developmentally appropriate way in association with families and the wider community
- Systematically observe the development of individual children to inform own practice and planning on an individual basis
- Establish and maintain efficient management systems that ensure the effective functioning of the ECD site/class
- Promote effective communication links between the ECD site, home and wider community
- Produce and respond to accessible written and oral communication and foster communication skills to operate more effectively in the workplace/ECD site. It will also contribute to more effective communication within the workplace environment
- Present information in a public setting (SAQA, 2009).

Using the *Hourglass Process©*, contact sessions begin with reflection and move to dialogue. Sessions are balanced with significant periods of teaching and skills enhancement, interspersed with dialogue and *CreACTion*™. The facilitator's role is more one of facilitation and mediation, rather than lecturing. Dialogue engages students in looking beyond themselves to gain insight into other teachers' contexts, and the children they teach. Then the following questions are asked: 'What does this mean in my context? What does it challenge? How can I adjust, improve, change, enrich?'

Teacher training at Caversham seen through the eyes of its teachers: three case studies

As part of the course requirements, students are expected to provide evidence of competence in their portfolios. During the course, students complete assignments, reports, questionnaires, interviews, observations/assessments of children, research and present a paper, design posters, write letters and lesson plans, undertake classroom practice and maintain a journal. The journal is the primary tool used for reflection, enabling students to engage with the concept of the hourglass and it is extracts from the selected students' journals that are used in this chapter. The extracts reveal the development of each student during the two years that they work through the course.

The responses are structured around the seven roles of educators as outlined in the South Africa National Education Policy Act 27, 1996: the teacher as Learning Mediator; Interpreter and Designer of Learning Programmes and Materials; Leader, Administrator, Manager; Scholar, Researcher, Lifelong Learner; Community, Citizenship and Pastoral Role; Assessor; Subject/Discipline/Phase Specialist. It is these roles that inspire the teaching profession.

The pastoral role of the teacher in the classroom and the community

Nowhere more than in the early years classroom must teachers be cognisant of their learners' backgrounds, home situation, family and health problems. The early years teacher needs to develop a close bond with her charges, helping to bridge the gap between home and school and providing a supportive environment in case of need. This is particularly important in South Africa where many children come from single-parent families, are looked after by grandmothers or older siblings or are orphaned from a young age (National Scientific Council Centre on the Developing Child, 2007). Early in the training programme, students are tasked to describe the children they teach, and their families.

> **Sheri:** *Eight to fourteen children with not every child attending five days a week. All children come from middle to higher socio-economic groups and two-parent families. The general level of education of the parents is good, the languages spoken are English and Afrikaans, the predominant faith is Christian. One child has been diagnosed as hearing-impaired. The school is in a village, established privately, has sufficient space and equipment, local access to doctors, clinic sisters, psychologists, library, churches, and police. The parent body is supportive, attends functions.*

> **Suzy:** *Twenty learners come from diverse backgrounds, half from single-parent families, very mixed socio-economic backgrounds, majority are Christian but also Hindus and Moslems, most are transported by bus. The special needs include asthma, epilepsy, speech delays, ADD and ADHD. Three different languages, access to speech and occupational therapists, remedial help. The class is well-equipped.*

> **Khani:** *Of the 27 children, 16 have two parents; 4 are from single-parent families; 3 have step-parents; one child is cared for by father and grandmother; 3 orphans. Parents come from middle to lower income groups, are Zulu, mixed races and white. The dominant language is Zulu, the faith Christian. The school is well-established, with a primary school, police station, clinic, church in the village.*

This activity, early in the course, combines reflection and dialogue (Bolton, 2001). It provides the opportunity for students to engage at a deeper level to become more sensitive and empathetic teachers (Gardner, 1997).

The teacher as a scholar and lifelong learner

To deepen the students' understanding of the influence they have on their children's lives, students are tasked to write a letter to a teacher who influenced them. These letters are shared in group contact sessions to demonstrate the positive or negative impact a teacher can have on a child's life.

> **Sheri**
> *My early school years did not always hold fond memories, as my parents divorced … my class one year was difficult, as my class teacher did not understand what I was going through and did not connect with me on an emotional level. Standard 3 was a wonderful year as I remember feeling stimulated and interested, enjoying the warm connection I had with you. I blossomed and came to know my strengths and to feel like a worthwhile individual. My confidence grew as a result, I was able to speak and relate to people with relative ease and familiarity that can only have resulted from a sense of belonging and acceptance, which you allowed me to feel.*

> **Khani**
> *Thank you very much for being positive to me to all the things I was facing telling me it will be o.k. one day, sharing with me your experiences when you were my age. I remember when I didn't have bus fare to come to school because my dad was so irresponsible but you turn it into a good opportunity to be independent, to think other ways to make life goes on and I end up selling sweets at school with your help. I pay the bus for myself never again bother anyone or excuse not to come to school. Even today I'm still carrying your independence you taught me.*
>
> *This piece of paper seems so small for the things you did for me: independence, patience, respect and trust.*

This activity helps students take ownership and responsibility for their lives. It develops knowledge and skills and uses a combination of reflection, dialogue and *CreACTion*™, the taking of creative, innovative action. Ownership is grown through recognising the past, being rooted in the present and taking full ownership of the future.

The teacher as manager and administrator

The *Hourglass Process*© is repeated during sessions throughout the course and is consolidated in the assignments, each of which begins with reflection. Some tasks are required for credits, but many are simply for personal growth. For example, whilst examining the roles of the teacher they explore their own personal and professional roles, how to prioritise, plan and manage time.

Sheri

Urgent and important

Sorting out fights or disagreements/bullying in the classroom

Dealing with a distraught child

Sorting out wounds or dealing with high temps/illness

Khani

Urgent but not important

Interruptions – phone calls from parents

Some meetings

Reference reading

The teacher as a learning mediator/subject/discipline/phase specialist

By reflecting on the characteristics that make effective teachers, the following excerpts evidence personal thoughts on how to become a better teacher. This reflection comes at the end of a section of the course in which the students engage with the content of the Learning Programmes and the methodology used to teach and assess them (Department of Education, 2002).

Sheri

Task: Identify three things to inspire yourself to become a better teacher (Sheri identified four)

Doing more daily planning and learning to assess children at shorter intervals.

Becoming more involved with parents, a huge problem as I seldom see the parents as the children arrive at school by the school bus service.

Working more closely with the speech and occupational therapists.

Bringing the problem areas that each child is working with into the class-room and therefore implementing more stringently.

Task: Identify three things to inspire others to become better teachers

Share knowledge and teaching experience.

Be passionate about teaching young minds.

Always do it right and with love.

The teacher as interpreter and designer of learning programmes and materials

After reflection and dialogue, there is often an opportunity for *CreACTion*™ and, finally, further reflection. These segments are flexible and interchangeable, depending upon the content and purpose. Here are some examples when exploring the topic of special needs.

The session starts with a group discussion using a case study of a child who has a barrier to learning. The groups consider and share their own personal feelings for this child, and then what they think the parents and finally the child would feel. After a formal presentation on different barriers to learning, a practical session follows in which the students consider ways of supporting children with barriers to learning in their classrooms. The final task asks students to reflect in their journal how they would feel if they had a major barrier to learning (Davin and Van Staden, 2005).

> **Suzy's response:** *One thing I am so grateful for is that I am healthy. This task has made me really think about what would be the worst handicap for me. Can you imagine not being able to hear? A world of silence … how lonely you must feel. I think with great courage I could learn to live with it. At least you can still do everything for yourself. But being blind would be the absolute worst. A life of total darkness. Not knowing where you were going, being lead around. I would hate it but I suppose I would learn to live with it and become a humble person, but how happy would I be? I thought about being a paraplegic and decided that must be worst and I don't think I could do it. I am a very independent person and don't like anyone doing anything for me. This has made me see handicapped people in a totally different light. And I think that when I deal with a handicapped person from now on I will show them a whole lot of respect.*

These reflections lead into the next section on vulnerability and ways to develop their own and their children's resilience through their teaching.

The teacher as researcher and leader

The following excerpt from the Facilitator's Notes outlines the activities around supporting and fostering resilience in vulnerable children. They provide a good example of the *Hourglass Process*© in action, combining all four aspects – reflection, dialogue, *CreACTion*™, ownership. Formal presentations linked to the topic grow the students' knowledge base and support their deepening awareness.

These opportunities to learn, explore and share underlying beliefs and prejudices develop compassion, understanding and empathy for others and help the students to apply these traits in a classroom context.

TIME	ACTIVITIES
5 min	**WORKSHOP** Present outcomes for the workshop
20 min	**INTRODUCTION** **What is vulnerability?** … a situation where we can be hurt, harmed or attacked **What is resilience?** • What does it mean? • What are the characteristics of resilience? • What are the capabilities of resilient people? • How can we cultivate it in ourselves and our learners – some simple tools?
10 min	**REFLECTION: GROUP ACTIVITY** Give each group a number of squares of coloured paper. Ask each participant to take three pieces of paper and record one thing that 'I can do', 'I am' and 'I have' to contribute to the group. Keep the pieces of paper.
20 min	*CreACTion™* Give each group one of the following scenarios: A preschool child from a home where: • both parents have alcohol abuse problems • the father physically abuses the mother and the older son • there is a single mother living in an inner-city building, surrounded by violence, neighbours are being robbed, raped, assaulted • both parents are unemployed, father is in the advanced stages of HIV and AIDS The groups are requested to create a story about that child in that given situation. They should give the child a name, a sex, a personality, a home with siblings, a family and a community, and outline some of the things that the child experiences on a day-to-day basis at home.
20 min	**PRESENTATION** • Environmental factors impacting on the vulnerability of the child • The overarching impact of poverty • Socio-economic factors: crime, violence, substance abuse, addiction • Child abuse: physical, emotional, sexual • Family disruption: HIV and AIDS with its resultant death and loss, death and bereavement, divorce • Other: bullying, punishment, conflict
30 min	*CreACTion™* Based on the story created for the child: • list the factors that make this child vulnerable • list some practical examples of ways to develop this child's resilience at school • list ways in which you could help this child's family and community
40 min	**PRESENTATION AND FEEDBACK** • National policies and legislation • Classroom/school policies
10 min	**CONCLUSION** The groups take the coloured squares on which they recorded their contributions and paste them onto a single sheet to a make a 'quilt'. Use this to summarise that each person is important and can make a difference.

Figure 12.1 Facilitator's notes

The teacher as leader and assessor

Assessment of children is integrated into every facet of the course and provides a thread throughout the programme. Assessment skills are extended to include the self in both personal and professional life. Students begin by setting goals, reflecting at intervals on their attainment.

Two components in the course require scrutiny by peers and an external assessor. One is a 5-minute presentation to the class in the first year, and the other is a workplace visit by an assessor to evaluate classroom competence. This assessment takes place near the end of the second year. The two sets of excerpts from the journal entries reveal the students' growth in confidence and experience.

First-year task for assessment: making a presentation

Sheri: Topic – The Importance of Music for Preschool Children

I feel challenged, excited, confident and anxious, unsure and daunted.

Advantage of acquiring presentation skills:

Knowledge that is achievable, a new skill for my portfolio, new information to use in my career, feeling of satisfaction, proving that I could do what I knew I could do all along.

Khani: Topic – Race and Culture
I feel confident

The topic fits me. I think I am going to help lots of people to understand … I'm more comfortable after I've seen other presentations.

Advantage of acquiring presentation skills:

Confidence to talk in public, learning skills to prepare and present, developing skills for using flip charts, developing skills for doing presentations in time limits, developing research skills.

Second-year task for assessment: writing a letter to the assessor

Suzy

I plan to make the assessment go as smoothly as possible.

I will remember to continuously ask open-ended questions, encouraging learning, not instructing. Listening to the learners and giving individual support where needed and, very importantly, keeping control using a variety of ways.

Khani

I want to be a good role model for Caversham students. This course has given me a lifetime gift. Even if I don't get through the first time I am not going to give up. I owe it to myself. This course has been a blessing to us, educating us to be the best teachers and most of all growing confident as women and mothers.

 Summary

The image of the individual as an hourglass highlights the importance of 'filling' the 'container' in order to make a more effective contribution. It is a cyclical process of filling and giving, enabling teachers to become agents of transformation in their lives and the lives of others. The approach used throughout the training combines structured reflection – pausing in order to gain a deeper understanding of self and others – dialogue, *CreACTion*™ and finally ownership. At the start of the course, students were requested to articulate their goals and later to reflect on these. These excerpts show clearly the personal and professional growth achieved by these teachers.

Sheri

The start of the journey:

By the end of this year I would like to:

• *Have found some direction in my working career.*

By the end of this course I would like to:

• *Feel comfortable with my qualification and abilities to teach/counsel children.*

The end of Year 1:

I have found this course more than just interesting and informative. For me it has been a journey that has tested my personal ideas and perspectives, my time management, my rusty brain cells (!) and my creativity.

I have felt at times stretched beyond my limits but at other times totally fulfilled.

Suzy

The start of the journey:

By the end of the year I want to:

• *Have readied the children in my class enough to enter Grade 1 confidently.*

• *Have a permanent position.*

By the end of the course:

• *I will have paid for my lectures.*

• *Have all my assignments completed and marked higher.*

• *I expect to complete this course successfully and feel more confident in my sharing and teaching.*

(Continued)

(Continued)

The end of the journey:

How wonderful it is to go back to the first page of my journal. I remember writing my outcomes, doubting whether I would achieve them.

It is such a satisfying feeling to write this now. I have achieved all I expected and more.

I have become far more sharing of my ideas and planning with Grade 1 teachers. I feel refreshed and inspired all over again – must be the hourglass process.

Thank you for sharing and helping me grow and meet all my expectations.

My Personal Outcomes have all been achieved with a fantastic 5!

Khani

The start of the journey:

By the end of the year I want to:

• *Definitely pass and do good in my studies.*

By the end of the course:

• *I would like to have more knowledge of working with kids and as a teacher.*

Six months later:

I have learnt so much from this course like knowing who I am so I can be able to be the best that I can be. I have learnt that if you want to help somebody you have to help yourself first. (To) know where people come from is very important it helps you understand them, and to have a goal to reach. I am definitely going to adjust/change the way I see myself (negative).

The end of the journey:

Little did I know this was my first door of a new life. In the beginning I didn't understand but now I know who I am and I know where I want to go. Caversham has brought back my confidence as a young black woman. I know I can make a difference to young children and women. Caversham has taught me first to love myself: in doing so I am able to understand children's minds.

I would also like to teach other women from my experience and work with people with knowledge of Caversham. They have played such a big role because they have been so understanding about where my life has been. It has been like someone has taught me to walk again ... and to have people who can tell you that at least once you are doing good!! Now I know I am going to be something someday. I can be proud of my son too, not only just us but all women and children of South Africa.

The need for highly competent teachers is more critical now than ever. An ongoing debate is taking place on how best to prepare students for a career in the classroom. It is hoped that this chapter will provide a window for further dialogue around alternative models for teacher training.

 Questions for discussion

1. Are the lessons learned from this chapter relevant only to early years teacher training or can they be adapted for other training programmes?
2. Can teachers use a similar approach in their classroom teaching?
3. Do other training institutions use a similar model and with what success?
4. Are the benefits gained limited to personal growth or is there a spill-over to improved results in the cognitive sphere?

References and suggested further reading

Entries in bold are further reading.

Bolton, G. (2001) *Reflective Practice: Writing and Professional Development.* **London: Sage.**

Chapman, P. and Chisholm, L. (eds) (2004) *Changing Class: Education and Social Change in Post-apartheid South Africa.* HSRC Press. Available online at: www.hsrcpress.ac.za/product.php?productid=1937andcat=0andpage=1 (accessed 20 November 2010).

Christie, P. (2008) *Opening the Doors of Learning: Changing Schools in South Africa.* **Johannesburg: Heinemann.**

Davin, R. and Van Staden, C. (2005) *The Reception Year: Learning through Play.* Johannesburg: Heinemann.

Department of Education (DoE) (2001a) *Report on National ECD Policies and Programmes.* Pretoria: Government Printer. Available online at: www.education.gov.za/dynamic/dynamic.aspx?pageid=326anddirid=3 (accessed 27 November 2010).

DoE (2001b) *Education White Paper 6: Special Needs Education: Building an Inclusive Education and Training System.* Pretoria: DoE.

DoE (2001c) *Education White Paper 5 on Early Childhood Education: Meeting the Challenge of Early Childhood Development in South Africa.* Pretoria: Government Printer. Available online at: www.education.gov.za/dynamic/dynamic.aspx?pageid=326anddirid=3 (accessed 1 December 2010).

DoE (2002) *National Curriculum Statement Grades R to 9 (Schools) Policy.* Pretoria: Government Printer. Available online at: www.education.gov.za/Curriculum/GET/GETstatements.asp (accessed 24 November 2010).

Education and Training Development Practices: Sector Education Training

Authority (ETDP SETA) (undated). Available online at: www.etdpseta.org.za (accessed 27 November 2010).

Gardner, H. (1997) *Extraordinary Minds*. New York: Perseus Book Group.

Ministry of Education (2003) *Revised National Curriculum Statement Grades R-9: Foundation Phase*. Pretoria: Ministry of Education.

National Scientific Council Centre on the Developing Child (2007) *The Science of Early Childhood Development: Closing the Gap Between What we Know and What we Do*. Harvard University.

Office of the President (1995) *South African Qualifications Act No. 58*. Pretoria: Government Printer. Available online at: www.acts.co.za/ed_saqa/index.htm (accessed 4 December 2010).

SAQA (2009) South African Qualifications Authority Registered Qualification: Higher Certificate ECD No. 64649. Available online at: www.saqa.org.za (accessed 2 December 2010).

13

International student experiences: influences on early childhood practice

Carolyn Silberfeld

Overview

This research explores the influences on early years practice, experienced by early childhood studies undergraduate students, from diverse cultural and socioeconomic backgrounds, who participated in an academic exchange programme between three higher education institutions in Europe and three higher education institutions in Canada, in 2005. Fieldwork was a compulsory component of the exchange programme and the participants all worked in early years settings. Some of the students were experienced practitioners, whilst others were not. For most of them the practical experience contributed to their developing knowledge about childhood and children's learning. Experiencing different approaches to practice was exciting for the students as well as challenging, not only with regard to the new practices but also with regard to their own opinions and beliefs about children's learning and development. The majority of students could articulate certain benefits of practising in an early years setting in a different country and contrasting culture. However, some students perceived that their experiences abroad had little influence on their previous or subsequent practice.

The focus of this chapter is the Education for Global Competencies (EfGC) exchange programme between six institutions and its relationship with transformative learning – the process of making meaning of one's experience. EfGC was a well-funded academic exchange programme between three higher education institutes in Canada and three in Europe. From September 2005 to January 2006, 27 students from three HE institutions in Canada (Vancouver, BC, Fraser Valley, BC and Montreal) exchanged with 27 students from three HE institutions in Europe (London, England; Stockholm, Sweden and Abo, Finland) for one semester. All students were undertaking undergraduate programmes in early childhood studies or early childhood education.

All 54 students involved in the project followed a similar programme during the three months of the exchange. The curriculum included a course about advanced child development, a module linked to early years practice and a new module for the project and adopted by the other five institutions, about children, culture and globalisation. All students experienced working in an early years setting during the exchange programme. Although the students were following a similar curriculum, it was evident from the evaluations that this curriculum was being delivered differently in different institutions yet there was commonality in many of the experiences of the students.

Transformative learning

The concept of transformative learning was introduced by Mezirow who described it as:

> the process of becoming critically aware of how and why our assumptions have come to constrain the way we perceive, understand, and feel about our world; changing these structures of habitual expectation to make possible a more inclusive, discriminating, and integrative perspective; and finally, making choices or otherwise, acting upon these new understandings. (1991: 167)

This process of critical awareness, however, will be different for different people depending on the way that they engage with transformative learning. Self-perception about the transformation that is taking place and the assumptions and presuppositions that are being questioned will also depend on cultural background, prior knowledge and experience and deeply held attitudes, values and beliefs. These will all influence how new experiences will be interpreted and evaluated and, as a consequence, will influence any new meaning perspectives. Mezirow (1991: 43) has identified three types of meaning perspective: epistemic (the way one knows and the uses one makes of knowledge); sociolinguistic (the way in which society, culture and language shape and limit perception and understanding); and psychological (the way in which people have learnt to protect themselves from traumatic events in their childhood).

The focus of this study was to explore the relationship between the educational exchange and transformative learning – the process of making meaning of one's experience – and the perceptions of the students after they had returned to their home institutions and familiar environments, when they would have had time to reassess their experiences during the change and time to develop new meanings and perspectives about their personal and academic development as well as their practice with young children. I also wanted to explore what the students meant by what they expressed, in order to better understand the way they had conceptualised their experiences.

The student exchange programme

This was an exploratory case study with the cohort of 54 students, chosen for ease of access. They were a volunteer sample which included both Canadian and European students. Interviews were conducted with a sample of 17 students to capture a holistic articulation of their experiences. Other information came from student evaluations throughout the exchange.

Four months following the exchange, students were asked about their perceptions regarding the impact and influence of the exchange. They were asked to describe how it has influenced them personally, how the exchange has influenced their academic development and how their practice with children and understanding of practice with children has been influenced since their return to a familiar environment. There was recognition and awareness, prior to the study, that the experiences of the students may not necessarily have made positive differences.

About the participants

The participants included eight female students who went to Canada from London and nine students (eight female and one male) who came from Canada to London. The eight from London went to institutions in Vancouver, Fraser Valley and Montreal (respectively) exchanging with nine Canadian students from these institutions. The students were contacted by email and telephoned to be informed about the study and to ask if they would consider participating in the research. Surprisingly, 16 out of the 17 agreed and seemed extremely enthusiastic.

It is important at this point to make clear the differences between the Canadian and British students and the differences between the higher education institutions from which they came. In general, the students from Britain tended to be more diverse with regard to their age and life experiences. The Canadians were all under the age of 30 years because part of their funding came from a youth grant, which specified that students participating in the exchange should not be older than 30 years. The British University is in London and is renowned for the diversity of its student population. The sample reflected this cultural, socio-economic, academic background and life experience diversity. The students were aged between 20 and 53 years. They had entered the degree programme via different admission criteria, which included traditional A Level results, vocational qualifications, qualifications from a different country and access to higher education courses for the students who had no formal qualifications. They were also diverse in their country of origin, their culture and their ethnicity.

The students from Canada also came from different backgrounds, usually depending on the location of their home institution. The three home institutions were very different in nature. One was in the centre of a city (Montreal), where the student population was similar to the university in London; one was on the outskirts of a city (Vancouver) in a community college; and the third was a university college in a rural, predominantly mono-cultural population, although there were international students in other parts of both this institution and the community college in Vancouver. The students from all three institutions were aged between 20 and 25 years and were all Caucasian students, born in Canada. They came from different socio-economic and cultural backgrounds, usually related to the environment in which they grew up. The differences between the UK and Canadian students appeared to influence the findings, particularly when the interview data was reconstructed.

Emerging issues

It was evident from the end of exchange evaluations that there were clear similarities and differences between the experiences of the Canadian and European students. The major differences were related to travel, study, grades and accommodation. Whereas the European students in Canada seemed to appreciate the opportunity to study in a different environment, the Canadian students seemed to appreciate more the travel opportunities that the exchange would enable them to experience. The Canadian students were very anxious about the grades that they received from the coursework because of the different system of grading in Canada. Financial difficulties were common to all students who found that they had underestimated the cost of the exchange and the impact of more debt. Other similarities included the self-confidence, independence and self-awareness that were developing towards the end of the exchange.

Without exception, the students spoke about having a greater awareness of themselves and their own needs, capabilities and capacities but not really understanding how this had occurred. The main differences and, therefore, greater range in interpretation and conception were related to the positive and negative reflections on learning and practice discussed below.

Approaches to practice

Fieldwork was a compulsory component of the exchange programme and all the participants enjoyed this aspect of the curriculum. Some of the students were experienced practitioners, whilst others were not. Students were placed in a variety of settings. In Vancouver and Fraser Valley, these placements were in preschool settings. In Vancouver, the UK students experienced the majority of their fieldwork practice in the university childcare centre. They also spent some time in an urban centre in one of the most deprived parts of the city and in an independent semi-rural setting. In Fraser Valley, there was an urban childcare setting and two rural settings, one of which took place in a community centre. In Montreal, the students were placed in kindergarten settings with children aged 5–6 years. Canadian students' placements in England were mainly in reception and Year 1 classes of local primary schools, although they differed in geographical location and demographic details. Three of the students had childcare placements in a local centre for refugees and asylum seekers. For most of them, the practical experience contributed to their developing knowledge about childhood and children's learning:

> I've never ever thought that you could learn from children in that sort of respect, you know, that you could set up a theme and then just feed off the children and that sort of thing. (Lara, UK)

The main variables seemed to be regarding the status of children, communication with children and families and communication with other professionals and practitioners. However, differences in perception could have been related to wider and more complex issues. For example, the students were experiencing change in general, not just in their practice. They may also have been looking at new experiences of practice with fresh eyes. The differences in their perception of working with children may also have been related to their level of experience, such as the number of years they had previously practised in early years settings and/or the diversity of practice they had experienced within these settings. Without doubt, their perception of approaches to practice was strongly linked to the other categories of description, such as disequilibrium, self-confidence, self-awareness and differing education systems.

Experiencing change

It is important to understand that the students experienced change in general, not just in their experiences of practice. They needed to learn how to live differently in a new environment with strangers. In doing so, they developed different relationships with others, both personally and professionally. For some, it meant letting go of longheld beliefs about children and learning, as well as adapting to new approaches to childcare and education. There was a realisation of the strong links to theory and practice by both groups of students, particularly on first experiencing a new approach to childcare and education.

> I remember going to the nursery and being very impressed with how they ran things, because everything I learned in Canada I saw put into practice in the school. I remember at home, in Canada, looking through theory and believing in it but not necessarily seeing it in practice here. So I thought, wow, that is significantly different from what I have seen at home, I can see that people in other places can do things differently with different perspectives. (Ian, Canada)

> I don't think it would have impacted on me as much as seeing it. It was actually seeing ... because you could read something in a book and you thought oh that sounds really interesting, but to actually see it in practice ... (Lara, UK)

All the students experienced what Pyvis and Chapman (2005) describe as cultural acclimatisation – the adjustment to the disorientation of being in a new environment. Faye, aged 25, who was a fairly experienced practitioner, sensed this disequilibrium at the beginning of her placement.

> ... when you're taken out of that, it's like a comfort zone. I was really comfortable, willing to be taken out, and to be put ... and I thought that'll be okay. And then the first day in the class I was like, oh, this is so different ... And, you know, even the accents ... they had difficulty, especially with mine, understanding my accent ... (Faye, Canada)

For some of the students, this disequilibrium triggered some form of culture shock, in that they found themselves in a very different cultural environment to their own. Pamela, aged 23, came from a semi-rural part of Canada, mainly bicultural. She had rarely seen a black or Asian person, so having her placement in a children's centre with children and families from many cultures and ethnic groups, was something she had not expected.

> We get Asians going through and stuff, but I've never been around that many cultures before. (Pamela, Canada)

Although Lisa experienced 'culture shock' – surprise, disorientation, uncertainty or confusion which can occur when 'an individual is forced to adjust to an unfamiliar social setting where previous learning no longer applies' (Pederson, 1995: 1) – she was interested by her new environment. Patricia, aged 25, experienced a similar culture shock in a primary school reception class and was fascinated that even though, for a large percentage of the children, English was not the first language, there appeared to be few communication barriers.

> ... especially the classroom, I was in, too, was ... I remember, of the, I think, 50 students that I saw between the two groups, there was maybe three, whose first, you know, whose mother's tongue was English, and I remember thinking how did ... I mean, there were no problems, none of the kids even cried when their parents left and I remember thinking this is amazing what they are able to do in this classroom. (Patricia, Canada)

Having previously thought that communication was problematic if the children spoke different languages, she began to see how this diversity was valued. It gave Patricia an insight into how she could adapt her practice when she returned home by bringing similar values of communication she had observed into her classroom.

Adapting to new practice

In general, the difficulties of adapting to new ways of practice appeared to be related to the relationships between the adults, rather than the practice itself. There was one exception to this and it was experienced by Fiona, aged 22, in the centre for refugees and asylum seekers. The majority of the childcare staff either held an NVQ2 or NVQ3 qualification which they had obtained whilst working at the centre. Their knowledge and understanding was somewhat limited in certain areas. One of these areas related to safeguarding children and children's rights.

> I'm always aware of what's happening and that you know a child can always say, someone touched me this way, or someone's hit me this way and you just have to be aware of it, but if the child needs a cuddle or they want to sit with you I'm not going to say no. That would sound really hard, because especially if they're crying and when we were there, they said, you can only hold their hand. And here you just want to hug them, hold them or just let them fall on you and you can hug them and hold them, and it's not a big deal. (Fiona, Canada)

When querying this approach, Fiona was informed that adults were not allowed to have physical contact with the children. Surprised by this, I checked with the manager of the centre who told me that one of the staff had undertaken a professional development day, organised by the local authority, on behalf of the centre and had cascaded the information down to the other staff members. What the member of staff had omitted to say was that adults should not have any physical contact with a child unless the child wanted that contact. In this instance, the manager had not questioned what the member of staff had reported back. One can only assume that the staff member did not really understand the rationale behind the safeguarding children policy. Unfortunately, Fiona was labelled as a 'troublemaker' by the manager, for having asked a very reasonable question. This can sometimes happen when someone feels threatened by higher qualified staff whose critical questioning (often based on greater knowledge and understanding) is perceived as challenging the status quo (Chandler, 2006).

Transforming relationships

The students had little difficulty in establishing good relationships with the children, families and practitioners whom they met within their placement settings. In general, the students' contributions to the settings were highly valued. This increased their levels of confidence as well as their knowledge and understanding of practice. On return to their home country, the students could reflect on their experiences abroad and could articulate how these experiences had influenced their practice since returning home. Relationships with the children appeared to have developed more with the students who went to Canada than with those who came to the UK. This seemed to relate to the way in which the students had observed the children's relationship with other practitioners.

> I think the children in Canada seemed very approachable and it made me more open and approachable too. Before I was a little bit scared – I was doing volunteering work at a school and I was not really sure how to get around things, what to say; it made me a better practitioner. (Lucy, UK)

Natalie, aged 24, had been a teaching assistant prior to the exchange and felt she had a good rapport with the children. However, in Canada, children are encouraged to ask questions of the adults, in the same way that they themselves are asked questions. Since returning to London, her relationships with children now reflect her experiences in Canada. Natalie's perception is that her relationships with children now are much more mutually respectful.

Lara, 39, recognised another way in which her approach to practice had gone through a form of transformation. She was another very experienced nursery nurse, who had worked in a variety of settings prior to the exchange.

> ... one of the things that I actually developed in Canada, one of the things that I realised, I don't think I ever did when working with children in those fifteen years, was actually listening to children.

The transformative catalyst for her was a programme called *Children Teaching Us* in the university childcare centre in which she and the other two students in Vancouver did their placements. Instead of the adult guiding the children in their learning and use of resources, the children made these decisions for themselves. When she first heard of the programme, Lara thought this approach would not engender a good learning experience for the children.

Negotiating with children to support their learning was another theme that was discussed during the interviews, particularly with the UK students. Rosemary, aged 53 years, completely re-evaluated her approach and learnt to give children more independence. Her own children, who were now adults in their 20s and 30s, were, in her own words, 'over-protected'. She was an experienced nursery worker in London and thought it was very important to show children what they should and could do. She discovered in the kindergarten in Montreal that being given more independence can enhance children's learning and development.

> Yes, I think sometimes we have to give children the freedom, you know, we have to give the children a lot ... too much ... we shouldn't overprotect them, because the more we give children, children can ... you know, if children are more independent, children can learn plenty, you know, and find out things for themselves. (Rosemary, UK)

Increased confidence in their ability to practise was another theme linked to the categories of description. This was particularly so with Lucy, who did not have so much experience of working with children as several of the others:

> Before, I'd interact with the children, but I wouldn't be as confident introducing something new to them because they're young and I'd be scared that I didn't want to confuse them. But going over there and seeing how it is done, through observations ... Because, as I've implemented it here, I've found it a lot easier and they have actually warmed to it a lot more and are a lot calmer than I thought they would be. (Lucy, UK)

Even the more experienced practitioners found they gained increased confidence, both with the UK and Canadian students. The students were eager to share their new understanding of practice with others when they returned home. Their perception was that these new developments would be welcomed by other professionals and practitioners. However, implementing some of these developments since the participants have been home has not been quite as straightforward as the students would have thought.

Natalie tried to develop strategies within the classroom to make the curriculum less rigid for the children, by making what she considered helpful suggestions to the class teacher. However, her suggestions were not taken up by the teacher who was very anxious about making sure she followed the recommendations of the EYFS. The teacher was fairly newly qualified and trying to meet her responsibilities through a very structured approach.

When Sandra returned to the school in which she worked, she was also eager to discuss her recent experiences with the class teacher. She was not expecting the response she received:

> ... what shocked me, what just really threw me ... the second week I was trying to have a conversation with the class teacher about *Emilia Reggio*. She didn't know about it. She did her training some years ago and I'm thinking, as early childhood educators, how can we ignore what's going on around us, in the academic world? But she told me ... 'Well once you get into practice, you can forget what you did at University'. I was horrified ... I was totally horrified. (Sandra, UK)

Even though Sandra found this reaction very worrying, she felt there was little she could do about the situation, other than to use strategies with which she could influence practice. Sandra was used to doing as she was told by the teacher.

Lara, too, experienced unexpected resistance from her colleagues on return to the UK, full of enthusiasm to implement some of the good practice she had been engaged with in Canada.

> It was very challenging when I came back, trying to help the others look at practice in a different way. I realised that when you are working in an environment, like I did for 15 years, you work in a particular way, and think why should things be changed if they work?

However, she recognised why there was resistance from other professionals and practitioners. She also recognised that she would have felt similarly to them had she not taken part in the exchange.

Transforming practice

There is no doubt that, to some extent, all the students interviewed had experienced some form of transformation relating to their professionalism and practice. For some, this transformation manifested itself in adapting practice by having a deeper understanding of effective practice. Pamela described herself as being much worldlier since her experiences in London.

For other students, the changes they spoke about appeared to be more embedded in their perception of good practice, were more long-term and ultimately more transformative. Previously, Patricia had focused on having sufficient resources to do what she considered to be a good job. After her experiences in London, she realised that having sufficient resources was only a part of providing an optimum learning environment:

> Well, it's given me a new perspective in that when I go into classrooms now and I see, I think, it's not impossible. And teachers talk a lot about time management, and not having enough resources and, and I think now, well, that's not necessarily all that's, that's lacking, you know, a lot can be done. It's a question of just having the right systems and planning properly and ... so it influenced me in that I think I learnt a lot of strategies there that I would implement into my own classroom. (Patricia, Canada)

Lara's approach to practice had also changed quite radically. Before going to Canada, she had not realised how constraining the curriculum could be. Her focus on good planning for children's learning experiences appeared to be quite rigidly structured and adult led. She had not realised that what she had considered to be good practice in London was more to do with meeting the required outcomes rather than the process of learning. Lara's experience helped her to recognise that outcome measures she had used when following the UK curriculum tended to focus on observing if the children were experiencing any difficulties, whereas in Canada, the emphasis wasn't on what the children couldn't do, it was more on what the children could do. This recognition changed the way that she herself thought about children's learning and development as well as transforming her approach to practice.

Summary

The interview transcripts identified the students' increased under-standing of the development of children as well as an increased understanding of how to support children's learning and develop-ment. The importance of specialist staff in the early years with an understanding of child development and learning has been advo-cated by early years professionals and practitioners for many years (Owen, 2006; David, 2001). Teacher training in the UK was per-ceived by both groups of students as having a greater focus on teaching practice than on an understanding of children's develop-ment and learning. What the students also seemed to have grasped is that becoming a better practitioner includes questioning and thinking about their own practice (Cranton, 1996). The more expe-rienced practitioners found the adaptation process more difficult but the transformation was longer lasting, whereas the less experi-enced practitioners took on board new ways of working more readily as part of developing their practice.

 Questions for discussion

1. Which strategies could/do you use to reflect on your practice?
2. How can you reflect on your practice in an informed way?
3. How has reflection influenced any transformative approach to thinking differently about your practice or practice issues?

References and suggested further reading

Entries in bold are further reading.

Chandler, T. (2006) Working in Multi-disciplinary Teams. In G. Pugh and B. Duffy (eds) *Contemporary Issues in the Early Years: Working Collaboratively for Children* (4th edn). London: Sage.

Cranton, P. (1996) *Professional Development as Transformative Learning*. San Francisco, CA: Jossey-Bass.

David, T. (2001) Curriculum in the Early Years. In G. Pugh (ed.) *Contemporary Issues in the Early Years: Working Collaboratively for Children* (3rd edn). London: NCB.

Mezirow, J. (1991) *Transformative Dimensions of Adult Learning*. San Francisco, CA: Jossey-Bass.

Owen, S. (2006) Training and Workforce Issues in the Early Years. In G. Pugh and B. Duffy (eds) *Contemporary Issues in the Early Years: Working Collaboratively for Children* (4th edn). London: Sage.

Pederson, P. (1995) *The Five Stages of Culture Shock*. London: Greenwood.

Pyvis, D. and Chapman, A. (2005) Culture Shock and the International Student 'Offshore'. *Journal of Research in International Education*, 4(1): 23–42.

14

Transformation of early years provision using discourses for professional development for practitioners

Christine Such, Julia Druce and Hazel Jennings

Overview

This chapter begins with a review of the changing policy in early years and how this is linked to professionalising the workforce with the focus on graduate leadership. We shall show how evidence on effective pedagogical practice is now part of the discourse promoting professional development using the Early Years Professional Status (EYPS) role as the focus of our inquiry. We examine the role of higher education in supporting early years practitioners' professional development. Here we seek to explore models of professional development drawing upon evidence from our practice as lecturers and trainers in a post-1992 university in England. In this part of the discussion, we shall provide examples from our own practice to identify networks of support which both help to create and sustain a community of practice (Wenger, 1998). Here our focus is on the use of an online forum which encourages shared learning.

Our focus is aspects of leadership of practice in early years settings and how this can be developed. We are interested in how communities of practice (Wenger, 1998) can be used to encourage shared learning and how using the online environment may promote constructive interaction and knowledge creation. Brooks identifies the importance of the online forum to promote development of a 'personal sense of connection with fellow group members' (2010: 263) and we feel that this can provide space for socialisation between members whose work and personal commitments may make face-to-face interactions more difficult. It is not easy to find that quiet space in which to think and perhaps having a forum where you can share with others can provide a meeting place for ideas to develop. We show how the online forum has been used by practitioners, and how they feel its use has supported their own professional development.

The drive to professionalise the workforce to increase the education and qualification levels is closely tied to the success of early years provision (Moss, 2006). In 2006, *The Early Years Professional Prospectus* (CWDC, 2006) was produced, setting out proposals and guidance on how to develop practice and create a new kind of professional (Jones and Pound, 2008). The consultation on Early Years Professional Status role (EYPS) was embedded within a wider review of the *Children's Workforce Strategy* (CWDC, 2005) seeking to raise staff qualification levels. The quality of the staff and the quality of provision are interwoven into government policies on early years. This has led to further training opportunities in the Essex County Council (CC) region to promote graduate early years leaders. It is these developments which prompted the creation of an online forum for practitioners. Essex CC wanted an online forum to encourage professional learning between different early years providers and their staff. Its content is largely determined by these users.

Changing policy context and workforce agenda in early years

In the literature produced by the Children's Workforce Development Council (CWDC) from 2006 to 2010, there is an emphasis on developing graduate leaders who can play their part in transforming early years practice. The qualities, skills and knowledge these leaders will show are couched in language which is inspirational. For example, the graduate leader (EYPS) will 'be able to change, shape and innovate practice and, by doing so, you will make a real difference to the lives of babies, young children and their families' (CWDC, 2008b: 1). In 2007 detailed guidance was produced on the standards which specify the skills and knowledge which candidates seeking to achieve EYPS have to meet. Following consultation with providers of EYPS training, this guidance was revised in 2008 to emphasise aspects of the leadership role and how it can be demonstrated by candidates in their practice.

Two themes have been derived from an analysis of the literature produced by the CWDC: the first covers the agenda on professionalising the workforce to create graduate leaders; and the second the professional identity of these graduate leaders. Urban has identified the close union between scholarly discourse and policy documents on the need to professionalise the early years workforce (2008: 137). It is this union which is apparent in the discussion on the necessity for developing a graduate-led profession in English early years settings. The graduate would assume the role of a teacher and lead practice on the Early Years Foundation Stage (EYFS, DCSF, 2007) curriculum to promote the care and education of young children. Policies which drive this development have articulated what is needed and why, and these appear to be a dominant theme in the publicity literature produced by the CWDC (2005, 2008a, 2008b). Research evidence has been used in these documents to show the relationship between the quality of the early learning environment provided and increased level of staff qualifications (Sylva and Pugh, 2005). Early years settings led by staff with an informed knowledge of child development, able to work in partnership with parents, and able to develop effective relationships with children, provided a more stimulating and enriching learning environment (Siraj-Blatchford, 2007).

Moss (2006) explores the dominant discourses on professionalism to consider how certain ways of thinking about the present workforce situation in early years settings and its future role have shaped practice. The emergence of a discourse based on the need for early years practitioners to adopt a more developmental and educational role to lead and transform practice is present in the standards on the EYPS role. Here, it is possible to see why, and how, a particular kind of technical role emerged based on the principles of developmentally appropriate practice and embedded within the EYPS standards (Yelland and Kilderry, 2008). Discourses can legitimise and shape our understanding of what is normal and desirable. It appears that leadership in early years settings is being closely tied to the developmental model of practice. What has emerged is a highly prescriptive specification on how graduate leaders would provide and conceive of ways to transform practice in early years settings. Yet the space for professional engagement to transform practice seems limited because of the dominance of more powerful agencies in determining the workforce policy agenda, to the exclusion of alternative and less influential voices, including those of practitioners (Cheeseman, 2007). We consider that an online forum can provide space for professional dialogue: at its best, it promotes collaboration across work boundaries and creates an environment for socialisation to encourage professional identity (Osgood, 2006).

We have sought to link national policy on professionalism to local initiatives on professional development to show how our work in higher education encourages graduate practitioners' professional learning. Miller provides a critical review of policy developments leading to the creation of EYPS. She outlines the parallels with previous workforce development which led to the creation of 'Senior Practitioner status achieved through an early years sector-endorsed foundation degree (EYSED), a vocational qualification designed to integrate academic study with work-based learning' (2008: 257). She shows how the government agenda on professionalising the workforce creates tensions and challenges when developing new professional roles.

McGillivray (2008) focuses on professional identity to further explore the implications for practitioners. She asks whether the mission to introduce a new graduate EYPS role will lead to a revaluation of the professional identity of early years practitioners, or whether it will flounder because of the lack of improved pay associated with the higher status work role. She notes that the voice of the practitioner is missing from the review on workforce reform. Thus, she argues that 'there may need to be a period of introspection and reflection, in order to create a model of a workforce that belongs to the workforce itself, with constructs of professional identity informed by a shared vision and understanding' (McGillivray, 2008: 252).

What is the Early Years Professional Status role?

In England, early years practitioners work in a wide range of settings, including full daycare, nursery and primary schools, preschool groups and children's centres, as well as in home-based childcare and family support. These settings include a range of different providers from the maintained, private, voluntary and independent sectors. The model of leadership introduced in the EYPS role is intended to cover all these different kinds of provision. Targets were set by the government to have an EYPS working in all children's centres offering childcare by 2010 and in every full daycare setting by 2015 (CWDC, 2008b).

In the *Early Years Professional Prospectus* (CWDC, 2006), the approach to the award of the EYPS to support the development of a new early years professional role is described in full. The government wanted to create a graduate-led profession to establish a leadership role which would be pivotal in raising the quality of early years provision. They would act as agents of change helping to raise standards in early years settings, and, in particular, to lead practice in the EYFS curriculum (Miller, 2008). They would show that they can exercise leadership in making a positive difference to children's well-being, learning and development (CWDC, 2008a). They would support and mentor other practitioners. Support for this new role was based on research evidence from the Effective Provision of Pre-school Education project (EPPE), a longitudinal study that followed the progress of 3000 children in 141 English preschools (CWDC, 2006). It provided case study evidence of specific pedagogies employed in good to excellent preschool settings. The use of this evidence to promote graduate leadership also encourages discussion of pedagogical practice.

Forms of professional development

We have sought to contextualise professional development within higher education. Apple and McMullen describe 'professional development systems as the interconnecting agencies, organisations, and higher education institutions that provide professional development and those power brokers who determine ECEC professional qualifications' (2007: 255). Whereas their review of the American system includes professional development based on formal, credit course and degree requirements as well as informal non-credit courses, ours is a narrower focus examining how experience in higher education supports students' opportunities to learn and engage in professional development leading to graduate leadership in early years provision. It does focus on what Leathwood and O'Connell characterise as the 'new' student in higher education who is more likely to be motivated to pursue studies which 'have currency in the job market and prepare them for work' (2003: 611). The students we teach are aiming to enhance their career prospects and employability. We wanted to set their experience as students, and ours as teachers, in the context of professional development systems.

The workforce agenda on professionalising the workforce in England has emphasised the link between graduate leaders and quality of provision in early years settings. April 2008 saw the DCSF publication of *Building Brighter Futures* (2008a) and the *2020 Children and Young People's Workforce Strategy* (2008b). The latter strategy aimed to build upon the existing 10-year childcare strategy to ensure the recruitment, retention and development of a quality workforce which could make a real difference for children in their earliest years. Urban observes that 'many countries have set ambitious policy goals to increase both the quantity and quality of provision' (2008: 137) which perhaps sets the agenda for professional development systems. It can be argued that the English strategy has been based on a commitment to professionalise the workforce. The 2020 strategy, for example, described the support needed to deliver on this vision and the reforms required to help drive it forward. The main thrust being: qualifications, training and progression routes – ensuring these are accessible, of high quality and that they provide not only skills development but also career progression.

Experiences of higher education: engaging in reflective practice

MacNaughton (2005) argues that professional development is more likely to be valued by early years practitioners if it occurs through collaborative inquiry and dialogue. Boud and Lee identify how the context for learning influences students' entry into communities of practice in higher education. Their research looks at the relationships which postgraduate research students may or may not choose to enter. They conclude that 'peers do not necessarily learn as a natural outcome of their being peers' (2005: 515) and therefore how opportunities are structured needs to be carefully considered. We have focused on how these opportunities can be encouraged within the university environment to promote collaborative learning which is meaningful to our students to develop their practice. Brooks identifies the value of using online communities of practice for professional development. They have the potential to create a forum which can cross institutional and geographical boundaries in higher education. What emerges as critical in this process is that online fora 'support constructive interaction and collaboration' (2010: 265). They help to develop a sense of 'personal' connection with a group of like-minded professionals; and may blur the boundaries between instruction and professional support.

MacNaughton (2005) invites students of early childhood to work together and engage with active learning within communities of practice. She thus identifies with new aspects of practitioners' discourses which question what is taken for granted to discover different ways of developing and leading practice in early years settings. This is more closely aligned with conceptions of the practitioner as researcher rather than as technician (Moss, 2006). We argue that this would better prepare students to become graduate leaders of practice and conceive of this role as the opportunity to develop and change practice in early years settings. The concept of 'community of practice' can be instigated for a variety of analytical purposes, but the origin and primary use of the concept has been embedded into learning theory. Three main characteristics identified by Wenger are *domain, a community* and *a practice* and it is the combination of these three elements that constitutes a community of practice (1998: 45). Therefore, it is by developing these three elements in parallel that one cultivates such a community. Wenger (2007) further discusses that new technologies such as the Internet have extended the reach of our interactions beyond the geographical limitations of traditional communities, but the increase in flow of information does not obviate the need for community. In fact, it expands the possibilities for community and calls for new kinds of communities based on shared practice.

The CWDC provided funding to facilitate the development of Early Years Networks both nationally, through Share Street (CWDC, 2010) and within local authorities to develop such networks of support (CWDC, 2008b). These fora may provide the kind of opportunities identified by MacNaughton (2005) and thus have the potential to develop alternative discourses on professionalism in early years settings. Osgood (2006) and Miller (2008) both subscribe to the idea of finding new ways to capture workers' perceptions and understanding of their role. We see this work as supporting an alternative paradigm of how practice could be led, and how innovation could be introduced, and is thus another way of viewing the EYPS role as a catalyst for change and innovation of practice in early years settings.

Online communities: supporting continuing professional development

An online community has been established in our university to encourage early years practitioners to remain involved and engaged in their professional learning. We feel that this does provide a useful forum for exchanging ideas based on the co-construction of professional knowledge to develop shared practice. The model of learning is based on Wenger's (2007) community of practice and the stages of engagement, and its use is based on Salmon's (2008) approach to online teaching and learning. Christine has used this approach to develop online learning tasks with early childhood studies undergraduate students. This has led her to establish a portfolio of online activities which have been successfully used with different student cohorts to provide blended learning opportunities.

The architecture of the online forum and how it frames practitioner inquiry is shown in Table 14.1. The domain is open to graduate early years professionals and early years advisors in the Essex county region of England. The site is managed by Hazel Jennings in her role as training and development officer to facilitate collaboration between professionals. She provides stewardship and it is this which helps to sustain the relevance of the forum to its members. The membership is fluid. Hazel continues to work with users but whereas her initial engagement was with early years advisors, it is now with frontline EYPs. Practitioners continue to provide a 'wish list' of their ideas. Their ideas include: free-flow play, cognitive and behavioural therapy, music therapy, baby yoga, Forest School and the natural environment, and helping children manage loss, separation and bereavement. Hazel feels that this is important because it creates a sense of ownership. Our review of the use of the site shows how it can contribute to professional identity which strengthens pedagogy based on practice inquiry. At its best, the workshops and the use of the forum can promote confidence and pride, as shown in the following quotes:

> Knowledge and skills gained from CPD has transformed my practice.

> ... has vastly improved my confidence and self-esteem. (Evidence from evaluation forms, 2009/10)

Regional online communities and the potential for professional learning

We see the development of the online forum as important in offering graduate early years practitioners opportunities to further their own professional development. We have sought to create a space which allows practitioners to develop their professional identity through shared engagement, to build relationships beyond the boundaries of their practice setting and to gain experience in sharing their expertise with other users. It is a medium for 'show and tell' and offers opportunities to visualise and document learning. We have provided illustrations of the site and explore its use as a network of support to create and sustain a community of practice (Wenger, 1998).

The opening page on the website invites participants to become involved and use the site to both access and share information, in other words to 'think something, change something and make something better' (Figures 14.1 and 14.2). The presentation is important in making it easy for users to navigate the site, and in many ways this page illustrates features of online social networking given the emphasis on ease of use which helps to promote early socialisation. Figure 14.1 is the old version of the opening page which has been updated to make navigation easier for users and the latest version is shown in Figure 14.2. Every EYP in Essex can be allocated a specific username and password (whether they are trained at Anglia Ruskin University or not), which gives them full access to the online resources, workshop information and booking. This part of the site covers content agreed with practitioners on their 'wish list' of training requests. There is also an open discussion area where practitioners can begin their own online conversations by posting ideas and responding to others.

Table 14.1 Online community for early years practitioners: supporting continuing professional development

Definitions of community practice	Using an online community for early years practitioners
The domain. 'A community of practice has an identity defined by a shared domain of interest. Membership therefore implies a commitment to the domain, and therefore a shared competence that distinguishes members from other people.'	www.mpowernet.anglia.ac.uk/eyps/inde. php Open to Essex Graduate Early Years Professionals, trainers and tutors (Faculty of Education, Anglia Ruskin University (mpowernet) Essex Early Years County Council Partnership members http://sharestreet.cwdcouncil.org.uk/ 'Share Street' a national forum (CWDC) www.foundation-stage.info/ 'The Early Years Foundation Stage Forum' – also a national forum with the option for private membership at local authority level *Welcome – outlines resources to use and invites members to join in*
The community. 'In pursuing their interest in their domain, members engage in joint activities and discussions, help each other, and share information. They build relationships that enable them to learn from each other.'	Workshops are structured and organised to promote sharing of information. Ideas are developed through online socialisation, exchange of information and developing knowledge in discussion. Collaborative inter-disciplinary learning is nurtured through shared goals *Interactive workshops provide opportunities for sharing new ideas, professional and personal learning*
The practice. 'Members of a community of practice are practitioners. They develop a shared repertoire of resources: experiences, stories, tools, ways of addressing recurring problems – in short a shared practice. This takes time and sustained interaction.'	Space for user engagement to network *Sharing of ideas, teaching and learning resources and experiences generated through face-to-face and online interaction are transferred to the setting and other practitioners*

Adapted from www.ewenger.com/theory (accessed 21 February 2010)

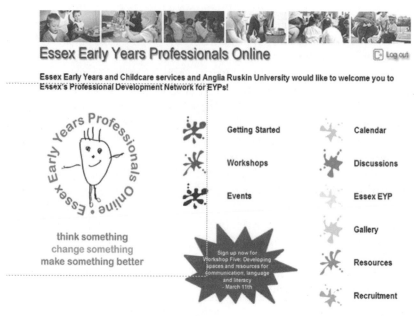

Figure 14.1 The website (1)

One of the first activities posted on the site was provided by Julia Druce in her role as tutor and workshop convenor on the effective use of persona dolls to support children's social and emotional aspects of development. Persona dolls are given a name, personality, family, cultural backgrounds and a history by the early years practitioner. They serve as a stimulus for discussion about issues to do with difference and diversity, and invoke feelings and emotions which can be used to examine issues in practice. Figure 14.3 shows the welcoming page used to promote this workshop. Practitioners

Figure 14.2 The website (2)

were provided with details of the workshop and invited to bring their persona dolls: the dolls continued to be used in online activities in which their characters began to develop 'personalities' and a 'life' beyond the workshop. Creating this link helps users to make sense of their practice and to help cascade expertise. Practitioners were able to report on the use of the dolls in their own practice and on how they encouraged others to consider their use with young children. The online forum provided a link to wider practice which is valued when collaborative learning is meaningful to users (Boud and Lee, 2005).

Welcome to: The Effective Use of Persona Dolls

The Persona Dolls can be used by practitioners in a calm and gentle manner to raise concerns and to address serious issues, such as the links between behaviour, safety, discrimination and cultural issues.

In this Unit you will be encouraged to work with the dolls. In doing so, you will realise the enormous potential for the dolls to help the children in your care to develop in all sorts of ways, particularly in the area of Social and Emotional Development. These dolls will encourage children to listen and to air their views calmly, in a safe and secure environment.

In this Unit we will look at how to provide more focussed activities and we will use the dolls to explore various issues and to help children understand the views and feelings of others. During the following weeks we will discuss, why and how we can use Persona dolls; and create 'personalities' and histories for the dolls which can be developed further in the setting.

E-tivity 1   Sharing Experiences

Figure 14.3 The welcoming page to promote the workshop

Further contacts with practice settings are encouraged through the use of newsletters and provision of an online gallery where images from workshops are stored. Users are encouraged to post their own images and this provides another commentary on practice. Messages posted on the discussion board show that practitioners welcome these opportunities to develop ideas in their workplace:

> The units and the workshops have helped me focus on practice in the setting, and the opportunity to share ideas with colleagues from different settings and areas of early years has been helpful. (3)

> ... cascading some of the ideas at a relaxation and anger management cluster training; remembering to promote SEAD to the eight settings present and to explain about the importance of developing emotional awareness and literacy. (4) (*both messages were posted on 30 November 2008 following a workshop*)

The discussion area is an open forum for users. Practitioners can post and respond to each other's messages. Through peer collaboration, new knowledge can be generated. It also provides support for practitioners beyond face-to-face instruction to blend their learning with online discussion to develop their professional practice. The following quotes illustrate these ideas:

> Becoming a EYP has definitely been supported by having this online forum. (1) (*posted on 24 November 2008*)

> I found the forum wonderful and will be sharing the ideas and activities discussed with my staff ... I particularly enjoyed networking with new colleagues. (2) (*posted on 8 December 2008*)

Summary

The chapter has shown how the use of the online environment can promote professional development for early years practitioners. We have explored the use of persona dolls to support training to promote children's social and emotional development. More workshops have taken place and Hazel's 'wish list' of what to provide to facilitate peer learning continues to be used. Here, we have tried to capture how the experience of using the online discussion forum encouraged peer collaboration. Creating the right space, an environment in which shared learning can develop, is important. We have discovered that the use of the forum lends itself to more bespoke training: being able to cascade ideas between users offers the potential to share practice between settings and identify new possibilities. We believe this is important in providing a space for practitioner inquiry: here users can discuss practice issues in a safe environment.

This is just one part of an otherwise complex professional development system (Apple and McMullen, 2007). There is a role for higher education to provide opportunities to share practice between providers and the use of online forums helps to provide just such a niche. Government initiatives on workforce reform did promote the use of online forums (CWDC, 2010) but their success is dependent on creating a community that works for its users. Each of us has played a different role in supporting this development and, in this chapter, we have explored its value to our practice in how we can develop practitioner inquiry. The university does provide an online environment for its taught undergraduate and masters' courses for early years students.

Questions for discussion

1. We make more use of the online environment in our work and social life. Consider how you might use this space to discuss ideas from your practice.
   - Write yourself a 'wish list'.
   - How could you encourage sharing with others in practice settings?
2. How can you take action for your own professional development and start to use one of the online forums listed below? Make sure that you become part of the community and remember to 'think something, change something and make something better'.

Useful websites

www.foundation-stage.info/ – useful information on all aspects of the foundation stage, its curriculum, profile of assessment and general information.

www.mpowernet.anglia.ac.uk/ – information on courses and other aspects of mpowernet's work.

www.facebook.com/pages/Anglia-Ruskins-EYPs/113192778696408 – this is self-explanatory!

http://sharestreet.cwdcouncil.org.uk/ – an online forum for all early years practitioners.

http://forums.nurseryworld.co.uk/ – discussion groups on different aspects of the English early years curriculum and pedagogy based on the magazine's website.

References and suggested further reading

Entries in bold are further reading.

Apple, P. and McMullen, M. (2007) Envisioning the Impact of Decisions Made About Early Childhood Professional Development by Different Constituent Groups. *Contemporary Issues in Early Childhood*, 8(3): 255–64.

Boud, D. and Lee, A. (2005) Peer Learning as Pedagogic Discourse for Research Education. *Studies in Higher Education*, 30(5): 501–16.

Brooks, C. (2010) Toward 'Hybridised' Faculty Development for the Twenty-first Century: Blending Online Communities of Practice and Face-to-face Meetings in Instructional and Professional Support Programmes. *Innovations in Education and Teaching International*, 47(3): 261–70.

Cheeseman, S. (2007) Pedagogical Silences in Australian Early Childhood Social Policy. *Contemporary Issues in Early Childhood*, 8(3): 244–54.

Children's Workforce Development Council (CWDC) (2005) *Children's Workforce Strategy: A Consultation*. London: CWDC.

CWDC (2006) *The Early Years Professional Prospectus*. London: CWDC.

CWDC (2008a) *Guidance to the Standards for the Award of Early Years Professional Status*. London: CWDC.

CWDC (2008b) *Introduction and Information Guide*. London: CWDC.

CWDC (2010) *Share Street: Sharing Integrated Working Experiences and Practice*. Available online at: http://sharestreet.cwdcouncil.org.uk (accessed 15 March 2010).

Department for Children, Schools and Families (DCSF) (2008a) *The Children's Plan: Building Brighter Futures*. Available online at: http://publications.dcsf.gov.uk/eOrderingDownload/The_Childrens_Plan.pdf (accessed 10 March 2010).

Department for Children, Schools and Families (DCSF) (2008b) *2020 Children and Young People's Workforce Strategy*. Available online at: www.everychildmatters.gov.uk/.../childrenandyoungpeoplesworkforce (accessed 10 March 2010).

Department for Education and Skills (DfES) *The Early Years Foundation Stage*. Nottingham: DfES.

Jones, C. and Pound, L. (2008) *Leadership and Management in the Early Years from Principles to Practice*. Maidenhead: Open University Press.

Leathwood, C. and O'Connell, P. (2003) 'It's a Struggle': The Construction of the 'New Student' in Higher Education. *Journal of Education Policy*, 18(6): 597–615.

MacNaughton, G. (2005) *Doing Foucault in Early Childhood Studies: Applying Poststructural Ideas*. London: Routledge.

McGillivray, G. (2008) Nannies, Nursery Nurses and Early Years Professionals: Constructions of Professional Identity in the Early Years Workforce in England. *European Early Childhood Education Research Journal*, 16(2): 242–54.

Miller, L. (2008) Developing New Professional Roles in the Early Years. In L. Miller and C. Cable (eds) *Professionalism in the Early Years*. Abingdon: Hodder Education.

Moss, P. (2006) Structures, Understandings and Discourses: Possibilities for Re-envisioning the Early Childhood Worker. *Contemporary Issues in Early Childhood*, 7(1): 30–41.

Osgood, J. (2006) Professionalism and Performativity: The Feminist Challenge Facing Early Years Practitioners. *Early Years*, 26(2): 187–99.

Salmon, G. (2008) *E-moderating: The Key to Teaching and Learning Online* (2nd edn). Abingdon: RoutledgeFalmer.

Siraj-Blatchford, I. (2007) The Case for Integrating Education with Care in the Early Years. In I. Siraj-Blatchford, K. Clarke and M. Needham (eds) *The Team Around the Child*. Stoke-on-Trent: Trentham Books.

Sylva, K. and Pugh, G. (2005) Transforming the early years in England. *Oxford Review of Education*, 31(1): 11–27.

Urban, M. (2008) Dealing with Uncertainty: Challenges and Possibilities for the Early Childhood Profession. *European Early Childhood Education Research Journal*, 16(2): 135–52.

Wenger, E. (1998) *Communities of Practice: Learning, Meaning, and Identity*. Cambridge: Cambridge University Press.

Wenger, E. (2007) Communities of Practice: A Brief Introduction. In *Communities of Practice*. Available online at: www.ewenger.com/theory/ (accessed 24 February 2010).

Yelland, N. and Kilderry, A. (2008) Against the Tide: New Ways in Early Childhood Education. In N. Yelland (ed.) *Critical Issues in Early Childhood Education* (2nd edn). Maidenhead: Open University Press.

15

From parent to practitioner: alternative pathways to professionalism

Hazel R. Wright

> **Overview**
>
> This chapter presents research evidence that reveals how, in the UK, training and working in childcare may be undertaken for personal reasons but, nevertheless can generate a range of benefits for society that could not have been anticipated; benefits that are small-scale but play an important role in strengthening the social fabric. In exploring the unplanned social payback consequent upon this instance of adult education and demonstrating how personal motivation can ultimately create public good, it seeks to remind policy makers that educational second chances and diversity matter, and that practices that work well on the ground may be damaged by a rigidly instrumental pursuit of workforce professionalization. In making this claim, it is not arguing against progress in the childcare sector but arguing for a more sensitive approach to change that recognizes human values.

In June 2008, four eminent British scholars[1] sent a letter to *The Independent* newspaper, complaining that 'government policy is no longer the solution to the difficulties we face but our greatest problem' and expressing concern that the 'permanent revolution' was endangering the very policy objectives being pursued. Their fears focused on the demise of lifelong learning opportunities with the decimation of adult educational provision in further education colleges, but the reasoning could apply equally well to the early years sector in the UK where Margaret Hodge's 'silent revolution' continues to address the quality agenda[2]. Spurred on by the Every Child Matters legislation (DfES, 2003), the early years sector is subjected to reforms at a pace that threatens to overwhelm the voluntary sector, where preschool education is serving the needs of local communities in ways that have not been fully acknowledged.

The research project underpinning this chapter (Wright, 2010) set out to study the educational experiences of a number of mature women training to work in childcare, mostly within the voluntary sector. It found that their motives and indeed their learning biographies were more complex than initially assumed and that, for these women, education was just one strand of their very busy lives; lives that were firmly embedded in their local communities and that privileged the needs of their children, partners, extended families, neighbours and other community users. Being able to train to work in childcare carried more significant consequences than the government vocational agenda presupposes, allowing the women to choose to fulfil a range of different needs and desires, many of which related to their present lives rather than their future aspirations. Indeed, the students were closely focused on their current 'beings' and 'doings' rather than their future aspirations, a pattern that can be related to Sen's *Capability Approach* (1999) (see Wright, 2011).

The research found that, at the micro-level, the childcare workers were making individualized choices that suited their families and their personal lives, regardless of the policy framework, but also that managing continual change was cumulatively stressful and many women were beginning to tire and to consider alternative occupations. It is this process of attrition that may eventually lead to the loss of the little recognized but important social consequences of this area of training and work.

Women in childcare training

One hundred and seventy mature women were enrolled on a preschool Supervisor Course in an English Further Education (FE) college and 150 were persuaded, retrospectively, to complete questionnaires detailing their personal characteristics and the expectations and consequences associated with their studies. The women predominately but not exclusively claimed white British ethnicity and most were married or cohabiting (80%) and parents (70% had children of primary school age on enrolling on the course). Despite sharing certain core characteristics, the students were not a homogenous group. In terms of class, age, prior qualifications and work experience, their backgrounds were highly differentiated. One major commonality was their pathway into childcare training. There were significant exceptions but the majority, rather than pursuing a clear career path, had drifted from parent to volunteer in a preschool to part-time paid assistant, taking on additional hours and responsibilities as their children grew older and needed less dedicated parenting. It is mainly these former parents that I aim to discuss here.

Assessing the views of childcare workers

A representative sample of 33 students were selected for further investigation, using open-ended conversational-style interviews asking the participants about the significance of education for themselves and their families. Conscious of my prior knowledge of some of the events they described, I adopted a form of free-association interviewing technique (Hollway and Jefferson, 2000) more common to psychology, whereby I listened closely for contradictions, hesitations and odd juxtapositions of ideas in their narratives and challenged these 'disfluencies' when they arose, often taking the discussion to deeper and more satisfying levels of explanation. Thus, I developed a role that was both co-constructor of knowledge and realizer of hidden truths, using myself as an additional research tool to clarify rather than simply accept the students' subjective experiences as retold (see Wright, 2009). On transcribing the conversations, I needed to make these nuances visible within the text and, therefore, adopted the coding techniques used in conversation analysis (Ten Have, 1999), to highlight such patterns and to evidence my consequent interpretation. Throughout the project, I worked iteratively, adopting a flexible, emergent design as befits this type of interdisciplinary, real-world research (Robson, 2002).

The motives and experiences of childcare workers

One of the main findings of the research was that the pattern of transition (from mother to worker, paid or voluntary, to mature student) was common because it enabled the women to combine and balance personal, familial, vocational and educational goals. The study cohort comprises women who have experience of children and choose to work in childcare because it fits in with their families' needs. It is the concern to be around their own children that shapes the students' intentions and the desire to integrate their own lives that leads them to a career pathway where part-time work in the local community dominates their discourse; it is *not* a familiarity with children that encourages them to seek work in this field, although this is also an important factor.

Arianne, a preschool manager, makes claims on behalf of her staff that: 'All of these girls do this job because it goes well with their children', and Bethany states: 'I knew that I wanted to do something that would enable me to spend time with the girls'. Knowing about children makes this pathway possible. Indeed, for Emily this was a vital connection for she claims: 'I didn't have any knowledge, only my own son'. In the words of Heena, the Supervisor Course as a mature-entry qualification, characteristically 'captures the mum market, carers who have been out of work' ... as it is 'something they know because they've got their own children'.

Interestingly, all the students interviewed were positive about the choices they made; any negative feelings were attributed to unnamed others.

Holly, for instance, believes that some women stay in childcare because of inertia: 'For most women I would suggest that they are in childcare positions because it works for them while their children are young and then they get stuck in this rut and so they carry on' ... 'but a researcher overview suggests a more complex pattern'.

The overall evidence implies a much more agentive approach. The women are recognizing and actively forging a network of reciprocal links between the family, the workplace and the training course that enable them to live their lives at a pace where they can support their own children at school, earn some independent income to boost the family finances and refresh their intellectual skills.

> I'm not looking to go anywhere, not yet – I've still got a son that is still at home, it's nice to have a bit of time with him. (Barbara)

> As they get older I feel I can do more – extra at work ... It fits in really well, yes, it's perfect for what I want at the moment. (Gina)

> It's like a step into using their brain again. (Heena)

The students are balancing their responsibilities and avoiding restricting their choices. Evelyn clearly articulates this view when she insists:

> I want the best of both worlds. I want to be able to work and also I want to be at home with my children when they are at home. And childcare, teaching, working within that environment allows me to do that and it's rewarding ...

Carving a space for study

The importance of the family is apparent throughout the student narratives: an integrated life is one that values relationships. As Faye says: 'I still don't feel that you should compromise family life'. Although excessive work commitments were tolerated by some of the families, unpaid study held a much more marginal position yet this was a vital element as without a qualification the students could not expect to continue to work in childcare. Students found a range of ways of ensuring that they studied whilst avoiding drawing attention to their need to do this, making education both marginalized and a luxury. They worked at odd moments '... fitting the college work around everything else' (Frieda), late at night and early in the morning, occasionally relying upon help from friends, husbands or grandparents. The majority, like Bella, used 'windows of opportunity' rather than 'putting the vacuum round'; those 'times when you might have just sat down and have a cup of tea you just had to get on' (Beryl).

The benefits to the childcare sector

Although many of the women drifted into childcare work rather than seeking a definite career path, the sector benefits from the caring attitude that these women have towards children, characteristics difficult to instil in younger students if not naturally present. Daisy, a mother of four, extends her caring to all the children she works with: 'As a mother I can feel that all the children are like my own children. I love them like my own really'. Frieda enthuses that 'there is something about that age group that I still find exciting even though my children have moved on from it'. Greta, herself childless, is concerned 'never to cause any harm or crush a child in any way and always to encourage blossoming' and focuses on the children's happiness when working in the group, fearing that even observations are disruptive: 'Children know that they are being watched and written about'. Imogen, one of the youngest members of the group (and childless), is a natural carer, who loves 'figuring' the children out and is distressed by the staff behaviour in the day nursery where she works. She listens to and tries to apply 'the little things' that make a difference, but eventually, disillusioned with the profession, enrols for a psychology degree instead, using the Supervisor Course to complete the matriculation requirements. She does make sure her degree includes a child development module and still wants to work with children, but maybe in a position from which she can influence practice.

In addition to this natural caring, there is evidence that these students are receptive to further learning: 'I was fascinated by how children work ... no child's the same so every day in nursery is different so I think it just made me go deeper and deeper into it. I'm hooked!' (Cindy). Training brings out latent qualities and knowledge. Beryl describes how: 'I look at children differently, what they are learning, what they are doing, why they are doing it'. Ingrid was persuaded to help in the local preschool and was amazed to find that 'it was just so different from how I expected it to be' and insightfully claims that the course 'taught us to sort of look behind the behaviour' as an important step underpinning discipline. Heidi also believes that the Supervisor Course has 'made me look at children ... watch the expressions on their faces, and listen to what they are saying to each other' and claims that: 'you do actually start thinking and looking at them in a whole new light'. Somewhat controversially, she argues: 'I think you have to have your own to understand what children are really like because children are not textbooks', and whilst this viewpoint can easily be contested I think we should remember that the parenting experience is a useful asset when working with children, for it represents a long-term commitment far in excess of what we could expect from the low salaries paid to childcare staff. Heidi verbalizes the importance of such in-depth learning when she muses: 'If you tie it all in together there is no reason why you should ever have a child ever crying'.

The community aspect is important too. Danni, a sensitive worker, talks about the 'hope that you have done the best for them', not only for the children's sake but 'because being village-based you know that you're going to see them for the rest of their primary lives'. Frances describes them as 'little people that are going to grow into big people' and explains how 'we loved children and we wanted to help them and we wanted to help the community and the mothers that perhaps couldn't do that'. The women really do put the children first. Frances, who had enjoyed working with children, decided to move on when the supervisor training caused her 'to worry that I wasn't doing it quite right', in preferring adult-led to child-led activities. Fiona goes into paediatric nursing eventually, 'right to the heart of the problem', because she 'wanted to help children with learning difficulties so that's why I went into childcare'.

Many recognize that working with children requires superior skills and value the nurturing and playful elements over the managerial. Indeed, it is a concern that some of the trends associated with increased professionalization reduce their contact time with children that is causing some to leave the sector.

> I find the constant change of demands by the government and the powers-that-be utterly frustrating. (Celia).

> It was becoming more like a classroom and it was vital that we prepared them for school and I didn't really believe that, I thought they were too young and so we kind of started going our separate ways. (Diane)

> One [staff member] left because of the stuff that is coming in and she wasn't prepared. She said 'I'm not, I can't take it from here'. (Faye)

> I just feel it is drudgery now ... I don't think I would ever drift back into pre-school. (Greta)

Frieda, in particular, is angry that salaries and expectations no longer match up: 'A professional should be being paid by the government on a reasonable wage, not on a hourly rate that can be equalled by Morrison's' [supermarket chain]. Even those who stay express concern about the changes:

> Sometimes it just feels that we're not getting down with the children and learning through play. We're too busy writing things up ... I agree with observation because that helps the children's learning and progression – but some of the forms ... you know! (Emily)

Perhaps because of their transfer from volunteer to paid staff, perhaps because they are motivated by values other than remuneration, many of the women work significant additional unpaid hours, doing planning, preparation and record keeping in their own homes and own time. Sometimes it is possible to trace this commitment to a need to boost self-worth: 'Your confidence does get a bit of a knock when you've got children' (Evelyn); sometimes to altruism: 'My mum's ethos is that if you want to see something happen you get involved and that still is very much what I believe' (Danni); sometimes to status: 'Other people have said to me that I have made a damn good successful playgroup' (Bethany). Sometimes it is a desire to get on: 'I don't mind going through the ranks as long as I can see a quick progression' (Bella). Whatever the motivation, the extra work is often to the detriment of family harmony.

Gina admits: 'You do get a bit of grumbling, you know, at home'. Beryl's husband, like others, complains: 'You are doing more hours than I am working and you're getting a pittance'. Heena, on the other hand, finds that her husband tolerates her unpaid hours because she is 'getting the holidays with the kids' and he wants to avoid them going to a childminder.

We should take care to avoid dismissing the contribution of these women because their work patterns lack a professional orientation. The children, the families and the communities that use these voluntary-run preschools benefit from the efforts of these underpaid workers and so, ultimately, does society as a whole. Students who move on often seek jobs in school or go on to teaching, thus children continue to benefit from their knowledge and nurturing skills. Working in childcare or as a teaching assistant (TA) motivates some to train as teachers. Barbara and Irene are considering this possibility, as did Felicity. Bethany is often asked if she will go on to teach and says: '… maybe once [my daughter] is established in secondary school'. Conversely, several others seeing the profession close up decide *not* to teach. Beryl decides to remain an assistant 'after seeing all the heartache and hair-tearing that seems to go on'. Gina explains: 'I had thought of teaching as well but I'm not quite sure about that … I have a few friends of mine who have done a PGCE in teaching and often it doesn't sound as good as what we have here'. Evelyn, now a TA, says: 'I would not want to be a teacher for love nor money these days'. Aileen, also a TA, explains exactly why teaching is not an attractive option for many:

> When I go home at the end of the day, that's it. If I choose to take work home with me, that's my choice. Teachers don't get that – they've got reports to write, they've got IEPs, they've got work to mark and work to put together and planning and no, that's not for me.

However, we should not underestimate the role that these qualified and experienced childcare staff have in schools. Sometimes this is a result of taking up a teaching assistantship. Beryl, for instance, talks of supporting a foundation coordinator who has 'not actually been trained in early years'. Frances, in her new role as a subject coordinator in a secondary school, claims that her ability to reason with badly behaved children stems from her early years training. Bethany, however, remains in the voluntary sector, running an 'extremely successful' preschool that attracts parents into the local and very small village primary school that 'needs the playgroup children to filter into the reception'. Danni works closely with the local primary school and talks of the Head sending a newly qualified teacher who was 'really struggling' with her class, to visit the preschool 'to see what we do and to see how we operate'; implying that the mature worker can help the more highly qualified novice.

The Supervisor Course also turns students into informed parents who can both contribute to and challenge the system: Ingrid, as a result of childcare training, has developed 'the confidence to actually make a difference' and has joined her local school as a parent governor. Barbara claims: 'I'm more confident to ask and query things with schools now ... when they quote Ofsted and things at me I'm not afraid of them'. Irene has talked to her children's Head 'regarding self-esteem issues' and admits that 'I probably wouldn't have done if I hadn't have had this training'. This confidence could be transferred to other educational sectors. Alex, for instance, thinks: 'I understand a lot more how the school systems work from doing it' [the course] and uses this knowledge to support her teenage son: 'Now I know if I push and I push and I push I am going to get somewhere. You have to persevere'.

The benefits for the students

Despite drifting onto the childcare course, there is evidence that the students derive many benefits and that these extend beyond childcare knowledge. Many enrol on a vocational course because this is possible: over the years, it has been funded by local, national or European sources as part of the UK bid to improve standards in childcare and to dislodge the 'largely unqualified army' of childminders and playgroup staff (Hevey and Curtis, 1996, cited in Pugh, 1998: 12).

In part, the students choose the Supervisor Course because others before them have demonstrated that this part-time study route is both practicable and enjoyable. Colleges, aware of the work on barriers to learning (Coats, 1994; McGivney, 1993), have largely addressed such issues, running courses that recognize the needs of adult women. In my college, in particular, we scheduled recruitment, teaching hours, coursework deadlines, study and counselling support to mirror school attendance patterns; prioritized adult timetabling to provide students with a single base room in which they could eat and drink; and delegated administrative responsibilities to a few named individuals so that students knew whom to contact and when they would be available.

Despite generally favouring liberal educational values, several make it clear that vocational learning is all they currently have time for. Yet, once on the course, the evidence is that they take whatever they need from it and the more personal outcomes described – like confidence, self-esteem, status, sense of achievement – demonstrate that liberal values matter, too. Indeed, the students relate outcomes that span the entire educational spectrum and several focus on study skills whilst admitting that they would not have enrolled on skills-oriented training, demonstrating that a narrow focus on specific objectives is not necessarily the best way of ensuring that people acquire the skills the government believes they need. Embedded skills can be acquired through other practices – a form of unplanned social payback.

Certainly, two of the women who held the lowest levels of prior education used the Supervisor Course to learn the skills they needed for 20th-century living. For Irma, the entire study experience was novel. She describes learning note taking, word processing and basic grammar and claims that: 'When I started I didn't even know what an assignment was'. Barbara, having left school prematurely due to teenage pregnancy, talks of colleagues who would 'correct my spellings ... help me with my grammar which has improved considerably'. She is now deputy manager of a setting and studying for a foundation degree. As she claims: 'I'm doing it all backwards'. Ingrid, too, admits that writing essays was a new experience as her previous National Vocational Qualification (NVQ) had only taught her to 'write little sentences in the box'.

Broader benefits

There is evidence within the data that students freely transfer knowledge from one area of their lives to another. Ideas relating to young children in settings are transferred to issues affecting their own children: 'If I learn all this I can transfer it to my children, my children shouldn't go amiss. I'll be one stage ahead of some of the other wives' (Holly).

Students also pass knowledge on to other parents. Several talk of being able to advise other family members about their children and some about helping friends or parents in the setting.

> My sister-in-law is struggling with her youngest at the moment ... and I can advise her, I can say to her, that this is the way that he is developing. (Ilsa)

> Friends who had babies used to come up to me ... and ask me about child development so that was good. (Emily)

Collectively, this sharing of knowledge forms a flexible alternative to parenting skills classes, supporting young families who lack nearby relatives.

The caring curriculum also teaches lessons in tolerance and cooperation that should not be underestimated. Working on a Holi festival project as part of her coursework, Ingrid gets to really know some local Asian families and begins to see that understanding why people do certain things stops her seeing behaviour as 'strange' or 'weird'. She describes herself as 'a lot less judgemental now', and claims: 'I have much more confidence in looking at people as just people'. Ilsa also feels that involvement in childcare has made her more relaxed, claiming: 'I think working with children has calmed me down because I'm patient ... I've obviously grown to be more patient with the children. For the first few months I found working with them really hard'. Alex now works long hours in a local shop and extends her caring to the youngsters who attend the nearby drug dependency unit: 'I mean I have actually had some good old conversations with some of them and they have some hard old lives'. For Gina, too, her work involves contact with young adults. She runs a crèche for teenage mothers in a community centre as well as working in their preschool and this involves 'sort of modelling for the parents and that sort of thing but it's a delicate area because they are quite sensitive'. These students partly attribute their confidence in carrying out these roles to the experience of educational success and to the training that covers additional material on working with parents and other adults. So, their stories demonstrate how benefits accrue beyond the traditional childcare setting.

Underpinning the student discourse of commitment to the workplace is a strong sense of community, suggesting that childcare work contributes to the localized formation of social capital. Only a few mention taking on additional roles – e.g. Brownies, school governorships, out of school clubs – probably because their own lives are already so busy. Students develop friendships during the course. Some groups socialize with partners outside of teaching sessions; others enrol in pairs, travel together or form study partnerships. Being with others who share their aims and experiences is an important facet of the course; several talk of the importance of 'everyone being in the same boat'. However, this social contact soon falls apart after the course finishes, due, I think, to the other commitments in their lives. Aileen's comment that 'life takes over' is a commonly expressed view. Indeed, considering the limited amounts of time that students could make available for studying and the juggling acts required to achieve a threefold integration of family, work and education, we should not be surprised that casual friendships were difficult to maintain. Generally, however, the students were appreciative that they had contacts elsewhere in the county and individuals described incidental meetings with peers at other training sessions and at youth events.

Summary

These women may drift into childcare work and training but they are very motivated individuals who seek to meet their own needs whilst, for the main part, foregrounding those of others, their children and partners, the children with whom they work, their colleagues and others in the local community. The students integrate aspects of their lives to create a stable framework within which they can bring up their own families, choosing to juggle their own needs as parents, students and workers. Importantly, I would like to suggest that just as preschools serve as transitional spaces between the home and formal schooling for many children, they offer a similarly safe space for women wanting to go back to work. Like Gina, many women find that 'when you have been at home with children you do somehow think the world has gone on without you to an extent', and need a place in which to readjust. Thus, the voluntary preschool sector unwittingly supports British government initiatives to return women to the workforce and the coincidental provision of subsidized childcare training makes this possible. Too great an instrumental focus on training itself or on professionalization of the workforce could unintentionally destroy a system that works. Quite apart from those who go on to develop serious careers, all the women in this study make a valuable contribution to society, reminding us that policy makers should consider hidden benefits too, the wealth of unplanned social payback, when seeking to expand and professionalize the childcare workforce.

Questions for discussion

1. In your setting, do you agree that the sector benefits from the caring attitude that women have towards children?
2. Consider what hidden benefits you and your colleagues provide for society.
3. What 'juggling acts' do you engage in as a professional? What do you do to manage the balance between home life and work?

Notes

1 Emeritus Professor Frank Coffield, Institute of Education, London; Professor Richard Taylor, Director of Continuing Education and Lifelong Learning, University of Cambridge; Professor Sir Peter Scott, Vice-Chancellor, University of Kingston; Professor Stephen Ball, Institute of Education, London; 'Government education policy is damaging its own objectives', Letters: Education Policy, *The Independent,* 2 June 2008.
2 'Silent revolution' was a phrase used by Margaret Hodge as Minister for Education on the *Matter of Fact* documentary broadcast on 3 February 2000 on BBC1.

References and suggested further reading

Entries in bold are further reading.

Coats, M. (1994) *Women's Education.* Buckingham: SRHE and Open University Press.
Department for Education and Skills (DfES) (2003) *Every Child Matters* (Green Paper). London: HMSO.
Hollway, W. and Jefferson, T. (2000) *Doing Qualitative Research Differently: Free Association, Narrative and the Interview Method.* London: Sage.
McGivney, V. (1993) *Women, Education and Training: Barriers to Access, Informal Starting Points and Progression Routes.* Leicester: National Institute for Adult and Continuing Education.
Pugh, G. (1998) Early Years Training in Context. In L. Abbot and G. Pugh (eds) *Training to Work in the Early Years: Developing the Climbing Frame.* Buckingham: Open University Press.

Robson, C. (2002) *Real World Research* (2nd edn). Oxford: Blackwell.

Sen, A. (1999) *Development as Freedom*. Oxford: Oxford University Press.

Ten Have, P. (1999) *Doing Conversation Analysis: A Practical Guide*. London: Sage.

Wright, H.R. (2009) Trusting the Process: Using an Emergent Design to Study Adult Education. *Educate (Kaleidoscope Special Issue)*, December, pp. 62–73.

Wright, H.R. (2010) Integrating Lives through Adult Education: A Case Study of Mature Women Training to Work in Childcare. Unpublished Ph.D. thesis, Anglia Ruskin University.

Wright, H.R. (2011) *Women Studying Childcare: Integrating Lives through Adult Education*. Stoke-on-Trent: Trentham Books.

Endpiece: where are we now and where should we be going?

Lilian G. Katz

It is now 50 years since I became involved in what, in those days, we referred to as 'nursery education'. Over these many years, I have had experience of teaching young children and their parents and teachers and working with many of our early years colleagues in more than 50 countries. With increasing frequency just about everywhere, I am asked the question: where are we now in relation to early education and where should we be going? When I ask myself these questions, I seem to come up with many more. For example:

- Where are we going if we continue to do what we are now doing?
- Where do we hope we are *not* going?
- Why do we seem to be going where we don't want to go?
- What should we be doing if we want to go somewhere else?
- Where else would that be?

Obviously many more such questions could be raised – but the answers are not simple. I propose to address them under six main headings as follows:

1. the alignment of early education with the elementary years curriculum

2. the short-term versus long-term effects of early education

3. the implications of recent neurological research on development

4. the distinctions between academic and intellectual development

5. the critical period in the development of social competence

6. a summary of the main points: where we should be going.

The alignment of early education with the elementary years curriculum

The evidence is now compelling that any provisions for young children – whether within the home or outside of it – that are of less than top quality represent missed opportunities to make a substantial positive contribution to the rest of the child's life. Today, no one with serious educational and social policy-making responsibility for a community or even a country all around the world, would argue against the proposition that the experiences of the early years of life have a powerful influence on all later ones. However, considerable argument concerning what constitutes top quality for an early years program continues, seemingly endlessly (Lally, 2010).

The growing confidence in the positive role of early education has been accompanied by an increasing trend towards aligning the early years curriculum to that of the elementary school. The rationale has been based largely on the importance of 'school readiness', i.e. using the preschool setting to prepare children to conform to classroom routines and to perform the standard academic skills that are typically expected at the beginning of elementary school (Merrell and Tymms, 2010). This trend has led to widespread pressure on early childhood programs to start young children on formal didactic academic instruction earlier than ever and to downplay the role of spontaneous play in young children's development. The extent to which such formal instruction is developmentally appropriate for children during their early years is the topic of frequent discussion within the field (Finn, 2010). The overall issue taken up here is that there are several aspects of early development that suggest that formal instruction has potential disadvantages, in both the short and in the long term, and that there are other pedagogical approaches that can yield both short- and long-term benefits.

The early introduction of formal instruction often causes children to behave as though they understand something, when in fact they do not. In this way, their confidence in their own intellect may be undermined very early on. They may come to doubt their own observations and hide their own questions and ideas. One common example that comes to mind is the increasing frequency over the last dozen or so years of engaging even 3- and 4-year-olds in the daily calendar ritual (Beneke et al., 2008). During a recent visit to a preschool in London, I arrived a bit late and the children were getting ready to leave as parents and others came to take them home. One 4-year-old was the last child in the class to be called for by her grandmother. While she was waiting for her, she was sitting on the carpet facing the wall where the calendar was resting against a blackboard. I asked her if they had talked about the calendar that day and she responded readily, 'Yes'. I then asked, 'Oh, so what day is it today?' and she replied, with little hesitation, 'Rainy'.

I have had countless experiences of such confusion among preschoolers about the meaning of dates, days, weeks, months and years, the instruction of which often takes up nearly half an hour of their few hours of participation in the curriculum. On any given day, this type of activity is unlikely to seriously damage the children but surely there is sufficient indication that the facts and concepts are too advanced for them and their time could more profitably be spent on engaging their minds more fully and more meaningfully.

The short-term versus long-term effects of early education

Another concern about the increasingly early introduction of formal academic instruction is the relationship between its short-term and long-term effects. Several studies have indicated that early introduction of formal academically oriented preschool curricula and exercises tend to produce positive effects *in the short-term*, immediately following instruction. These early positive effects are not surprising when we realize that, in many of the cases studied, the curriculum prepares the children for the tests. Indeed, many teachers (at least in the USA and UK) report being under strong pressure to make sure their children do well on the tests – for the sake of the children as well as their own jobs.

However, when the children in such academically focused curricula have been followed up well into the elementary school years, these positive effects are no longer observed. On the contrary, it seems that the long-term benefits of intellectually oriented curricula, while they are not so evident in the early test results, appear to do better later than those from more academically focused curricula (Marcon, 2000). The long-term benefits of curriculum approaches like High/Scope and Montessori yield good long-term benefits for the children, though they are not as positive at the end of the preschool period.

In other words, the early positive effects of academically oriented preschool curricula can be largely due to the way we measure the effects of preschool programs when we use standardized tests. It is obvious that the closer the content and skills offered by the curriculum are to the tests, the better the children will perform on them. However, again, when these children are followed over a period of three or more years, the children who had early experience in more intellectually engaging curriculum approaches were more likely to do well in school *over the long-term* than their peers who had early exposure to academic formal instruction (Golbeck, 2001; Marcon, 2000).

Another interesting implication of the long-term follow-up studies is that early introduction of formal academic instruction seems to be more damaging for boys than for girls. It is not entirely clear why boys are more vulnerable than girls to excessive premature formal instruction. It has been suggested that the rate at which boys develop neurologically is known to be somewhat slower than that of girls. Eventually, the boys catch up with the girls at about the age of 8 years.

However, another hypothesis worth considering concerning the differential gender effects of early formal instruction is that academic instruction places the children in a passive and receptive role, rather than in an active, assertive and initiative-taking role. It is noteworthy that, in most cultures, and probably more so in those associated with low-income or disadvantaged communities, boys are expected to be assertive in many activities. In such cultural groups, boys are expected to be 'agentic', i.e. to take action and initiative and to demonstrate their strength rather than the easier passive and submissive role of the female in the formal classroom and in the culture in general. Furthermore, in such cultural milieu, girls learn early to be relatively passive as is required and adaptive in formal school teaching settings. However, this interpretation is only a hypothesis that needs further exploration.

The implications of recent neurological research on development

During the last dozen or so years, our understanding of the significance of the early years for neurological development has grown and deepened greatly, though not without controversy (Bruer, 1999). I want to emphasize that, thus far, no reports of the so-called 'brain research' can tell us specifically which pedagogical or curriculum approaches are most brain-compatible even though many have tried to suggest otherwise.

A major implication of recent studies is that the most important kinds of experiences young children need long before they enter traditional primary school are particular kinds of interactions mostly with significant adults (Blair, 2002). In particular, Blair emphasizes the important relationship between children's early experience of what he refers to as 'synchronous' interaction between them and their caretakers that consist of frequent sustained sequences of contingent interactions in which each participant's behavior is contingent on or related to the responses of the other. Blair suggests that early and frequent experience of such series of sequences of sustained interdependent interactions cause neurological links to be developed, and to grow between the midbrain and the prefrontal cortex upon which subsequent abilities to attend, to carry out tasks purposefully and to engage in executive actions depend. The implications of Blair's summary of this neurological growth cannot be over-emphasized. It is not just a matter of the infant or young child being 'stimulated' or 'provoked' by adults or other children. In fact, it is likely that many children most in need of good early education have more than enough stimulation – and not necessarily of a beneficial kind. What is of great importance in this recently discovered aspect of neurological development is that from very early on, children have frequent experience of sequences of contingent continuous interactions, especially with adults, but with peers as well. The participants do not necessarily have to talk; some contingent responses might be smiles or frowns or reaching out to another person in response to a comment or request.

This insight into early neurological development and the role of continuous sequences of interactions is one more reason why our young children could benefit greatly from being in mixed age groups (Katz, 1998). There is both experience and evidence to suggest that mixing the ages increases the chances of young children engaging each other, making requests of each other, making suggestions to each other and so forth. Mixed age grouping is still practiced in some countries – especially in Scandinavia – until about the age of 7 years, and there is no reason to doubt its potential advantages in the early years of schooling.

One of the important implications of the principle of sustained contingent interaction is that the children have to have something to interact about – something that matters to them and that is of interest and concern to them. Thus, the content of the curriculum should allow for mindful rather than mindless activities. I see far too many classes of young children in which the activities can best be described as mindless; too much cutting and pasting as well as the calendar rituals mentioned earlier. During one early spring (i.e. late March), I visited a preschool in the state of Wisconsin, one of our northern states known nationally as the 'dairy state'. All the children were seated in groups of about five at round tables. Every child had in front them a copy of the same printed picture of a smiling lamb on which they were expected to paste cotton wool balls placed on the table. It occurred to me, with some surprise, that, being early spring, perhaps even in the 'dairy state', there was some local sheep farming and that perhaps the children had been to see new baby lambs. So I asked one child, 'Have you been to see some lambs?' When he said 'No', I then asked 'So why are you doing this?' He thought for a minute and then said, 'Because lambs like to march!' He had made the best sense he could of the date, the month and the mindless task in front of him! This task was unlikely to be damaging but it did not appear to be intellectually engaging in any way.

The distinctions between academic and intellectual development

Many in positions of responsibility for educational and curriculum decisions for young children seem to believe that early years programs typically emphasize either 'school readiness' with formal academic instruction, or much of the children's time devoted to 'just playing', cutting and pasting, and other spontaneous activities with a variety of materials. These two different kinds of approaches to the early years curriculum are often assumed by those not familiar with the field of early education to be the only two main options (Finn, 2010; Bruer, 1999). However, I want to suggest that some of the children's time devoted to these kinds of activities could be justified. But what is typically omitted from these discussions is the importance of young children's intellectual development, i.e. curriculum practices that emphasize frequent engagement of their lively minds.

This mistaken and misleading dichotomy concerning curriculum choices in the early years may be due to the fact that while we tend to over-estimate young children academically, we underestimate them intellectually. I suggest that it is useful to keep in mind the distinctions between the term *academic* and *intellectual* aspects of development and learning. Academic goals are served by presenting children with formal lessons and instructions, worksheets, drills and other kinds of exercises designed to start them on basic literacy and numeracy skills. Academic tasks are small, disembedded items usually taught in isolation, requiring right answers, relying heavily on memory or rote learning versus understanding, and the regurgitation of specific items learned from formal instruction. In addition, academic tasks tend to be more devoted to learning *skills* rather than to deepening understanding and strengthening the important potentially lifelong disposition to seek understanding (Katz, 2010).

Furthermore, formal instruction in academic skills requires the learner to be in a passive receptive rather than an active expressive or assertive role. It requires the learner to be *in*structed, to accept what is given and told to them and to repeat and reproduce what is instructed, rather than to be encouraged to *con*struct ideas and hypotheses and questions. Again, I do not wish to imply that academic tasks and skills are never useful or appropriate. On the contrary, they have an important place in education, especially as children grow older. In this sense, the inclusion of academic instruction in the curriculum is not merely an educational or philosophical issue; it is a *developmental* one. The concept of development deals with the *when* questions, such as: *When* is formal academic instruction developmentally appropriate?

The formal definition of the term *intellectual* emphasizes reasoning, the processes of reflection, the development and analysis of observations and ideas. Intellectual activities include dispositions to theorize and hypothesize about, for example, cause–effect relationships, to make predictions and to check them, to pose questions and to snoop and pry and try to find things out, and so forth. These intellectual dispositions are in-born in all human beings – granted stronger in some than in others. Nevertheless, it would seem to serve children's intellectual development best if teachers approach them with the intention to strengthen these intellectual dispositions. Furthermore, I suggest that a good quality environment for young children is one in which their intellectual dispositions are meaningfully and purposefully applied in investigations, often referred to as projects (see Katz and Chard, 2000). Experience indicates that, in the course of project work, children are strongly motivated to acquire and make use of academic skills in meaningful and purposeful ways (see, for example, the description of a preschool project involving young children in an investigation of various properties of balls, (in Katz, 2009).

The critical period in the development of social competence

Social competence in the early years can be defined as the ability to initiate and maintain a few mutual or reciprocal relationships with peers. It is helpful to keep in mind – and to help parents be mindful of as well – the idea that the issue is not the quantity of peer relationships a child has but, rather, their quality. It includes having a sufficiently mutual or reciprocal relationship with one or two peers that is resumed and continued following a disagreement, an argument or a fight. The evidence has been accumulating for more than 25 years – primarily in North America – that unless a child achieves a minimal level of social competence by about 6 years old, plus or minus a half a year, the child is at risk of various difficulties for the rest of his or her life.

This critical period of the first six years is not due to any limitations of the brain and its development. Rather, the lasting effects of early social development are due to what can be conceptualized as the *recursive cycle*, namely that whatever pattern of social behavior a young child has, the chances are that others will react to him or her so that the pattern – whether positive or negative – will be strengthened.

If a child is friendly, approachable and, in other ways, responds to peers competently, they will welcome his or her company, engage and interact with him or her on the basis of which the child will strengthen his or her confidence as a social participant. These interactions provide opportunities to polish already available social skills and acquire new ones, and social competence will increase and strengthen in a dynamic fashion. In this way, a child who is easy to like becomes more likeable – in a positive recursive cycle. However, a child lacking such competences is likely to be avoided by others, and thereby loses opportunities to strengthen whatever social skills he or she does have, and to acquire new ones, thus being caught in a negative recursive cycle. It is important to keep in mind that evidence is accumulating which indicates that early social difficulties are associated with many later school problems including dropping out of school (Siegler et al., 2003).

Experience suggests that a child of 3- or 4-years-old with social difficulties can be helped in a matter of weeks. But if help is not provided before the child reaches 8 or more years old, professional specialist services will most likely be needed – and it still may be too late to break the negative cycle. Thus, those involved in the education of young children have a very significant role to play in this major aspect of lifelong human functioning.

Several basic teaching strategies have been shown to help break the negative cycle. For example, children who habitually approach peers referring primarily to themselves (e.g. 'I can make a bigger bridge than you made') can be helped by a teacher suggesting to the child that when addressing others they use what are referred to as 'other' references, e.g. 'What are you going to add next?' Another example can be when a child comes to the teacher to complain that a peer is refusing to let him or her have a turn with a desired toy or tricycle. When the teacher responds by asking the complainer, 'What have you tried so far?', she is teaching the disposition to try different strategies to solve the problem, such as to be experimental when confronting social difficulties. Very often, a child does not have a response to that question and the teacher can offer a suggestion, adding to it 'And if that doesn't help, come back and we can talk about some other things to try'.

It is also most likely to help in such situations when teachers speak clearly and matter of factly to children about what behavior they think is right, and to resist the temptation to preach to young children – for example, 'The others don't like it when you do that!' – a fact generally known to the child who is at fault. These and many more basic peer relationship skills are life skills the acquisition of which must be well under way in the early years. Teachers of the young can contribute greatly to getting them on the right track.

☐ Summary: where we should be going

It seems that, with increasing frequency, in the USA and the UK, discussions about the goals of education, at every level including the early years, are discussed in terms of performance standards and outcomes. Inevitably, such conceptions of the effects of children's education lead to the development of increasingly frequent testing, even during the early years.

However, I would suggest that, especially during the early years, it is more appropriate for us to examine the quality of provisions for our young children in terms of *standards of experience*. An important emphasis in the suggested list of possible standards below is on engaging children's minds, i.e. their intellects, much of the time. These standards should address the basic and fundamental question: *What does it feel like to be a child in this environment day after day after day?*

A preliminary list of possible and appropriate answers to such a question is suggested as follows:

- being frequently intellectually engaged and absorbed

- being intellectually challenged

- being engaged in extended interactions (e.g. conversations, discussions, exchanges of views, arguments, group planning, etc.)

- having sustained involvement in investigations of aspects of my own environment worthy of understanding more deeply, more accurately and more fully, more knowledgeably, etc.

- taking the initiative in a range of activities

- accepting some responsibility for what is accomplished

- having the satisfaction that comes from overcoming obstacles and set backs and from solving problems

- having some feeling of confidence in my own questions and intellectual powers

- helping others to find out things, to understand some problems and issues better

- making suggestions to others and expressing appreciation of others' efforts and accomplishments

- applying developing basic literacy and numeracy skills in purposeful ways

- having feelings of belonging to a group of peers

- and so on.

This preliminary list is based on general considerations of what kinds of experiences we have good reasons – philosophical as well as pedagogical and empirical – to believe that all children should experience during much of the time that they spend in our early education settings.

References and suggested further reading

Entries in bold are further reading.

Beneke, S.J., Ostrosky, M. and Katz, L.G. (2008) Calendar Time for Young Children: Good Intentions Gone Awry. *Young Children*, 63(3): 12–16.

Blair, C. (2002) School Readiness: Integrating Cognition and Emotion in a Neurobiological Conceptualization of Children Functioning at School Entry. *American Psychologist*, 57(2): 111–27.

Bruer, J.T. (1999) *The Myth of the First Three Years: A New Understanding of Early Brain Development and Lifelong Learning.* New York: Free Press.

Finn, C.E. (2010) Targeted, Not Universal PreK. *Phi Delta Kappan*, 92(3): 12–16.

Golbeck, S.L. (2001) Instructional Models for Early Childhood: In Search of a Child-Regulated/Teacher-Guided Pedagogy. In S. Golbeck (ed.) *Psychological Perspectives on Early Childhood Education: Reframing Dilemmas in Research and Practice.* New

York: Erlbaum.

Katz, L.G. (1998) The Benefits of the Mix. *Child Care Information Exchange*. Available online at: www.childcareexchange.com/catalog/product_info.php?products_id=5012446&search=&category= (accessed 25 March 2011).

Katz, L.G. (2009) *All About Balls: A Preschool Project*. Clearinghouse on Early Education and Parenting. Available online at: http://ceep.crc.uiuc.edu (accessed 15 January 2011).

Katz, L.G. (2010) Knowledge, Understanding, and the Disposition to Seek Both. *Exchange*, November/December, 32(6): 46–7.

Katz, L.G. and Chard, S.C. (2000) *Engaging Children's Minds: The Project Approach*. **Stamford, CT: Ablex Publishing Co.**

Lally, J.R. (2010) School Readiness Begins in Infancy. *Phi Delta Kappan*, 92(3): 17–21.

Marcon, R. (2000) *Impact of Preschool Models on Educational Transitions from Early Childhood to Middle Childhood and into Early Adolescence*. Poster session presented at the Conference on Human Development in Memphis, TN, 16 April.

Merrell, C. and Tymms, P. (2010) Changes in Children's Cognitive Development at the Start of School in England, 2001–2008. *Oxford Review of Education*, 36(6): 1–13.

Siegler, R., Deloache, J. and Eisenberg, N. (2003) *How Children Develop*. New York: Worth.

Name index

Subject index